A CHOICE OF
WEAPONS

A CHOICE OF WEAPONS

Gordon Parks

MINNESOTA HISTORICAL SOCIETY PRESS

ST. PAUL

*Borealis Books are high-quality paperback reprints
of books chosen by the Minnesota Historical Society Press
for their importance as enduring historical sources and their value
as enjoyable accounts of life in the Upper Midwest.*

∞

The paper used in this publication meets the minimum requirements
of the American National Standard for Information Sciences—
Permanence for Printed Library Materials, ANSI Z39.48-1984.

Minnesota Historical Society Press
St. Paul, Minnesota 55102
800 647 7827
www.mnhs.org/mhspress

International Standard Book Number 0-87351-202-2
Manufactured in the United States of America
10   9   8   7

Library of Congress Cataloging-in-Publication Data
Parks, Gordon, 1912–
    A choice of weapons.
    Reprint. Originally published: New York: Harper & Row,
1966.
    1. Parks, Gordon, 1912–   .
    2. Afro-American photographers—United States—Biography.
    3. Authors, American—20th century—Biography
    I. Title.
TR140.P35A3   1986   770′.92′4[B]   86-17993
ISBN 0-87351-202-2 (pbk.)

PICTURE CREDITS
Front cover: *Self-portrait*, 1945;
back cover: *Norman Jr. Reading in Bed*, 1967;
both photographs © Gordon Parks.

TO
GORDON,
TONI,
DAVID
AND
ALAIN

PREFACE
TO THE REPRINT EDITION

Seldom do I go back to read a book of mine. The letters from so many readers, both young and old, forced me back to *A Choice of Weapons*. My experience seems to have touched them in a way I never expected — but in a way that leaves me grateful. Their remarks come genuinely from the heart; their questions are asked with a sincerity of purpose. I didn't set out to preach sermons or deliver profound messages. I simply wanted to get a few things off my chest that weighed heavily upon it for too many years.

The inevitable question. "Are you still angry?"

No. I am not. My experience — though I would never wish it upon anyone else — has helped make me whatever I am and still hope to be. If providence were to will me the choice of starting all over — as a rich black or white boy — I would choose the way I have come. Indeed the road was rougher to travel, but one with a kind of learning no other road might have lent me. Time was too precious to waste in anger and hatred. It was so much better used to confront those obstacles that I encountered. Furthermore, I have never known anyone important enough to consume me in anger beyond a few hours. Better to depart their existence before they poison your own.

As a child I was poor, miserably so, but so beautifully rich with the love of my mother and father, as well as that of fourteen brothers and sisters. What they gave is now what I attempt to give. I have come to understand that hunger, hatred, and love are the same wherever you find them, and it is that understanding that now helps me escape the past that once imprisoned me.

When I started writing this sequel to *The Learning Tree* my thoughts jumped immediately to the first hard, cold winters I spent in St. Paul, Minnesota. It is most significant to me because it was in this impersonal north country that I had to become a man at 16 — or perish. Also it was the beginning of the true worth of my mother's teaching, those teachings that enabled me to survive. This was the real proving ground — the cold, the hunger, the frustration and fear. But from here came the strength that would sustain me in the giant worlds outside that I would later encounter. I value the experience.

Gordon Parks

New York City
May 1986

PROLOGUE

WE ARE standing silent in the safe quarter of this pale green gas chamber. There are twelve of us and a cocky young guard; his orders splinter my thoughts: "Don't move around—don't gesture—don't talk aloud—obey commands promptly." Now, for some unaccountable reason, the guard is motioning me down front—to within three feet of the waiting chair. From here, only a thick glass will separate me from the death we have agreed to witness. Close behind us a minister leafs his Bible for words to say at the appropriate time.

The color of the walls seems so incompatible with the occasion. Why not a somber gray or, better still, black?

The door to the death cubicle is opening. The quiet is heavy, and I damn myself for accepting the warden's invitation. But it's too late for that now; the doomed man is already coming, ashen and shaking, flanked by three beefy guards. He is dressed in blue prison denim, wears gray flannel bedroom slippers and moves with a hesitant shuffle as they guide him through the door. Only the compassionate whispers of the minister stir the silence—*that the saying of Jesus might be fulfilled, which he spake, signifying what death he should die.* The prisoner observes us through tears; and, for a curious moment, his eyes seem to question our presence. He is turning slowly, using up every precious second before surrendering his body to the chair, realizing, as he must, that he will never through his own strength rise again. *Then said Pilate unto them, Take ye him, and judge him according to your own law. The Jews therefore said unto him, It is not lawful for us to put any man to death.* Obviously they have fed him well; the guards strain to secure the straps around his sagging belly. Obligingly he inhales deeply as they snap the buckle and strap down his shoulders and legs. Two of the guards are leaving but one lingers to adjust the stethoscope over the heart. There must be a precise moment of death to enter into the record. *The Lord is my shepherd; I shall not want. He maketh me to lie down in green pastures: he leadeth me beside the still waters.* The guard is advising him, or warning him, to inhale "it" quickly, to get it over with fast. And, as he is leaving, he pats the man's back. But wait: the condemned man is asking for something and there is a flurry of movement outside the door. It must have been a Bible that he asked for; one is being thrust into the cubicle and the guard is placing it firmly in his hands. The guard is out now, closing the door. And at last he sits alone, head bowed, thumbing the Bible—awaiting death. I must assume the reporter's obligation and remember the passage he finally selects. They are sealing the door. What are his thoughts? A tear is rolling down the man's cheek as he thumbs on—Samuel, Kings, Chronicles, Ezra, Esther, Job, Psalms —*he restoreth my soul; he leadeth me in the paths of righteousness for his name's sake.* In the glass I perceive my own image emerging from within his. Interestingly abstract, the two images, one over another; and there, distorted in the reflection, the other witnesses, chalk-white in the nauseous green. Proverbs, Isaiah, Jeremiah (the warden's arm is rising), Lamentations. *Yea, though I walk through the valley of the shadow of death, I will fear no evil: for thou art with me; thy rod and thy staff they comfort me.* The warden's arm drops. The pellet drops. The gas should be rising. Yes, his head just snapped backward. The thumb digs into Lamentations and the Bible, falling free, snaps shut. His image is parted from mine now, and there is intense quivering from the top of the head to the neck. His nervous system is being eaten away. *Thou preparest a table before me in the presence of mine enemies: thou anointest my head with oil; my cup runneth over.* The quivering reaches his belly, his hips, his knees, his legs; and there is one final spasm of protest as it reaches his toes. He is still. *And I will dwell in the house of the Lord for ever.*

It is over. Without reason he murdered a stranger dispassionately; his judgment was served as dispassionately. How useless now, for him slumped there in death, that I fail to distinguish the profanity of one act from the profanity of the other. It seems, to my disordered thinking, that one evil, cloaked in cold judicial morality, has just fed upon another. As we file out, I sense that our young guard is pleased with the pain on my face. He wants to know if I enjoyed the show. Incredible. I won't answer. "Too bad you wasn't around a few weeks ago when two colored boys went at the same time. One cut his jugular with a razor blade before we could strap him down and blood was all over the windows, guards and chairs and he was crying, 'Don't kill me, don't kill me,' and the other one was laughing like a hyena and hollering, 'Come on, man. Don't let whitey think you're scared'—and he kept laughing right up to the end."

Life, so precious, seems for the instant so absurdly cheap.

I keep walking, hearing, holding the silence we have been instructed to hold. Now, fleeing through the gate, my own scarred past stretches out before me. I recall that elaborate conspiracy of evil that once beckoned me toward such a death, and I am afraid. For, having finished off that man back there, I know it will be dogging my footsteps again. I can feel it. And I am almost frightened into running, but I will not, call it vanity, bravado, pride or whatever. Only I know it to be something different—a faith in the weapons I hold to rout such fear. Years ago I found them, one by one. I remember so vividly. They were all half hidden in obscure cubbyholes stretching along the labyrinthine corridors of my earlier life. But I found them. And I chose them slowly, with pain and infinite caution. Here now, in the chill of this frightful morning, their presence comforts me: how fortunate I was to have had the privilege of choosing them.

A CHOICE OF
WEAPONS

ONE

THE FULL meaning of my mother's death had settled
over me before they lowered her into the grave. They
buried her at two-thirty in the afternoon; now, at nightfall,
our big family was starting to break up. Once there had
been fifteen of us and, at sixteen, I was the youngest. There
was never much money, so now my older brothers and
sisters were scraping up enough for my coach ticket north.
I would live in St. Paul, Minnesota, with my sister Maggie
Lee, as my mother had requested a few minutes before she
died.

Poppa, a good quiet man, spent the last hours before our
parting moving aimlessly about the yard, keeping to himself and avoiding me. A sigh now and then belied his outer
calm. Several times I wanted to say that I was sorry to be
going, and that I would miss him very much. But the
silence that had always lain between us prevented this.
Now I realized that probably he hadn't spoken more than a
few thousand words to me during my entire childhood. It
was always: "Mornin', boy"; "Git your chores done, boy";
"Goodnight, boy." If I asked for a dime or nickel, he
would look beyond me for a moment, grunt, then dig
through the nuts and bolts in his blue jeans and hand me
the money. I loved him in spite of his silence.

For his own reasons Poppa didn't go to the depot, but as my sister and I were leaving he came up, a cob pipe jutting from his mouth, and stood sideways, looking over the misty Kansas countryside. I stood awkwardly waiting for him to say something. He just grunted—three short grunts. "Well," Maggie Lee said nervously, "won't you be kissin' your poppa goodbye?" I picked up my cardboard suitcase, turned and kissed his stubbly cheek and started climbing into the taxicab. I was halfway in when his hand touched my shoulder. "Boy, remember your momma's teachin'. You'll be all right. Just you remember her teachin'." I promised, then sat back in the Model T taxi. As we rounded the corner, Poppa was already headed for the hog pens. It was feeding time.

Our parents had filled us with love and a staunch Methodist religion. We were poor, though I did not know it at the time; the rich soil surrounding our clapboard house had yielded the food for the family. And the love of this family had eased the burden of being black. But there were segregated schools and warnings to avoid white neighborhoods after dark. I always had to sit in the peanut gallery (the Negro section) at the movies. We weren't allowed to drink a soda in the drugstore in town. I was stoned and beaten and called "nigger," "black boy," "darky," "shine." These indignities came so often I began to accept them as normal. Yet I always fought back. Now I considered myself lucky to be alive; three of my close friends had already died of senseless brutality, and I was lucky that I hadn't killed someone myself. Until the very day that I left Fort Scott on that train for the North, there had been a fair chance of being shot or perhaps beaten to death. I could easily have been the victim of mistaken identity, of a sudden act of terror by hate-filled white men, or, for that matter, I could have been murdered by some violent member of my own race. There had been a lot of killing in the border states of Kansas, Oklahoma and Missouri, more than I cared to remember.

I was nine years old when the Tulsa riots took place in 1921. Whites had invaded the Negro neighborhood, which turned out to be an armed camp. Many white Tulsans were killed, and rumors had it that the fight would spread into Kansas and beyond. About this time, a grown cousin of mine decided to go south to work in a mill. My mother, knowing his hot temper, pleaded with him not to go, but he caught a freight going south. Months passed and we had no word of him. Then one day his name flashed across the nation as one of the most-wanted men in the country. He had killed a white millhand who spat in his face and called him "nigger." He killed another man while fleeing the scene and shot another on the viaduct between Kansas City, Missouri, and Kansas City, Kansas.

I asked Momma questions she couldn't possibly answer. Would they catch him? Would he be lynched? Where did she think he was hiding? How long did she think he could hold out? She knew what all the rest of us knew, that he would come back to our house if it was possible.

He came one night. It was storming, and I lay in the dark of my room, listening to the rain pound the roof. Suddenly, the window next to my bed slid up, and my cousin, wet and cautious, scrambled through the opening. I started to yell as he landed on my bed, but he quickly covered my mouth with his hand, whispered his name, and cautioned me into silence. I got out of bed and followed him. He went straight to Momma's room, kneeled down and shook her awake. "Momma Parks," he whispered, "it's me, it's me. Wake up." And she awoke easily and put her hand on his head. "My Lord, son," she said, "you're in such bad trouble." Then she sat up on the side of the bed and began to pray over him. After she had finished, she tried to persuade him to give himself up. "They'll kill you, son. You can't run forever." But he refused. Then, going to our old icebox, he filled a sack with food and went back out my window into the cornfield.

None of us ever saw or heard of him again. And I would lie awake nights wondering if the whites had killed my cousin, praying that they hadn't. I remembered the huge sacks of peanut brittle he used to bring me and the rides he gave me on the back of his battered motorcycle. And my days were full of fantasies in which I helped him escape imaginary white mobs.

When I was eleven, I became possessed of an exaggerated fear of death. It started one quiet summer afternoon with an explosion in the alley behind our house. I jumped up from under a shade tree and tailed Poppa toward the scene. Black smoke billowed skyward, a large hole gaped in the wall of our barn and several maimed chickens and a headless turkey flopped about on the ground. Then Poppa stopped and muttered, "Good Lord." I clutched his overalls and looked. A man, or what was left of him, was strewn about in three parts. A gas main he had been repairing had somehow ignited and blown everything around it to bits.

Then once, with two friends, I had swum along the bottom of the muddy Marmaton River, trying to locate the body of a Negro man. We had been promised fifty cents apiece by the same white policeman who had shot him while he was in the water trying to escape arrest. The dead man had been in a crap game with several others who had managed to get away. My buddy, Johnny Young, was swimming beside me; we swam with ice hooks which we were to use for grappling. The two of us touched the corpse at the same instant. Fear streaked through me and the memory of his bloated body haunted my dreams for nights.

One night at the Empress Theater, I sat alone in the peanut gallery watching a motion picture, *The Phantom of the Opera*. When the curious heroine, against Lon Chaney's warning, snatched away his mask, and the skull of death filled the screen, I screamed out loud and ran out of the theater. I didn't stop until I reached home, crying to Momma, "I'm going to die! I'm going to die."

Momma, after several months of cajoling, had all but destroyed this fear when another cruel thing happened. A Negro gambler called Captain Tuck was mysteriously killed on the Frisco tracks. Elmer Kinard, a buddy, and I had gone to the Cheney Mortuary out of youthful, and perhaps morbid, curiosity. Two white men, standing at the back door where bodies were received, smiled mischievously and beckoned to us. Elmer was wise and ran, but they caught me. "Come on in, boy. You want to see Captain Tuck, don't you?"

"No, no," I pleaded. "No, no, let me go."

The two men lifted me through the door and shoved me into a dark room. "Cap'n Tuck's in here, boy. You can say hello to him." The stench of embalming fluid mixed with fright. I started vomiting, screaming and pounding the door. Then a smeared light bulb flicked on and, there before me, his broken body covering the slab, was Captain Tuck. My body froze and I collapsed beside the door.

After they revived me and put me on the street, I ran home with the old fear again running the distance beside me. My brother Clem evened the score with his fists the next day, but from then on Poppa proclaimed that no Parks would ever be caught dead in Cheney's. "The Koonantz boys will do all our burying from now on," he told Orlando Cheney.

Another time, I saw a woman cut another woman to death. There were men around, but they didn't stop it. They all stood there as if they were watching a horror movie. Months later, I would shudder at the sight of Johnny Young, one of my closest buddies, lying, shot to death, at the feet of his father and the girl he loved. His murderer had been in love with the same girl. And not long after, Emphry Hawkins, who had helped us bear Johnny's coffin, was also shot to death.

As the train whistled through the evening, I realized that only hours before, during what seemed like a bottomless night, I had left my bed to sleep on the floor beside my mother's coffin. It was, I knew now, a final attempt to destroy this fear of death.

But in spite of the memories I would miss this Kansas land that I was leaving. The great prairies filled with green and cornstalks; the flowering apple trees, the tall elms and oaks bordering the streams that gurgled and the rivers that rolled quiet. The summers of long, sleepy days for fishing, swimming and snatching crawdads from beneath the rocks. The endless tufts of high clouds billowing across the heavens. The butterflies to chase through grass high as the chin. The swallowtails, bobolinks and robins. Nights filled with soft laughter, with fireflies and restless stars, and the winding sound of the cricket rubbing dampness from its wing. The silver of September rain, the orange-red-brown Octobers and Novembers, and the white Decembers with the hungry smells of hams and pork butts curing in the smokehouses. Yet, as the train sped along, the telegraph poles whizzing toward and past us, I had a feeling that I was escaping a doom which had already trapped the relatives and friends I was leaving behind. For, although I was departing from this beautiful land, it would be impossible ever to forget the fear, hatred and violence that Negroes had suffered upon it.

It was all behind me now. By the next day, there would be what my mother had called "another kind of world, one with more hope and promising things." She had said, "Make a man of yourself up there. Put something into it, and you'll get something out of it." It was her dream for me. When I stepped onto the chilly streets of St. Paul, Minnesota, two days later, I was determined to fulfill that dream.

I had never met my brother-in-law, and his handshake told me that I was to be tolerated rather than accepted. He was nearly white in color, big and fierce-looking. His whole person seemed formidable. His only words to me that first evening were about things I should not do in his house.

It was a nice house—two-storied, handsomely middle-class, with large, comfortable rooms. And that night, lying in bed, I marveled at the hundreds of deer leaping the bushes on the wallpaper around me, and my thoughts were charged with vague imaginings of the future. Yet I felt that whatever security lay ahead would be of my own making. There was no feeling of permanence in the softness of the ornate bed. I sensed that this was to be an uneasy stopover, and that it would be necessary to move on before long.

"Cut off your lamp! Electric lights cost money, boy!" It was my brother-in-law outside the door. I didn't answer, I thought it better to remain silent, but I switched off the light and listened to him lumber down the hall. But, in spite of the long coach ride, I was restless and couldn't sleep. A few minutes later, my sister sneaked in the door with a handful of gingersnaps and a glass of milk and placed them on my night table. "Don't worry. Everything will work out all right," she whispered, then she slipped back into the hallway.

Even on this first night, I had bad feeling for this man. It was the kind of feeling I had for the whites whose indignities had pushed me to the edge of violence, whose injustices toward me had created one emotional crisis after another, all because my skin was black. My mind shifted back to those mornings when I stood before the cracked mirror in our house and wondered why God had made me black, and I remembered the dream I once had of being white, with skin so flabby and loose that I attempted to pull it into shape, to make it fit, only to awaken and find myself clutching at my underwear. But now I knew I was black and that I would always be black.

At fourteen, in the black-and-white world of Kansas, anyone whiter than I became my enemy. I had grown rebellious and once, while in a fit of temper, I knocked my crippled brother Leroy, who was a couple of shades lighter than I, to the floor. Immediately ashamed, I reached down to help him. He smiled and waved me aside, and I ran from the room crying. It hurt to learn several days later that he had known for months that he was incurably ill. Just before he died, the following winter, he called me to his bedside.

"Pedro," he said, using his favorite nickname for me, "for the life of me I don't know why you're so mad at the world. You can't whip it the way you're going. It's too big.

If you're going to fight it, use your brain. It's got a lot more power than your fists." Before sleep came that night in St. Paul, it was clear to me that such reasoning was needed if I was to cope with my brother-in-law's hostility.

I awoke early the next day, dressed and went out of doors, eager for a look at the new surroundings. The morning was already brisk and alive, with sunshine full upon the big porch. The tree-lined avenue seemed clean and beautiful. The leaves, yielding to the first frosts, had taken on the golds and oranges of autumn. Stretching full length upon the steps, I was suddenly thankful to be in this bright new land.

People were now on the street, moving with the quickness that autumn mornings enforce. I thought that I too would have to move much faster here; otherwise I would be left behind. Maggie Lee had made pancakes and sausage for breakfast. We ate quietly, the three of us; then my brother-in-law, a Pullman porter, went away for a week—the only week that I was to know happiness in this house.

I enrolled in Mechanic Arts High School, and got an evening job bussing dishes in a diner, where I was paid six dollars a week and given one meal a day. My brother-in-law took two of this for my rent and meals, yet the four dollars left seemed adequate. It was more than I had ever had at one time in my entire life. The new friends I made kidded me about my country mannerisms and dress, my shyness with the girls and my "Kansas talk." But when basketball season came, my status grew. Their regulation hoops seemed a lot wider than the small barrel rims through which I had learned to shoot, and they were impressed when my shots swished through, hardly ever touching the rim. Not long after this, they invited me into the "Diplomats Club." Their team needed a good forward, and they liked my way of playing. My sister was much happier than my brother-in-law about this. "He should spend his extra time making a better living," he grumbled after she had announced my achievement.

Real winter came one Friday just before Christmas. A hungry north wind knifed down like a hawk. By seven o'clock that night, the temperature had dipped to ten degrees below zero. It was the night our club was to make arrangements for its Christmas party, and I was bundled up to go to the meeting. Maggie Lee, her friend Crystal Graham and my brother-in-law were sitting in the living room as I bade them goodnight and started out.

"Where you going, boy?" My brother-in-law's voice was menacing.

"To a club meeting."

"You ain't going no place. You were out two nights in a row."

I got hot beneath my clothes. Crystal cleared her throat nervously, and Maggie Lee's eyes darted back and forth between her husband and me.

"It's our last meeting before the party." My tone was guarded to avoid trouble, if only for my sister's sake.

"You heard me," he said, rising from his chair.

"Gordon! Gordon!" My sister was up between us. Crystal was behind her.

Perhaps if he hadn't shoved my sister against the wall, I might have gone back to my room. But, when that happened, I rushed toward him, swinging for his belly before he realized what was happening. But he was a powerful man. My blows only angered him. He pounced on me, crushing me to the floor beneath his two hundred thirty pounds. His hands were groping for my throat and, while my sister and Crystal screamed at the top of their lungs, he began choking me and banging my head against the floor. "Stop it! You're killing him! Stop it!" Now Crystal was beating his head with an umbrella. His hands fell loose and I scrambled from beneath him, and, as she continued to beat him, I rolled across the floor and ran out the door. Crystal grabbed her coat and followed me out.

Several minutes later I was picking up my belongings from beneath my bedroom window, where he had thrown them. Crystal was there beside me in the deep snow, helping. She still held the umbrella in her hand. And though it was brutally cold I sweated as we charged about in the wind, grabbing the garments and stuffing them into my cardboard suitcase. I could hear my sister still sobbing hysterically up on the second floor. The storm window opened above me, and my alarm clock sailed out and thudded beside me in the snow. Crystal dug it out, and we made our way to the street.

I stood there for several minutes, dazed and confused, tears welling up in my eyes.

"Where will you go?" Crystal asked.

"I don't know." She looked at me rather helplessly for a second or two, then hurried off.

At the club meeting there would be heat and food, but the suitcase and clock would have to be explained. And, since the Diplomats came from the "better Negro families," I felt it would be embarrassing to have to explain my situation. So, instead of going there, I decided on Jim Williams' pool hall, which was four blocks away.

I had been thrown out so quickly it was difficult to grasp the truth of it; but after two blocks the cold and the empty street told me that, for the first time, I was homeless and alone. Only a few months before my family and home had seemed to be something which would last forever. I remembered our potbellied stove, heated to redness; pans of chicken, cornbread, rolls, puddings and pies; my brothers and sisters eating at the oversized supper table. Now, as the stale heat of Jim Williams' pool hall hit my face, the sense of being and belonging seemed of another life, another time.

My hands and feet were stiff. I dropped my belongings, pressed against a radiator and blew on my fingers to kill the numbness. I only had two dollars and fifty cents left from my pay check; my brother-in-law had taken the rest. I anticipated the warmth of school the following week, then remembered it was already closed for the holidays. The diner where I worked would be shut until Monday. And, with a lump in my throat, my chest heaving, my stomach in knots, I watched the pool players drifting around and above the green of the billiard tables; but their hawking, spitting, cursing and laughter seemed detached from them. They were like ghosts.

After the pool hall closed, I rode trolley cars back and forth to the ends of the line between St. Paul and Minneapolis, sleeping most of the time, using my suitcase for a pillow, waking now and then to the sound of snow and sleet pelting against the trolley windows. I was aware of people getting on and off at different stops, knowing that they had someplace to go, knowing that I was only riding out the night. Once, when I awoke, the car was empty and dark, the doors were open and wind and snow swept in from both ends. I sat up, rubbed frost from the window and looked out. Except for the falling snow, there was nothing—no trees, lights or landscape. The car seemed suspended in the stormy blackness. Again I rubbed briskly at the window, and then there came a sputtering of bluish-white light. The trolley operator was swinging the contact pole to the power line from where it had slipped. The lights came on, and a railing came into view. We were on a bridge, high above the Mississippi River.

I rode the trolley between the Twin Cities for several weeks. The rent was reasonable, and there was always some heat. My food for those days and nights was the single meal I got at the diner, eked out by hot dogs and root beer.

Soon after the fight with my brother-in-law I became fully aware of the problems that I faced. And quickly enough I tried thinking of ways to survive. The distance back to Kansas was insuperable. I never thought of seeking shelter and food at the Salvation Army or some other charity. Yet there were some other things I considered; the worst was robbery. This I came closest to one dawn when I found myself alone on the trolley with an aging conductor. It was my birthday, and we were back in St. Paul. The trolley operator had already gone for coffee to a café across the street. The conductor poked me awake, saying that we were at the end of the line. He stood there, just above me, with a bundle of green bills wadded together with a rubber band. At the sight of them, my hand tightened about a switchblade in my pocket. I rose slowly, looking through the windows to see who was about. We were alone. His back was toward me as we walked to the rear of the car. Perspiration rolled from my armpits, and the anxiety of evil-doing must have shown on my face. I pressed the button, and the long blade popped out.

"Conductor!"

"Yes." He turned and looked calmly at the blade. I looked at him, trembling now, with all my mother's teaching coming hot at me.

"Conductor," I said, "would you give me a dollar for this knife? I'm hungry and I don't have any place to stay."

He watched me for a second. "You can keep the knife," he said. "Come on over to the café, and I'll buy you a meal."

I stood shaking for a moment, not knowing what to do, then I closed the blade. "I'm sorry," I said.

"It's all right," he answered, peeling off two dollar bills. "Go where you want and get some grub."

"It's okay. I can manage."

"Take it," he insisted, "and keep yourself out of trouble." I refused the money, jumped out of the car and hurried off, more frightened and ashamed than I had ever been in my life. The poolroom would be opening soon and it would be warm there. I scurried through an alleyway, hoping the conductor had lost sight of me. It was a long walk but Tee Vernon, the rack man, was just opening up when I got there.

I began each day assuming the worst. Sometimes, after walking long distances I would stop in a restaurant, movie house or department store and try for a better job. All I got was indifference and, at times, scorn. The six dollars a week hardly kept me in hot dogs and carfare; and the windows filled with roast hams, turkey and other holiday fowl sharpened my hunger unbearably. It was hard not to smash them.

Momma had always held such high hopes for me. I wondered what she would have felt had she seen me there freezing and starving. Until her death I hadn't known we were so poor. In the early protected days poverty seemed for the old and the helpless. I was naïve and carefree, loving a particular pair of overalls, a certain stocking cap, rifle, pocketknife, spinning top or some such thing. It hardly touched me that my parents went without to give me these simple pleasures. Only when she lay dying did bits of gossip reveal that her sickness had resulted from overwork. So now, in a way, poverty seemed new to me. And its embarrassment was as painful as the hunger it brought.

Some Minnesota Negroes I encountered were as indifferent to my condition as the whites. But it was my brother-in-law who served himself up as the individual to whom I would prove something. And I let him know it one afternoon when I saw him on the street. "You'll see!" I shouted at him. "I'll make it! You'll see!" He pursed his lips, spat in the snow and continued on his way. Perhaps he did me a favor by pushing me out. Early manhood, after all, was my inheritance; the sooner I began it the better.

Tee Vernon, aside from being the rack man at the pool hall, was also its bouncer. He was contentedly fat, kind and good-natured; but he was tough. His huge belly and his head were his weapons. One night I saw him slam an unruly patron into the wall with one and butt him into unconsciousness with the other. Big Jim, the owner, oversaw the gambling, moneylending and bootlegging on the floor above. Each morning when I returned to get warm, Tee would watch me from the corner of his eye. Now and then he would push an empty box by the radiator for me to sit on, or hand me part of a sandwich, saying it was too much for him to finish. Then sometimes he would ask me for a game of rotation, at which he was an expert, and allow me miraculously to win the ten cents we agreed to bet. One day I asked him if I could leave my suitcase with him.

"Sure," he said, and he stuck it in a closet in the back. "How's it goin'?"

"So-so," I answered.

"Need anything?"

"Nope—everything's okay, I guess. If only I could get a better job some place at night—playing a piano or anything to make more money."

"How long have you been playing the piano?"

"I don't know. For as long as I can remember."

"I'll keep my eyes open for you," he replied and waddled off to rack some balls.

Freddie Conners, my boss at the diner, was the opposite of Tee. He was thin, pasty-white and pimply, with a longish red nose that he constantly wiped on his apron. And he was vile smelling and mean. I could never do enough work for him, no matter how hard I tried. My job was to sweep the floor, wash windows, bus and wash the dishes and clean the counters. There was also a mysterious basement, but I was ordered to keep away from that. The one meal he gave me was skimpy and, if I didn't watch him closely, it would be the leftovers from a customer's plate. I caught him at this one night and complained. He called me a liar and threatened to fire me. In spite of my hunger, I dumped the food into the garbage and finished my chores. Then later, while his back was turned, I slipped four raw wieners and a container of milk into my pockets. In answer to my "Goodnight," he wiped his nose on his apron and snarled, "Go to hell." I wanted to quit, then and there; but common sense buttoned my lips. And I left without another word.

TWO

THE EVENING before Christmas, I was sweeping the floor when four policemen walked in and started pushing Freddie and me around the place. "You ain't keeping this joint servin' one meal a day! Come on now, where's the stuff hidin'?" Freddie whined his innocence, but the big policemen kept shoving us to the back. One officer went down to the basement. Another bolted the front door, then walked over to me. His face was kinder than the others', and I felt his hand on my shoulder.

"Look, son," he said in a fatherly tone, "we know there's a lot of hot stuff in this place. You can save yourself a lot of trouble and lead us to it."

"What's hot stuff?" My question was sincere, and I thought that the one with the kind face thought so. But another one observed me with disapproval.

"It's stolen goods!" he snarled, shoving me against the wall. "You know damned well what it is!"

"Bring 'em down here," hollered the one who had gone below.

We went down. "Open it up," they ordered Freddie, pointing to the locked room that he had forbidden me to enter.

It was true; Freddie was a fence for stolen goods. There was everything imaginable in that room: jewelry, furs, guns of all kinds, golf bags, fishing rods, even a couple of naked clothing-store dummies; and also automobile tires, paintings, radios, a rack of suits and overcoats, ties, shirts, shoes and underwear of all sizes and colors.

The police asked me a few more questions. Then Freddie grudgingly convinced them that I didn't know anything about his "other business." After that, the one with the kind face let me go.

"How about my week's pay?" I asked Freddie, as they led him away.

He shrugged. "I got troubles; you got troubles." He climbed into the paddy wagon and they roared off; and I buttoned up and headed for the poolroom.

The spirit of Christmas had, by now, come full upon the city. The sidewalks were crammed with late shoppers. Little Salvation Army groups sang and played carols on the corners, and the streets sparkled with Yuletide decorations. I walked through the downtown area, ignoring the carolers, the Santa Clauses with their bells; rejecting the joyfulness and the real meaning of the holiday festivity about me. I short-cut up over Cathedral Hill and, looking up, recognized the great church of St. Paul, its medieval beauty thinly veiled by the falling snow, passed it, then turning right toward the lower Rondo section, saw that even here candles lit the windows of the poorer Negroes. I walked on, barely hearing my footsteps in the quiet of the evening. Several children whizzed by on their sleds. A car turned into the street, and they veered off into the curb, piling onto one another. They scrambled up, laughing and shouting, and the car's light shining against them revealed a small boy with only one leg. He balanced himself, took a couple of hops with his sled, fell forward and slid off into the darkness with the others.

Approaching Jim's, I could hear the loudspeakers from the skating rink blaring Christmas carols. It was somehow easier to listen to them here in the Rondo section. Humming, I crossed the street and entered the pool hall.

Tee was about ready to close up when a tall, thin, brown-skinned man walked through the door. He was nattily dressed in a black chesterfield coat, derby and white spats over patent leather shoes. He talked to Tee for several minutes, then they both walked over to me.

"This is Jimmy," said Tee. "He's from Pope's over in Minneapolis, and he needs a piano player. I told him you could play. You interested?"

"I don't know if I'm good enough. I've only played at little parties and around home."

"You play the blues?" Jimmy cut in. I noticed now that his face was powdered and that he wore a pencil-line mustache. His delicate nostrils flared when he spoke.

"Yep. I feel around with them a little bit."

"You git two bucks a night and tips." His speech was clipped and he looked at my clothes as if he thought they needed overhauling.

"Where?" I was beginning to dislike his manner and looks.

"Pope's. A house—a place on the north side. You can start tonight. I'll take you over." Any place would beat sleeping on a streetcar. "I'll try it," I said.

The "place" turned out to be a four-story ramshackle house in the night-life district. Jimmy led me up two flights of stairs, then stopped at a landing which was lit by a single red bulb. He tapped a code on the door, and the man who opened it squinted at me just as curiously as I looked at him. He was chalky-white, an albino, with a mop of fuzzy hair. His eyes, tiny and red, danced nervously behind bifocal lenses, and he held two drumsticks in his hand.

"Here's your new plunker, Red," Jimmy said, ushering me into a room furnished with two gaudy sofas and a half-dozen chintz-covered chairs.

Red nodded to me with a grunt.

"What do we call you?" Jimmy asked.

"Parks—just Parks is okay."

"Okay. Red'll take care of you from here on." Jimmy then disappeared through a side door.

The piano was a Kimball upright with a naked woman drawn across the full length of the front. Most of the ivory had vanished from the keys, and liquor had burned a lot of the varnish from the top and sides. The bench's feet were four crudely-carved lion heads, and the seat, made from two planks of wood, stretched the length of the piano.

Red cleared his throat and sat down behind his drums and turned a switch; multicolored lights began blinking behind the front skins. "Wanta try something?" he asked.

My foot reached for the pedals. There was only one, and it wasn't working. "Anything special?" I inquired.

"Anything, anything to warm up with," he mumbled.

"There ain't nobody around now. Who do we play for, anyhow?" I asked. I was stalling for time and confidence. The only time my playing had been taken for entertainment was back home when a gramophone had broken down at a teen-age party. Then a set of cowbells and a Jew's harp had accompanied me.

"It's early. The cats will start comin' about one or two, soon as the legit joints close up." I didn't know what a "legit joint" was, but I accepted Red's terminology as if I did.

His drumming was as bad as my piano playing. And, after several horrible warmup numbers, including "Five Foot Two," "Sweet Georgia Brown" and "Dardanella," I no longer even regarded him as my peer. Finally he decided to rest, but I needed practice, so I played on a bit. I felt melancholy and started singing "Street of Dreams." Red listened. Then, after I had finished, he asked me to sing it again. I did, and halfway through the number a woman walked in. She was scantily clad, with a silk kimono around her shoulders, and she was honey-colored, willowy and pretty. Her black hair was combed straight back and matched her large eyes, that were as melancholy as the song I was singing. A snake-shaped ring of gold coiled about her finger; I could see its ruby eyes glistening as she held the kimono in place just below her breast. She looked about twenty-two. I finished my song with a sound that must have resembled that of an ailing pup. I smiled at her, then struck a grace note with my pinky.

She didn't smile back, but looked at me for a moment. "That was nice; wanta play it again sometime for me?"

"Any time you say," I answered. She tossed a quarter in the kitty, turned slowly and went back through the door.

A grunt came from Red. "You got Casa going there, man," he informed me, "and she ain't easy to move."

"Who is she?"

"Casamala, one of Pope's old ladies," Red answered, lighting a cigarette.

"One of them?" I asked. "How many has he got?"

Red laughed and his laugh was like a hen's cackle. "That's something all of them would like to know." Then his voice was very soft. "Casa's a wonderful girl." He said "Casa" with such tenderness that I knew he liked her. Before the night was over, and after the "cats" had come, enjoyed themselves and gone, I knew, indisputably, that I was a piano player in a whorehouse.

Christmas Day was gloomy, but it was not without some good fortune. Tipping, the night before, had been rather generous, and Red and I split a kitty of nearly ten dollars. This amount, plus the two-dollar salary, left me with a healthier pocketbook and a much brighter outlook. There was no reason to return to St. Paul, so I decided to rent a room in Minneapolis and eliminate the carfare. School wouldn't start until after the New Year, and this problem could be solved when the time came.

Red got me a room only two doors from Pope's place; it was tiny and dark, but there was heat and the landlady seemed amiable enough. The rent came to three dollars a week, and Red explained that it would be nice because most of Pope's employees were also staying there. "You won't get lonesome," he promised.

After sleeping most of the morning, I went out to telephone my sister. It made her happy to know that I was all right, working and had a place to sleep. Then I went to a corner restaurant, which also belonged to Pope, and ate. And it was here that I first saw him. He was alighting from a big cream-colored car, one that was resplendent with wire wheels and white sidewall tires. "Here comes Pope," a waitress chirped. A woman was seated in the front, and when she turned around my heart skipped. There was Casamala of the honey skin, black hair and doe eyes. But, sitting there in the harsh daylight, a cigarette hanging from her heavily rouged lips, she seemed older and tougher. The tenderness of the night before was gone. Now, with smoke curling up into her nostrils, she looked the role she had chosen to play.

Pope had none of the sartorial dash of Jimmy or his other hirelings I had seen the night before. He could have been a minister or a clerk. His face, however, was evilly fixed. It seemed to express an icy contempt for anyone who might look into it. He was light brown, lean and of medium height, and he moved in the manner of one who definitely had everything under control. And he did. Most of the rackets on the north side were controlled by him, and he went about, adequately armed, and personally picked up the lion's share of the take. As he entered the restaurant, I noticed that he was slightly pigeon-toed and wore sharp-pointed yellow shoes.

Walking back to the rooming house, I wondered at the great change in Casamala. She had seemed almost angelic as she listened to the poignant lyrics—". . . dreams broken in two can be made like new on the street of dreams." Her look had haunted me, and I had finally gone to sleep warm in the memory of it. But daylight had robbed her, as morning robs an empty cabaret of its darksome glamor. It would be easy enough to forget her after this.

As I walked back to my room, my thoughts turned to Christmas. It would be the first one I had ever spent alone. I thought about my brothers and sisters now, and I wondered how akin their problems were to mine.

On Christmas night, Pope sent in a case of booze and sandwiches and gave his employees the night off. And for the first time I got a chance to see all the "girls." There were Cleo, Caroline, Myrtle, Babe, Claudia, Kitty, Sadie and, of course, Casamala. And again tonight she had that look that set her apart. Obviously, she was a nocturnal beauty who faded in daylight. That night I played her another song:

> Butterfly be careful of your wings,
> Be careful of the tears tomorrow brings . . .

This, she assured me rather drunkenly, was even better than "Street of Dreams." She said, "Just a minute. I want you to play that song for Carmanosa." She rocked through the door, humming the tune. Then in about two minutes she returned with Carmanosa: Carmanosa of the same honey skin, eyes, lips and hair of Casamala! They were identical twins. And they both belonged to Pope.

During the party, Casamala hung around the piano requesting songs and feeding me sandwiches and liquor. As night wore on, she grew increasingly melancholy and eventually her arms went easily about my shoulders. And the feel of them helped me to forget the misery of the previous weeks. Flattered by her attention, I played constantly so that she would stay beside me. Sometime that evening, I played her a part of "Bittersweet," a tune I had begun writing that afternoon, and she said that I should become a composer. Long after the whiskey had dulled her reasoning she insisted, "You're gonna compose, compose and compose, sugar. I mean it, you're gonna compose. . . ." And I mumbled drunkenly that she was too good for this place and that she must become a great movie actress. I began imagining my name on all the theater marquees from Kansas City to New York. And I was before an orchestra, elegantly dressed and directing the musicians in a medley of my own compositions. And Casamala, the great actress, floated in and out of the fantasy.

I passed out about four in the morning, Red told me later, and I finally came to the next afternoon in the warmth of Casamala's bed. For the first few moments I lay still trying to remember how I had gotten there—and I couldn't. But it seemed natural enough lying beside her, listening to her gentle snoring, feeling her softness against me. I touched the loose hair, then her face. It looked so calm in the light filtering through the window. Casamala was attractive, even in her hungover condition, and my resentment began rising against those who called nightly to see her. After she had awakened, and we had made love, I asked her how she could give herself to so many, night after night. And why did she sell her body for a guy like Pope, knowing he had others, even her own twin sister, doing the same thing?

"First off," she replied, "I don't give them nothing. They pay for what they get." She paused for a moment, then went on, her eyes wandering over the ceiling. "It's not like being here with you. They don't mean nothing to me. I make myself think they're not really there." Her voice had become slightly defiant, and though her explanation seemed plausible her manner hinted at disillusion. I looked about the shabby room. On an ancient dresser, covered with graying lace, were soiled powder puffs, open pots of rouge, lipsticks, a bottle of perfume and a withered red rose. A brush, its metal frame dented and tarnished with time, held a broken comb in its bristles. A badly tinted photograph of Casamala and Pope was propped up against a talcum powder can. They stood somberly, arm in arm, by his car, staring down at me. There was one chintz-covered chair and a faded hassock. A few dresses hung behind a calico curtain that was stretched on a string across one corner of the room.

"But how can you?" I insisted.

"I never asked for it." Her voice was filled with distress now. "Pope and my sister got me into it."

"But you've gotta think for yourself," I argued. "You're young and pretty enough to be married to some nice guy."

Casamala reached for a cigarette, struck a match on the dresser and lit it. She turned toward me, squinting through the smoke. "Like who?" she asked softly. "Who would have me?" I wanted to say that I would, that I would take her away from Pope and all this. And she observed me ruefully, waiting. And I didn't say anything. Tears came suddenly to her eyes. "What the hell are you trying to do, anyhow," she asked, "make me something I ain't? I'm a whore. It's a living . . . it's all I've got. It's the only thing I know." She began to cry.

"But you can learn other things," I protested feebly.

"If you think I'm so god-awful, why are you laying here with me, making me worse? You're no better than Pope. Are you?"

I didn't have the answer; and for this reason, more than any other, I pulled her to me and held her until her tears subsided. Then we both realized the folly of such talk. Casamala rubbed the fire from the cigarette, wiped her eyes on the sheet and then buried her face in my neck. Before long she was asleep.

But I lay awake thinking. She was right; I was no more honorable than Pope. He at least paid her rent and bailed her out when she was picked up by the police. At least he was someone to whom she could say she belonged. But I did like her. I even had a wild thought of taking her away, perhaps to New York, Chicago or maybe Kansas City. I was thinking this as I listened to the footsteps in the hall . . . the knock on Casamala's door.

She sprang awake. "Who is it?" she called, rising on her elbows.

"Me. Open up."

"My god," she whispered, "it's Pope!" She switched on the light.

I looked about, bewildered. "What'll I do?"

Casamala faked a yawn. "Just a minute, honey. I've been

sleeping." Then she grabbed my clothes and threw them under the bed, and I lost no time in following them. I watched her bare feet move toward the door, and with fright saw the door open and Pope's pointed-toe shoes enter and stop at the bed, about three feet from where I lay. Then the mattress sagged under his weight.

"My back's aching like hell. It's killing me," Casamala complained.

"What's the matter with it?"

"Christmas week is rough."

"Things'll slow up after the first. Best to git it while we can."

"Yeh, but my back's killing me."

"Try and hold out till after New Year's Eve. That's a big night. I'd hate to lose it."

"I think I can make it."

"You need a doctor?"

"Let's wait. See how I feel tomorrow."

"Try'n hang on."

"I'll try, but my back's killing me."

"You got the last two nights' take, Kitten?"

"The last three. You ain't been around since Wednesday." Casamala's feet moved toward the dresser. The drawer squeaked open, shut and her feet returned to the side of the bed. "It's about a hundred and fifty here."

There was an awful silence while Pope counted the take. "Okay, Kitten. Take care of yourself."

"So long, Pope."

"See you, Kitten." The door closed, and his footsteps faded down the hall.

I waited a few minutes, then crawled from under the bed and began to dress. My conscience had tormented me as I lay there listening, knowing she was deeply embarrassed.

Now, remembering the conversation I had just forced upon her, it was hard to speak. The ugliness of the room, the smell of powder, the wasted beauty of this sad woman all caught in my throat. More than ever, I was sorry for her; but now I was wise enough not to express it. I glanced quickly at her, breathed heavily and left without a word.

My job at Pope's ended abruptly at the dawn of the new year. Someone plunged a butcher knife through a customer's neck and pushed him three stories down into the alley. As the police arrived, I escaped through a rear exit. Running out, I saw the bloody corpse sprawled in the snow; his face looked very young.

Common sense, and panic, told me to quit Minneapolis's north side as soon as possible. And when I left the rooming house I knocked lightly on Casamala's door. There was no answer. The police had probably taken her to jail. I felt sad about that. But there was Pope; he would go her bail. I took an envelope and pencil from my pocket and started writing: "Dear Casamala . . ." A woman's scream pierced the quiet, then came a man's curse and another scream. I crushed the note, dropped it on the floor and left.

Ten minutes later, my life closed to Casamala, I hopped a trolley for St. Paul.

THREE

WE CROSSED the frozen Mississippi just before day-break; and an icy wind blasting up from below shook the trolley car, recalling my earlier journeys along this route.

In St. Paul I rubbed frost from the window and looked out over the unmarked countryside. Dawn was coming full upon the houses, and I watched their chimney smoke curl up into the white-flaked air and wished for the comfort and warmth inside those walls. Farther on, two men in black were carrying a casket to a hearse; and under the weight they seemed to float through the whiteness. I thought back to the murdered youth, stiffening in the alleyway under this snow, and shuddered at the awfulness of death, especially to one who, at most, had seen twenty winters before being cut down. I shivered at the imagery of him decaying into dust in the airless blackness. Perhaps old age would make death easier, but the important thing now was some-how to stay alive, by any means.

Dusk and several inches of snow had fallen before I found a rooming house that I could afford. It was a leaning, two-story clapboard in the poor section on lower Rondo Street. A sign written in bad longhand was nailed into the siding and advertised cheap rooms by day, week or month.

The door opened when I touched it, and I stepped into a dark hallway where a light shone from beneath another door. A drunk, drifted in from the cold, lay upon the floor. I stepped over him and went to where the light shone and knocked.

A pretty brown-skinned girl of about twelve opened the door and asked me what I wanted. I didn't answer immediately. My eyes went beyond her to three men and a woman, playing cards at a table in the center of the room. The four of them looked in my direction, but it was the woman who spoke. "What do you want, sonny?" she asked.

"A room."

She looked me up and down for a moment and drank from a whiskey glass before answering. "Let him in, Lottie," she said, turning back to the game. She motioned me to a chair. "I'll take care of you after we finish this hand. Rest yourself. Lottie, get back to your school work."

Lottie went to a small box, which turned out to be her desk, and sat down on a smaller box and began to write. Then she was up beside her mother with a book, pointing to a word. "What does it mean, Momma?" she asked. The woman, who looked to be in her mid-thirties, took another swallow and squinted at the word.

"What does p-e-d-e-s-t-r-i-a-n-s mean?" she inquired of her companions. None of them ventured an answer, and the mother rather nervously shooed the daughter back to her desk, saying she would help her later. Lottie dropped the book to her side and started back.

"Can I help you, Lottie?" I asked.

She looked at me with surprise and grinned. "Maybe, in a minute," she answered. She wrote something on paper and her smile widened, then she came over to show me what she had written. "Pedestrians means people who walk," it read. Now we both smiled at her secret. I could only guess that she was mischievous or wanted attention.

Lottie's mother observed me closely; and I saw that she was shapely and attractive. While her eyes were still on me, she ordered Lottie to bed.

"But it's early, Momma," the girl complained.

"Do as you're told. Get to bed. Now." She gave the order in an even, final tone.

Lottie, obviously hurt, collected her books, left through a side door and banged it shut behind her.

"Hot-tempered little bitch," the woman muttered, shuffling her cards. Then turning to me she said, "I'll show you a room right after this hand." I explained that there was no need for her to hurry, but even then I was about to fall asleep; only by forcing my attention upon the card players did I hope to keep awake.

Two of the men, wearing hats, were brutish and quiet. Powerful muscles bulged their coat sleeves. The other, a skinny, "high-yellow" man with a poker face, prattled on constantly about things which seemed of no importance to the others, who watched their cards with seriousness.

I finally went to sleep, but the landlady didn't disturb me for an hour or more. When she eventually shook me awake, several other people were around the gaming table, but in my weariness they seemed like shadows. She led me back through the hallway and up one flight to a cold, windowless room that was hardly wider than the bed. I couldn't have expected much more; the two dollars I handed her was the week's advance.

She had gone, and I was already out of my pants when the door reopened and she stood eying me. "Thanks for helping Lottie tonight," she said.

"But I didn't do anything for her," I mumbled, holding my trousers awkwardly before me.

"Yes you did. I could tell by her looks." She stepped fully into the room and closed the door behind her. "How old are you, anyway?"

"Twenty-one . . . just about twenty-one," I lied.

"You go to school?"

"Yes, mam."

"My name's Jenny."

"Yes, Miss Jenny."

"Just plain Jenny."

"Jenny."

"That's better." She sat down on the bed beside me. "It's going to be nice having a smart young man like you around." She reached over and started unbuttoning my shirt. "Here, let me help you. You're all pooped out."

"It's okay," I protested weakly, realizing now why I had advanced my age.

"You've got skin like a baby. You sure you're twenty-one?"

I tried an experienced smile, but in that moment I could only manage to grin nervously. She pulled my shirt from me and dropped it to the floor, bolted the door and snapped out the light. Soon we were interlocked in a kind of passion I had never known before.

She left sometime during the night, but at least twelve hours passed before I sprang awake, in what seemed untrackable space, sweating a dream of the murdered youth, not knowing for several moments who I was or where I was. Then suddenly feeling the teeth marks on my neck and body, I remembered and fell back upon the bed. Sometime later my hand touched some bills that had been tucked under my pillow; they were the same bills I had paid toward my rent.

The money I had made at Pope's soon dwindled away. I returned to school after the beginning of the new year, but Jenny, who fed as well as housed me, made demands on the time I needed for study. I got to sleep late every night, but even then the noise of those gambling below kept me from getting my rest. School became an ordeal. I slept through most of the classes and very often I was sent to the principal's office for not having done my homework. Mr. Long, the principal, was short, pale and white-maned, with an awful temper toward anyone who didn't study. One morning he pounded his desk with his pallid fist and shouted, "You land in this office just one more time and you're expelled!" He meant it. It was either Jenny or school. I chose school.

Instead of going home that evening, I hurried through the February cold to the downtown section and tramped from place to place, asking for work.

It was nearly ten in the evening when I reached Jenny's, and I was cold, hungry and tired. She had been drinking, and when I entered she started complaining about my being late. The gambling room was crowded, but she kept pressing, demanding heatedly that I tell her where I had been. I chose this moment for a showdown. "Since when," I said, "do I have to tell you where I've been?"

Her reaction was quick and unexpected. She snatched a glass of whiskey from the table and splashed it into my face. Then, cursing at the top of her voice, she charged and began beating me with her fist. Half blinded by the liquor, I grappled with her for an instant, but her teeth cut into my arm, and I shoved her against the gambling table. She screamed, tottered, then fell to the floor. Then the little high-yellow man's fist smashed into my jaw and spun me into the wall. I ducked another blow, grabbed a chair and started swinging, trying to back my way out of the room. Jenny got up and aimed a whisky bottle at my head. The bottle missed me, but fragments of it struck my neck after it broke against the wall. "Momma! Momma!" Lottie was screaming. The high-yellow man was coming at me again, so I flung the chair in his direction, grabbed my books and ran through the hallway into the street.

Later at Jim's pool hall, disheveled and exhausted, I collapsed near my favorite radiator and welcomed the friendlier noise of the pool players and billiard balls.

My pulse eventually slowed down, and my jaw started to ache; but Mr. Long's warning still rang in my ear and I began thumbing my books for the next day's homework. At first the notations I had made in class seemed blurred, but after a while the letters and words began taking shape, and I studied until the pool hall closed. Again I rode the streetcars all night between St. Paul and Minneapolis; and I managed to complete my homework before leaving the trolley in St. Paul at dawn.

Walking across town toward school, I watched a flock of pigeons swoop down between the buildings; they twisted, turned and, as they shot upward, one struck the cornice of a building. Stunned, it fell to the snow just a few feet ahead of me. I bent over to pick up the bird, but a growl, coming from behind a truck, sent shivers up my spine and I drew back. A large dog, hunger showing at his ribs, was inching toward the bird. We eyed one another for a moment, each measuring the other's courage; then suddenly he lunged for the bird and I threw a book at him. He had managed to mouth the bird, but with the blow he yelped, dropped it and fled back into the street.

The pigeon was still, and its head fell to one side as I picked it up. The dog had broken its neck, and now he stood in the street, growling as I smoothed the ruffled feathers. I picked up my books, stuffed the pigeon into my pocket, then continued across town.

At a clearing near the school, I took the bird from my pocket and looked at it closely. It was dead, freshly killed, and I was hungry. I looked about for firewood and paper, and in less than an hour I had plucked the bird's feathers, gutted it with my knife, roasted and eaten it.

When I reached school, I went to the back of the building and pounded on the boiler room. The caretaker, a kindly man, let me in, and I curled up on a box in the corner and went to sleep watching him stoke the furnaces. He shook me awake about a half hour before my first class and offered me a biscuit and hot coffee.

"You ought to tell Mr. Long about your problems," he advised when I left.

"Why?"

"He might be able to help you," he answered.

I promised that I would, knowing all the while that a ridiculous pride would violate that promise.

Sometime during the third-period class, I began thinking about the morning's experience. The dog's needs had been the same as mine. We were both hungry. My stomach churned as the thought grew. And then, feeling the worst coming on, I bolted past Mrs. Ginsburg, my English teacher, and ran into the hallway, where I lost my breakfast.

FOUR

THE HARDER times became, the more determined I was to stay in school. The shelter from the cold was, perhaps, a considerable motive, and I loathed the bone-chilling and lonely weekends. I would drift through them, missing the desks, the musty gymnasium, the oil and sawdust odor of the floors, the inflexible voices of the teachers and the warm halls and classrooms. It seemed that Monday never came quickly enough. But there was more that compelled me to classes with such regularity. The necessity of learning came with the first pangs of hunger, with the first homeless night. It wasn't enough to trust to chance or street learning. Already I had been refused several jobs because I didn't have a high school education. Perhaps a diploma would deprive people of such excuses.

So I hung on, preying upon waste receptacles for newspapers that carried the daily ads. And I answered them. But it was always my "youth" or some other fabricated excuse that disqualified me. I hunted for the warm spots where there was light so that I could work on new lyrics and melodies; my ragged notebook was crammed with titles and ideas. And the futility of those days was so well reflected in those lyrics and songs my friends began to call

me "Blue." Every line in that notebook spoke of heart-
break and hard luck. But melancholy served me well at
times; twice I got one-night jobs at an after-hours joint
called Sperling's, where people with the blues didn't want
to hear anything but the blues. And at Sperling's, especially
during the late hours, a drunk, a dejected lover or even a
lonely stranger would empty his pockets when a tune
lamented his fate.

My sister got what small change and food she could to
me by a plan we worked out over the telephone. I would
slip in through the alleyway at night and whatever she had
she left in the milk box. Even when my brother-in-law was
away he had an effective spy system; so all my excursions
to the milk box were made well after dusk. My mother's
brothers, Charlie and Pete, lived somewhere in St. Paul.
Uncle Pete was a Pullman porter who ran to Chicago and
Seattle. He was a short, round, amiable man with a wall-
eye. I had only seen him once since I had been north. He
was running then to catch a streetcar. "Come by and see
me sometime," he had hollered, but I didn't have his
address. Uncle Charlie didn't work at anything. I saw him a
couple of times but he was too tipsy to recognize me. Each
time I had spoken, but he had smiled blandly and gone on
his way.

In time I became a master of self-exclusion. And it was a
lonely business. When my schoolmates asked me where I
went every night, I told them tales that made them envy
me. I had either met some glamorous woman with a big car,
or played the piano at a wealthy party, or met some
publisher from New York or Chicago. Unfortunately, the
lies were never justified by my appearance; yet I squan-
dered my dreams freely. They were my only possessions;
and I used them as a cover-up for my loneliness. But there

was one boy I never tried to fool. His name was George Berry. He was lean, tall and soft spoken, with a special kind of warmth and understanding. I trusted him with my desperation; and many times that awful winter he brought me to the warmth of his home. And every time I came his mother would ask, "Are you hungry, son?"

"Well—no, mam. I guess not," I would answer.

"You don't sound too sure, son. You'd better eat—just in case," she would answer. I would pretend not to hear, knowing she had already gone to fix me something. It was always the same.

FIVE

MARCH CAME and held at fifteen below for several days; then a warm front pushed in and brought relief. But a big snow followed. It started around eight one evening, and by the next morning the city was buried beneath its whiteness. Twenty-foot drifts blocked the highways. Stores and schools closed and nothing moved but snowplows and trolley cars. I borrowed a shovel from George and in two days I made over twenty-five dollars—enough to get a room for a month and a few meals. It was Friday when I moved into the rooming house, and I had bought a newspaper and gone to bed when I saw the ad. The Stumble Inn near Bemidji, Minnesota, wanted a piano player. The salary was eighteen dollars a week—and tips. The room and board were free and the hours from eight until two in the morning. I reasoned that I could stay in school with a job like that. I stood in the dimly lit room trying to decide. I had paid five dollars toward my rent, which I knew I couldn't get back. And it would mean leaving St. Paul. But the prospect of eating and sleeping regularly made it seem worthwhile. I got up, dressed, stuffed the paper in my pocket and hurried to the Western Union office.

My telegram naïvely advised that I would take the job and

they could expect me within two days. And at six the next morning I was at the outskirts of town trying to thumb a ride to Bemidji. Car after car passed; and I stamped about in the snow trying to kill the numbness in my feet. The cold wind rose and began to whip fright into me and I was ready to turn back when a big truck slid to a stop. I jumped up on the running board, but my hands were too cold to turn the handle. The driver leaned over and opened the door and I jumped up into the cab.

"Where you headin'?" His accent was Southern.

"Bemidji."

"You're lucky. Goin' within fifteen miles of it."

We rode the next few miles in silence. Now and then he would curse the drifts as we approached them, gun his motor and burst through, sending flurries in every direction. The silences were awkward and I finally told him I was glad that he had picked me up.

"It's okay," he drawled, " 'cause I git sleepy on long hauls. A little comp'ny keeps me goin'." Another drift was coming up. "Damn useless snow! I cain't see why people settle in ass-freezin' country like this anyhow. Cain't figger it out." We plowed through and snow shot high above the cab, blinding us for a moment or so—then the road was before us again.

I wanted to ask him where he came from, but he was a white Southerner and this might have led to some uncomfortable North-South talk. He had done me a big favor, and I was in no position to argue in case his views opposed mine—and I was sure they did. Then, as if he were clairvoyant, "I got a boy 'bout your size back in Florida, and I bet you a hound's tooth to a dollar he's lazyin' 'neath a orange tree in the back yard."

"He's lucky," I said.

"Maybe yes. Maybe no." I didn't know how to take

that, so I kept quiet, waiting, so that he might clarify himself. "He ain't exactly a good boy, and he ain't exactly a bad one. Main thing wrong is he's got a lot of screwed-up ideas."

"Like what?"

"Well, he got us into a peck of trouble 'bout a week ago. We ain't out of it yet. It's not that my wife and me is against you people, but there's a time and place for everything. Well, my boy he gives a birthday party last week, and right in the middle of it a nigra boy who he invited walks smack through the front door, and my boy starts feedin' him cake and ice cream. Well, you don't know the commotion it started."

"What happened?"

"One of my boy's pals called him a nigga, and my boy hit him for doin' it. His own friend, mind you. Now every white boy in town wants to beat up on him. He's got hisself in a peck of trouble. He should never done such a thing in the first place. You think so?"

"I don't know."

"Would your paw like it if you invited a white boy to your birthday party?"

"I never had a birthday party."

"But s'pose you did . . . you think he'd like it?"

"He wouldn't care one bit."

"How do you know if you never had a birthday party?"

"I just know my poppa, that's all."

"Well, what you are saying is my boy don't know me."

"I didn't say that."

We were silent for some time after that. His manner told me he was thinking deeply. "You ever sleep with a white girl, boy?"

"Did you ever sleep with a colored girl?"

"Yeh, I did. And it was good. Now how 'bout you?"

I stiffened and got ready to thumb the rest of the way to Bemidji. "Yessir, I have," I lied, "and it wasn't so good."

To my surprise he roared with laughter. "Just wait till my boy hears what you said. It'll kill him. By god, it'll kill him." He continued laughing for almost another mile. After that I went to sleep, deeply puzzled by his reaction.

Sometime later in the night he nudged me in the ribs. "I quit you here. Bemidji's about fifteen miles down the road. Market trucks'll be goin' in for the weekend. You oughta git a lift 'fore long."

I rubbed sleep from my eyes and peered out. The high-way marker, caught in the glare of the headlights, fixed my destination as exactly fifteen and a half miles. I thanked him and jumped down to the snowbank. As the truck roared off, I watched the whiteness swirl upward and around it, obscuring the only thing moving through the blackness. The sound of the motor gradually faded, and I turned and started down the road. The wind had died, but the temperature this far north was still far below zero. Past Kansas winters had taught me in such instances to keep moving, not too fast, not too slow—just enough, as my dad used to warn, to keep the blood running hot. A few market trucks did come along, but they didn't stop, and I made the whole distance on foot, reaching the outskirts a little after one o'clock in the morning. I saw a garage and stopped there to get warm.

The white garage keeper was kind. He gave me a cheese sandwich and three cups of coffee and, as I sat in the heat of his pot-bellied stove, I remarked that it was the same type as we had back in Kansas. He asked me where I was going, and I proudly mentioned the job I had come to take at Stumble Inn.

"When you starting?"

"Soon as I can find the place."

"Why, didn't you come down the main road?"

"That's right."

"Good Lord, fellow, you passed it about three and a half miles back." My expression must have been most lamentable, for he immediately asked me if I would like to sleep there until morning. Wearily I accepted. There were two bales of hay in the corner, and I collapsed on them. The garage keeper threw me a horse blanket. I covered myself with it and slept as soundly as I had ever slept in my life.

As far as the owner of Stumble Inn was concerned, I could have remained in the garage forever. When I knocked at his place the next morning, he came to the door in his long underwear. I had awakened him and he regarded me impatiently as I explained who I was. "Hell," he said, "that job's already taken." Then he slammed the door in my face.

I went back to town and looked about for work all day, without success. By eleven o'clock that night a blizzard raged. The streets were deserted. I went back to the garage, but it was closed. Through the driving snow I saw a lighted sign that said EAT. Already weak, I felt faint as I was pushed along by the strong gusts. I reached the door and went inside.

"What do you want?" the waitress asked.

"A cup of coffee," I said, then I collapsed on a stool. Three white men and a woman sat at a table alongside the wall. They had been drinking. "Well, ah declare!" one of the men said in a heavy Southern drawl. "Ah seen eva'thing now. A nigga eatin' in the very same place as white folks. Ain't nothin' gonna happen like that down where ah come from."

I ignored him. He went on. "Black bastards'll be wantin' to git in our beds next!"

Suddenly my control was gone. I grabbed my cup and

dashed the scalding coffee on him. He yelled. The woman next to him screamed. I began throwing sugar bowls, salt and pepper shakers, ketchup bottles, anything that I could get my hands on.

All at once the waitress shouted a warning, but it was too late. A chair knocked me unconscious. I came to while being hauled from the diner by two policemen. They took me to jail.

When they released me from jail the following morning, there was a soreness where the chair had struck my temple. The day was cold but clear, and I started walking toward the highway. As I passed the café, it appeared innocent of the violence that had erupted there only a few hours before. It was like passing a tombstone one had defaced, and I hurried on. Soon Bemidji and Stumble Inn were far behind me, and two hours later I was picked up by another trucker. Luck was with me. He was going all the way to St. Paul. It was easier to relax now, for I would be back in time for school on Monday morning, and I had a room— for at least the rest of the month.

As the truck bumped over the highway, I thought back over the fruitless journey. I couldn't understand that Southern truck driver. Had he picked me up out of kindness, or was he trying to expiate his feeling about Negroes? Why, after asking such a question, had he roared with laughter at my flippant answer? Was he trying to understand his own son through me, or maybe understand me through his son? I didn't know. It was impossible to judge him in terms of his actions. Then there were the garage man and the innkeeper, both white, but as different as summer and winter. Next, the other Southerner with whom I had fought in the café. He had obviously deserved his lumps. But had I handled that situation the way my mother would have wanted me to? No, she would have found some other way to defeat him and yet maintain her dignity and pride. But this man's tongue had hurt worse than a fist, and I had reacted out of an impulse fed by despair. My conscience told me that my actions were wrong, but my heart approved them. Momma used to say that strength came through prayer. I prayed these nights, but I was beginning to wonder about a God who would test me so severely.

I had come north to prove my worth, and I was discovering that there was a lot more to it than just the desire for recognition or success. The naïveté of youth, the frustrations of being black had me trapped, and achievement seemed almost impossible. It was becoming more and more difficult to live with the indifference, the hate, and at the same time endure the poverty. But even then I knew I couldn't go on feeling condemned because of my color. I made up my mind, there in the cab of that truck, that I wouldn't allow my life to be conditioned by what others thought or did, or give in to anyone who would have me be subservient. We rolled into St. Paul about three in the morning. The disappointing trip had left me tired and wounded; I was glad to be back.

Finally after a month, the snow was gone, and spring was over the land, but the memory of this first winter stayed with me. Yet, as I stood on a corner warming beneath the sun, I was glad I had stayed in school, and thankful that somewhere I had a family. My father, sisters and brothers were scattered, but at that moment they seemed as close to me as the poverty. I hadn't heard from any of them, but I felt that somewhere they were extending their hopes and love.

I could no longer consider myself just a boy. I knew that youth as it should be at seventeen was not for me, and that full manhood must come quickly if I was going to make it. There wasn't much good to extract from the memory of that never-to-be-forgotten winter. I had come out of it frightened and dispirited, stripped of nearly everything but hope.

SIX

SEVERAL THINGS happened that spring which would brighten the coming summer. Three older sisters—Lillian, Gladys, Cora—a brother Jack, and later my father came to live in St. Paul; I got a job as a bellboy evenings after school, at the Minnesota Club, an exclusive establishment for St. Paul's wealthier men; and I fell in love with Sally Alvis.

That March, Herbert Hoover, in his inaugural address, said that all Americans should be bright with hope, that we should have no fears for the future. And I began to think that my good fortune, as small as it was, somehow reflected his thinking. Now, happy at being part of a family again, of working and eating regularly, of tasting the indefinable warmth of a first love, I brightened considerably.

By this time Cora was divorced and working to support her two children. Lillian and Gladys were both married, with children. And Jack had just taken on a wife in Chicago. Poppa would stay with Lillian, and I would remain at the rooming house. I had gone with my sisters to the station to meet him the day he arrived, shrunken into himself, still grieving the death of my mother. He had lowered his chin and eyed me over the upper rims of his

47

spectacles. "Well, boy, how have things been going?" he asked. His manner and tone hadn't changed. It was as though he were inquiring about firewood for the night.

"Just fine, Poppa," I said, straightening, smiling, attempting to appear the embodiment of health and happiness.

"You're skinny as a jack rabbit. Been eatin' enough?"

I lied again and answered yes. I told Poppa about the new job I had, and he was very pleased. Then we all went to eat supper at Cora's.

The world inside the Minnesota Club was one of spacious rooms with high-beamed ceilings, of thick carpeting, of master and servant, of expensive wines and liquors, of elegant table settings and epicurean tastes. Influential men like Frank Kellogg, Justice Pierce Butler and Jim Hill of the Great Northern Railway sat about smoking long cigars and ornate pipes in the overstuffed high-back chairs of the mahogany-paneled library. And I, dressed in a suit of blue tails, white tie and striped red vest, would stand near them discreetly listening to their confidential talk of financial deals, court decisions, their wives and children, boats, politics, women, the Stock Exchange—and the weather. To most of them, I was invisible and unhearing, a sort of dark ectoplasm that only materialized when their fingers snapped for service. I used to stand at the door and take their coats; and the camel's hair and the velvet-collared chesterfields felt good to my callused hands. Their suits were well cut and well pressed, their oxfords and grained brogues discreetly shined. Their faces looked scrubbed; their hair was always neatly trimmed and smelled of barber's soap and bay rum.

In time I got to know all their mannerisms. The way Justice Kellogg's teeth clipped his cigars intrigued me. He measured and bit in one quick motion. And I, timing that motion perfectly, would have the match lit; then I would nearly gag from the smoke as he puffed away. And Justice Butler's slumping in one of the mammoth leather chairs, his legs crossed and stretched out, his chin resting on his clasped hands, was, I thought, a picture of grace.

There was always the aroma of good food. The great silver platters of roast pheasant, duck and guinea hen banked with wild rice, the huge buttered steaks, served on planks of wood and garnished with steaming vegetables, the spicy cakes, rum sauces, ices and creamy desserts kept my appetite at its peak. And after such dinners, when the great sitting room filled with pipe and cigar smoke, I went about serving little toasted cakes and brandy. I was never hungry during those days.

There was a lot an unlettered black boy from Kansas could learn here. And what I learned I tucked deep inside, determined meanwhile to put each lesson into use whenever I could. I began to read more, slipping newspapers, novels and books of poetry from the club library. And soon a whole new world was opening up, one that would have been impossible to imagine back in Kansas.

One day I heard Justice Butler complain to another member, "I'll be damned if I can remember his name. He wrote *Arrowsmith*." And, before the other man could reply, I gulped and said, "Pardon, sir—if you don't mind—it's Sinclair Lewis."

"Lewis. Sinclair Lewis, that's it." And he went on speaking, I thought, without ever realizing where the name had come from. But a few days later he handed me a small package. "It's for you," he said.

I tore off the paper. It was a first edition of Edith Wharton's *The Age of Innocence*, dating back to 1920. I thanked him warmly. That book would always have a very special meaning for me. And I told him so. The rest of that week I walked around school with it, showing it to my friends.

George Berry and Woodford Mills were in most of my classes, and they soon became my closest associates in most of the things young men do. A few weeks before Easter, the three of us went to Ben Myers' tailor shop to be measured for new suits. Our forest-green outfits were to be exactly alike, even down to the double-breasted vests that I had seen some of the club members wearing. The suits cost thirty-two dollars and fifty cents apiece. I was only making fifteen dollars a week. Each of us paid ten dollars down; Ben would get the rest when he caught up with us. Meanwhile we scraped up the rest of the accessories: brown-and-white spectator oxfords, striped stiff-bosomed shirts, green ties and gray snap-brim hats.

On Easter the three of us met at George's house, where we spent at least an hour before the mirror. Then Woodford quipped, "Come on, fellows, let's go up to Dale and Rondo and give the world a break." And it would have been impossible to convince us that we weren't doing just that, standing there in the bright Sabbath sun like three peacocks. Everything went well until Woodford's shoes began to pinch his toes. But he was determined not to give up; propping himself up against a building, he stood for nearly two hours on his heels trying to relieve the pressure. But finally his heels gave out, and George had to go fetch his father's Essex to haul Woodford home. He walked from the car to his door in his stocking feet, the rest of his day ruined.

That same evening, through a blind date George arranged, I met Sally. She had a dimpled smile on her pale beige face when he introduced us. I smiled back and said that I was very glad to meet her. She had soft black hair that swept back into a knot at the nape of her neck. Her dress was powder blue silk. We didn't talk much as George drove time and again around Lake Como, whispering softly to his girl. At first I thought Sally looked like Claudette Colbert; then, after she had let me move closer, I decided she was prettier. She lived in Minneapolis. After George's Essex had finally chugged to a stop in front of her house, we sat there, not knowing how to say goodnight. When the front door of her house opened, she said, "It's Mom. I'll have to go now." She pressed my hand gently, quickly, got out and ran up the steps. And from that moment on I was in love.

Most of the boys I got to know in Minnesota had never hunted, trapped, ridden horses, watered circus elephants, raided peach and apple orchards, fished for perch and catfish, gathered walnuts, gone on hayrides, swum naked in rivers or done any of the wonderful things I had. When I talked about persimmon and mulberry trees, it seemed as foreign to them as the twang of my Kansas voice. And since they didn't know about such things, I often entertained them with tales that stretched far beyond the truth.

"Come on, Blue," using the nickname they had given me, "tell us about the time you caught a bear in a skunk trap," they would plead. "Hey, Blue, did you ever fight any real Indians?"

"Hell," I'd counter, "I used to fight along beside them. They used to call me Chief Blackfoot." And, while the laughter was at its height, I would concoct a roaring tale to back up my lie.

Yet seldom, if ever, did I recall the tragedies. A boyhood

friend of mine, Cleo Anderson, had gotten his leg cut off beneath a freight we used to hop back in Kansas. I remembered he had not cried as he lay alongside the track looking crazily at his amputated limb, that the accident never changed his wonderfully funny ways; it was as though the misfortune had not befallen him. But such truths were not for entertainment.

The Minnesota boys smoked, drank, shot pool, played cards—and even drove automobiles—things I had never attempted back in Kansas. No boy in our family had smoked until he had moved away and started a family of his own. Even then, when Momma was around, they stuck their pipes away. A cigarette was out of the question, at any age. Only Poppa was allowed a half pint of sweet wine once a year. "It's to wash out any evil that's got into your Poppa's soul," Momma used to say. Pool and cards were strictly for sinners. No self-respecting Christian would be caught playing such games.

Neither were these new friends as militant as we back there had been. The lack of racial conflict here made the difference. Minnesota Negroes were given more, so they had less to fight for. Negro and white boys fought now and then in the Twin Cities, but the fights never amounted to much. Some Negro boys dated white girls without any major outcry. The most resentment came from Negro girls who refused dates to anyone "slipping out with Paddy girls." The Negro boys indulged, now and then, in a sort of satiric gallantry. One night a white man approached a group of us at the corner of Dale and Rondo, our favorite hangout. He quietly asked us where he might find a nice-looking colored girl.

We all looked at each other solemnly for a few seconds, then Leroy Lazenberry, a tall, bespectacled boy, shook his head regretfully. "Well, sir," he said with disappointment in his voice, "we're terribly sorry, but we just don't know where to find you any colored girls"—a long regretful pause and more shaking of the head. "But I tell you," he went on, his face brightening up (the man suddenly more hopeful), "we know where we can get you several nice-looking white girls—without any trouble." The man flushed and took off hurriedly without another word. And we, our insides nearly bursting, could hardly wait until he was gone before breaking into laughter.

We weren't subtle with restaurants that used to burn our hamburgers, oversalt them and serve our drinks in unwashed glasses. The White Castle chain was probably the most notorious for this; but after ten of us dumped our sandwiches on the floor one night and doused them with water, the practice stopped, at least at that restaurant.

There were exceptions, but Minnesota Negroes seemed apathetic about the lynching, burning and murdering of black people in the South. The tragedy taking place down there might just as well have been on another planet. And they didn't press vigorously for rights in their own communities.

Until the late 1920's only one Negro, Bob Marshall, had played on the university football team. The thought of one playing in the backfield seemed impossible—the white boys just wouldn't block for him, everyone said. This seemed odd when white boys were already blocking for Negro boys on many high school gridirons in the state. What, I wondered, happened to the white linemen's attitudes in the three months between high school and college? And, though Negro boys played high school basketball throughout the state, and an iron-clad Big Ten rule prohibited their making the Minnesota varsity, scattered grumblings were the only protests.

One Negro newspaper existed, the *Minneapolis Spokes-*

man–St. Paul Recorder. It had a small voice and a small
Negro circulation. Its publisher, Cecil Newman, was as
militant as the climate would allow—but the climate wasn't
allowing much. My young friends didn't talk about these
conditions very often. They seemed at times content with
their lot. Or perhaps they were just awaiting the right
voice or situation to jolt them into action. Even I, who
only a few months before had faced starvation, had all but
forgotten the frightful winter. Contentment was the word
now, in the pleasant summer of 1929.

June burned into July. And July burned into August.
By September I had saved a little money, received a
two-dollar raise and fallen deeper in love; and on the ninth
day of that same month I enrolled at Central High School.
Working evenings and weekends at the club, I overheard
talk of Hoover, A. T. & T., General Motors, U.S. Steel,
General Electric, the Federal Reserve Bank and other such
names. And, though I didn't know what the conversations
really meant, I sensed a certain optimism in them.

On the fifteenth of October, I asked Sally if she would
marry me. She only blushed, laughed and explained,
"Why . . . I must finish high school before thinking
about such things." I felt a little crushed; but she hadn't
refused outright. Furthermore, common sense warned me
to finish high school too, before taking on a wife. I opened
a savings account, anticipating the day, a year later, when
we both would graduate.

The employees' locker room at the club was unusually
quiet when I arrived at work one Wednesday that same
month. Waiters who had known each other for years were
sitting about as though they were strangers. The cause for
silence was tacked to the bulletin board. It read: "Because
of unforeseen circumstances, some personnel will be laid

off the first of next month. Those directly affected will be notified in due time. The management."

"That Hoover's ruining the country," an old waiter finally said. No one answered him. I changed into my suit of blue tails, wondering what had happened. By Thursday the entire world knew. "Market Crashes—Panic Hits Nation!" one headline blared. The newspapers were full of it, and I read everything I could get my hands on, gathering in the full meaning of such terms as Black Thursday, deflation and depression. I couldn't imagine such financial disaster touching my small world; it surely concerned only the rich. But by the first week of November I too knew differently; along with millions of others across the nation, I was without a job. All that next week I searched for any kind of work that would prevent my leaving school. Again it was, "We're firing, not hiring." "Sorry, sonny, nothing doing here." Finally, on the seventh of November I went to school and cleaned out my locker, knowing it was impossible to stay on. A piercing chill was in the air as I walked back to the rooming house. The hawk had come. I could already feel his wings shadowing me.

SEVEN

BY MID-DECEMBER Hoover's promises were meaningless and hard times had settled in. My kinfolk had, like many others, lost their jobs and their credit. They were just hanging on. I had given up my room on my birthday, owing a month's rent, promising my landlady I would eventually pay. Now the days would be spent searching for work and going from one relative to another to sleep or, if there was enough food, to eat. Gladys' husband was keeping his family going by shining shoes. Cora cooked and sewed to feed her two children. Lillian's husband was finding it rough as a part-time waiter. My brother Jack, also a waiter, found himself the sole provider for his new wife's family. And now, at seventy, Poppa was the fading image of the man I had known as a child.

One chill morning I saw him sitting on a tree stump at the edge of a vacant lot, leaning forward, his hands clasped, looking into space. I approached him slowly, sensing his loneliness and thinking that so little time remained for him. His old felt hat was pushed back on his head. His eyes were watery from the cold and his spectacles, pushed down to the flat of his nose, were frosted over from his breath. His mustache, mixed now with gray, swooped down like oxen's tusks.

"How are you?" I said as he looked up toward me.
"Why, howdy, sir. Cold mornin' I'd say. Cold mornin'."
I was embarrassed for him. He hadn't recognized me.
"It's me, Poppa," I said before he could go on. And he
ducked his chin in that marvelous way of his and looked at
me over the top of his glasses. "Well, I declare, I must be
going blind," he said with a chuckle.

"Why are you out here in the cold like this?" I asked,
questioning an act of his for the very first time in my life.
He didn't answer until he had struck a match and lit his
pipe. "Well, boy, I was just sittin' here thinkin' back over
the years a bit." I remained silent, braced myself against the
cold and squatted down beside him, hoping he would go on
talking. We had never confided on such terms. He went
on. "Maybe I'm just an old man sittin' out my last days in a
place where I don't fit." He paused for about a minute. "I
hope I'm buried someday near the potato patches and corn
rows we used to plow in the spring. Maybe that's why I
won't sell the place."

"Aren't you happy here, Poppa?"
"It ain't the same without your mother."
"I miss her too."
"She was a good woman."
"Do you think she was right about my coming here?" I
was remembering the first winter, the hunger and frustra-
tion and the cold highway to Bemidji.

He took several puffs and stroked his mustache. "Cain't
rightly say, boy. She had a way of lookin' far ahead. She
was always pretty much right about things. Best you can
do is remember her teachin'. That's about all. You cain't
help but come out all right." He was quiet after that, lapsed
back into his old silence. I didn't push him, for in those few
moments there was more understanding between us than
there had been in our whole lifetime. I started to touch his

shoulder when I got up to go, but at the last instant I
shoved my hands into my pockets.

"You had better go in, Poppa. It's awful cold out here."

"My bones are too old for freezin'. You take care and
keep out of trouble. There's plenty of it up this way
too."

As there had been no turkey for Thanksgiving, there
was no good cheer or presents for Christmas. The new year
only rang in more snow and icy wind. During the last week
in January I decided, for some inexplicable reason, to try
my luck in Chicago. I had no idea of how I would get
there. That same weekend I met a trumpet player named
Jess Turner. Soft-spoken, tall and consumptive-looking, he
was stranded with an orchestra and wanted to get back to
Chicago to his wife and children. We were standing by my
favorite radiator in Jim Williams' pool hall trying to think
of some way to make the trip, knowing neither of us had
the necessary cash. It was Jess who finally thought of
hopping a freight. "With luck we'd make it in about two
days," he said.

"It would be awful cold."

"We'll wait till it warms a little."

We waited for nearly a week but the warmer weather
never came. So, according to plan, Jess and I met at Dale
and Rondo at six o'clock one Monday morning and took a
trolley for the freight yards. The same cardboard suitcase I
had brought from Kansas was filled with a few clothes, an
army blanket and several bologna sandwiches my sister
Cora had fixed for me; and I had two dollars. The weather
was well below zero, and I pulled on three layers of long
underwear, two pairs of wool socks and overshoes. Jess's
landlady had held his clothing for unpaid rent, and he was
poorly dressed for such weather in a chesterfield overcoat,
a thin suit and patent leather shoes. He had no gloves and

carried only his trumpet case. I was concerned for him and told him so, but the cold tight-fisted ways of Minnesota had numbed him into an almost suicidal indifference. He seemed to ignore the unmercifully cold wind as it pushed us along after we reached the freight yard.

"I wouldn't try it, Jess," I warned again.

"I've got to git back to my kids and wife. I ain't seen them in over three months. I'm more worried about them than this damned cold." The determination in his voice made any further warning futile. We wandered about the yard for nearly an hour, ducking railway police, searching for boxcars marked for the East. It was a hobo who finally helped us. He sensed our plight the moment he spotted us.

"Where you headin'?" he whispered as we climbed over a car coupling.

"Chi," Jess answered quickly.

"You're in the right lane. Just lay low for a spell. We'll board soon as they hook onto that line a couple of tracks over," he said.

"Why can't we get on now?" I asked.

"The yard dicks are still checkin'. Better wait a spell like I say." He motioned us down beside him in the snow beneath a flat car. "Keep low—out of sight."

We crouched and waited. Jess was already gray from the cold. But the hobo was right. In less than ten minutes a big yard cop, dressed in a red mackinaw, climbed into the car we would take and looked about. A club was in his hand. He swung down, slid the door shut and continued on his way. "They'll be hookin' on now. Then we'll run for it. Damn glad he didn't seal her up." I was beginning to respect this hobo. There was a banging in the distance. The cars on the next track lurched backward, shaking off the loose snow, then stopped.

Jess and I eyed the hobo nervously. He was getting to his

feet and motioning us up with him. "Take it easy," he whispered. He stuck his head around a boxcar, observed the tracks from both directions and signaled us. "Come on. Make it snappy." We scurried across, slid the door open and scrambled up and in. Then the hobo eased the door shut.

There was very little space inside the car. Large wooden crates marked for a dye factory in Philadelphia took up most of the room. The hobo, who gave his name as Joe, pushed against them. "Better be sure none of this stuff shifts on the turns. We'd be smashed like potatoes." Jess and I put down our belongings and started pushing. The thought of being caught under such weight was frightening. "Don't worry. It's solid," Joe said. Then the three of us settled down in a space suitable for four men and sat waiting. Joe was leathered from the cold. Overalls padded with newspaper stuck from beneath his worn army coat, and his feet were wrapped in pieces of old blanket. He hadn't shaved in weeks and resembled a dirty Santa Claus with the gray-matted hair flowing down to his neck from under a red-and-black stocking cap. His breath smelled of alcohol in the closeness. But I was glad to have him with us. At last the train jerked forward and we were on our way, and I took out my blanket and offered it to Jess.

Hour by freezing hour we rattled over the countryside and only the quiet of my mind, braced against the noise and incredible cold, assured me of reality. All the problems of the world seemed to be contracted into this small and impersonal space. We were three shivering strangers, sharing our gloom in terms of chance and hard times. Now and then the freight slowed to a stop. But, before we could adjust our ears to the silence, a passenger train would roar past and the freight, having paid its respect to luxury and speed, would rattle off on another leg of our journey. When I got hungry I took out the sandwiches and we ate. Joe pulled out a bottle of cheap red wine, and we washed down the food with it.

Sometime during the first night we hit an area of paralyzing cold, and although the three of us were huddled beneath the blanket, I felt a stiffness in my legs and arms. Jess, I knew, had to be freezing, but he lay there all night, his head on his trumpet case, without complaining.

The trouble came the next morning when we decided to stand for a stretch. Joe and I got to our feet but Jess could only move from his waist up. He kept pinching his legs and thighs, saying he felt like a rock. We pulled him to his feet but he began to totter. We tried to make him take a step but he couldn't move. Joe felt his lower limbs. "This ain't good," he said. "Your friend's got a bad frostbite. Better lay him back down."

After he was on the floor I doubled the blanket around his legs and started to rub them briskly, hoping to return the circulation. "Better not do that—his skin's likely to rub off in that condition," Joe warned. "We'll fix him up at the next stop. Better pray there's snow wherever we pull up." I prayed. And about an hour later, after we had stopped, Joe and I hopped out, filled the blanket with snow, and got back into the car.

"Pull his pants and shoes off," Joe said.

"What for?" I asked.

"Do as I say if you wanta save him." He was packing the snow into a solid form.

"Okay with you, Jess?" I asked.

"It's okay. I don't feel nothin' anyway."

I pulled off his shoes and pants, and we placed the blanket of snow beneath him up to his waist. Then, scooping up the loose snow, Joe covered the top of his legs with it and secured the blanket. "That oughta thaw him out slow," Joe explained. "If he ain't better by afternoon you're gonna have to git him off here and to a hospital someway."

"How do you feel, Jess?" I asked.

"I don't feel," he answered bluntly.

"You will after a spell," Joe assured him. "Now I'm gonna git some more sleep."

The morning seemed endless. I thought of Sally and the uncertain hours stretching ahead. Depressed and disillusioned, I had left without seeing her. There was only a hastily scribbled note mailed saying I would be out of town for a few weeks. I could give no address but I would write, I promised. Now, lying between two men in the odor of wine and filth, I thought back to the warm breezes of summer that had played at her soft hair, the long walks by the lakes, the smell of meadow and her delicately scented skin, the promises and the tender moments of our love.

Why was I running? It was as if I were trying to escape hardship by stumbling backward into an even worse fate. Yet whatever my mother had hoped for me was still far out in the crooked distance. I wouldn't forget the afternoon when she trudged into the yard weary and sick, her gingham skirts trailing dust, the fire and spirit gone, a market basket under one arm and a blood-flecked handkerchief at her mouth. I had helped her into the house and into a chair. "What's the matter, Momma? What's the matter?" I kept demanding as tears clouded my sight. We were alone. I sat at her feet sensing that our world together was ending. I could feel it. The very nature of her silence said so.

"I'm going to ask Maggie Lee to take you back north with her. And I want you to mind her and go to church like you was brought up to do." The handkerchief was completely red now. "It's a better world up there in the North—color won't work so hard against you." There was a long pause. "Do right and don't get in trouble, and make a good man of yourself." I was trying to remember every word, not realizing how soon I would be needing them. "You better go to the field and look for your father. I'm awful tired."

When I returned with Poppa, she was lying on the floor unconscious. A few weeks later she came to long enough to mutter a prayer over me. Then my brother Clem told me to go to bed. Early the next morning I was awakened and told that Momma was dead. Now the fear I had shaken off such a short time before had caught up. And it lay beside me, gloating over the intensity of my shivering.

When Jess began to stir I shook Joe awake. But soon the quiet that Jess had held during the night was replaced with agonized cries that went on for several hours. "You got to git him off," Joe said at last. "It's too bad—we oughta be near Chi by now."

"I'll make it in. Don't put me off out here. Take me on to Chicago," Jess pleaded through his groans.

"But I'll get an ambulance at the next stop. They'll take you to a hospital," I said—not knowing if what I was saying was true or not.

"No. Get me home; I've gotta see my wife and kids."

I decided to let him have his way. Joe agreed and we settled in for another miserable night. We reached the Chicago freight yards early the next morning. A sparse scattering of snow whitened the area but it was nothing like Minnesota. After the train had stopped I jumped out and ran across to a signal tower for help. The man inside listened to my story rather unsympathetically, then said he had work to do and couldn't be bothered with frozen bums. But I persisted until he telephoned the yard master. In about an hour they brought an ambulance to the edge of the tracks and brought out a stretcher to take Jess away. I asked to go along in the ambulance but the driver refused me. "You'd best git the hell our of here before they take you to the lockup," he warned. They gave Jess an injection, wrapped him in dry blankets and hauled him off. I went as far as the ambulance.

"So long, Jess," I said.

"So long, kid," he said as they lifted him into the ambulance.

When I got back to the boxcar, Joe was gone and so were my blanket and bag. The morning was cold and blustery, and I walked toward the skyscrapers I saw in the distance, staying close to the buildings to avoid the thrusts of cold air that swept the wide streets. I wound up on Wacker Drive and continued along the river toward Michigan Avenue. There the gales of the lake turned me about and I sought shelter in the lobby of a large building. And this was to be my tactic the rest of the morning until the chill began to leave my body. That night I found a flophouse on lower Wabash Avenue called the Hotel Southland. Rooms were advertised for twenty-five cents and up. The two dollars I had would provide eight nights of shelter. A young clerk with a badly pimpled face was on the desk. He eyed me curiously and in a very nervous voice asked me what I wanted.

"A twenty-five-cent room," I answered.

He looked at me as though I were about to draw a gun

on him. "I'm not supposed to take colored in here. I'm
sorry. It's the boss's rule, not mine. You understand, don't
you?"

"No, I don't understand. It's damn cold out there, and
I've got a quarter to pay for a bed." I glanced about the
dirty, smoke-filled lobby, at the despondent and broken
men sitting and lying about on the floor.

"Why don't you try the colored section out on the south
side of town?"

"Because I want work downtown here and I don't have
carfare back and forth."

"You're looking for work? Just a minute, maybe I can
do something for you." He disappeared behind a ragged
velvet drapery into an inner room. After a few minutes he
reappeared with a tall fat man named John. He chewed on
a cigar butt and tobacco juice coursed down his bulbous
chin. "Mike tells me you're looking for a room and work.
That so?" he asked, squinting down through the smoke at
me.

"That's right."

"You look like a clean-cut colored boy."

"I'm a boy. I don't know what my color's got to do with
it."

"Don't go gittin' your dander up. I think I got a proposition for you." I waited. "How'd you like to have a room
and a job both?"

"Where?"

"Right here. I'm needin' a boy to clean this place. You'll
git a room in the back and a half a buck a day."

Fifty cents a day would hardly keep me in food, and a
back room in such a flophouse would be pretty bad, I
thought. "Why don't you take it?" Mike urged. "At least
you'll be out of the cold and have a place to sleep."

"I'd like to know why I can't just pay and sleep here?"

"Look, I ain't no expert on race problems," the fat man said impatiently. "I'm just givin' you a proposition. Whyn't you try it and see how things work out?"

"Give me twenty-five cents more a day and some food."

"Hell, fellow, you'll be makin' a buck a day with all that. That's big dough round these parts."

"Sorry," I said turning as if I were going.

"Just a second." I had bluffed him into a decision. "Okay, I'll try it your way. Six bits a day and some grub." He threw up his hands and went back through the curtain.

"You shoulda held out for two bits more. He'd a paid it. This joint's dirty as hell—ain't been swept for a week," Mike whispered. He led me through the tangle of ill-smelling men and up to a tiny unheated room on the third floor. There was an army cot with a blanket on it and, like the other rooms in the place, it was separated from the hallway by meshed wire. The rooms resembled rows of chicken coops and had padlocks on their wobbly doors. They looked more like cages. As we walked along, I noticed that they were dark, the only light being from the bare bulbs in the corridors. And they were partitioned off from one another by thin plywood. The haggard men stared out from them evilly, reminding me of trapped animals. And after Mike left I stretched out on the cot, listening to their hawking and spitting and their snarling, incoherent voices until I went to sleep.

EIGHT

WHEN JOHN awakened me at seven the next morning, an awful stench was in the place. Because of the cold I had slept in my clothes so I didn't have to dress. He led me to a hall closet, which was larger than my room; it was cluttered with rags, brooms, buckets and dustpans. There was Lysol for the toilets and a bin of sawdust for sweeping the floor. When I asked him about food he said the kitchen would be open at eight but that I should have all the corridors cleaned by then. After a breakfast of an oily, nondescript soup and stale bread, I went up to clean the rooms and toilets. And I instantly learned that poverty in the big cities festered a special kind of filth.

Some of the men were up and moving about. Others still slept. Several of them had ignored the toilets and defecated upon the floor. One drunk lay face down in his own vomit and another, claiming to have been beaten and robbed during the night, lay groaning in his bed, his blanket matted with blood. The toilets were filthy beyond use. Our hog pens back in Kansas were antiseptic by comparison. Without doubt the Hotel Southland was the vilest piece of real estate in the entire city of Chicago. Cleaning the place was hard, but it was the washing of spittoons covered with slime and tobacco juice that made the work even more unpleasant. Plowing was backbreaking but it was much cleaner. The freshly turned soil had been cool and soothing to my bare feet. Keeping the plow straight in the furrows brought clean sweat. And there had been something wholesome about driving Charlie, our plow horse, the length of a field without stopping to rest.

But the Hotel Southland was a bad breath of smoke, alcohol, sour bodies and human excrement. Its pickpockets, alcoholics, bums, addicts, perverts, panhandlers and thugs were of the lowest order. They spoke with an intolerable vulgarity that was catching. Soon I was saying things of which I was ashamed. But it was the only way, I thought, to hold my own here, where profanity meant prestige and politeness invited abuse.

"Good morning," I said to a drunk on the third day.

"What's good about it, you black son-of-a-bitch?" he growled back.

I froze in anger, wanting to hit him, disgusted with myself for not having an equally ungracious reply. He stumbled on down the hall, urinating in his pants as he went, unaware of the emotions he had aroused in me.

Minutes later a scream spun me about. The same drunk, seized now with violent delirium, was trying to scale the wire partition. "Snakes!" he screamed. "They're all over the place!" He grabbed at his legs, neck and thighs as if they were biting him. "Snakes!" His screams must have only multiplied their numbers, for he gradually slipped down to the floor, shrieking and exhausted. And I imagined them curling over and under him as he lay quivering in silence. Several men came out and staggered toward his body, that twisted and contracted under the imaginary reptiles. They would help him, I thought. But instead one kicked him in the back; one searched his pockets for money;

one stuck a burning cigarette to his leg—he only flinched
—and another clamped a spittoon on his head. The slime and
tobacco juice, mixed with the viscous sweat of his halluci-
nation, soaked his hair, face and neck. Then the men joined
hands and danced weirdly around him to a drunken chant
of "He's a jolly good fellow." The man was hemorrhaging
from his mouth and nose and his eyes had frozen to a stare;
I was afraid he was dying. But after a while he came to and
pushed off the spittoon. He tried to stand but their feet
pushed him back down and he lay there cringing beneath
their mocking dance. He looked up to me, his hand extended, pleading for help. I stood there with a broom in my
hand, observing him, remembering that a few minutes
before he had called me a black son-of-a-bitch. The moment was mine and all I could bring to it was revenge. I
smiled at him scornfully and backed away. The others gave
him a final kick and staggered off to their cages, and
eventually he crawled away on his hands and knees.

This strange, indecent ritual had taught me that degrada-
tion was no respecter of color: the truth of the lesson fell
triphammer hard. And in a wordless way I felt exalted,
reassured—knowing that I would never sink to such a
depth. After it was quiet again I began sweeping up the
mess; and it was like clearing away the remnants of a
decayed animal.

Big John was tight the first Saturday I went into his
office for my pay. He was passing out cigars and corn
whiskey to Mike and a policeman who had stopped in to
get warm. His generosity, I learned, was seeded with the
joy of his wife's pregnancy. And the nature of his talk
swelled with adulterous boasting. "I'm fifty and I can still
hump four chicks a day. Not one, mind you, but four—
five if I'm pushed to it—'cause I take care of myself."

The cop's coat was open, and his winter underwear

needed washing. He didn't seem to be listening. He chewed the cigar and sipped the whiskey without taking his eyes from the floor. Mike, on the other hand, hung on to every word his boss uttered. Maybe he was thinking about his girl. But either the whiskey or the cigar—or maybe the talk—was turning him paler by the minute.

"And I don't mean git'n on and blow'n off like a schoolboy. I mean stay'n with it for a hour or so if I'm goin' good." His red eyes turned toward me. "How much you got coming, boy?" he said frowning.

"Four-fifty. You owe me for six days." I wanted to get out for the weekend and I tried to show my impatience by pretending to ignore his boasting. Now he ignored me.

"When's the last time you got a piece, Mike?" The younger man, seeming disturbed by the question, fidgeted the cigar and gulped down the last of his whiskey.

Big John persisted. "Come on, tell us. When'd you git your last piece?" A fiendish grin played around his jowls, and Mike's bad complexion was turning an ashen purple. His thin lips were almost colorless.

"I'm sick," he gulped and ran out the door.

Big John roared with laughter. "Sick, he says, sick. Hell, he ain't sick—he's a goddamned fruit. He likes boys—specially sailor boys—that's what he likes. He's a goddamned punk." Now he doubled in laughter and still laughing he pulled open a drawer and took out a half dollar and four greasy bills and tossed them at me. The cop's expression hadn't changed. He continued chewing the cigar, sipping the whiskey and gazing at the floor. I pocketed the money and fled the derisive laughter, the smoke and the smell of dirty bodies.

So Mike was a "fruit." What a hell of a place for him to work, I thought.

It was only five o'clock, and since I hadn't been to the south side I decided to go there for the evening. As I rounded the corner toward the elevated train a Negro youth stopped me. His car, he said, had stalled and he wanted me to help him push it to an incline several feet away. "Once I get rolling it'll start up," he said. We both pushed and near the incline he jumped in and behind the wheel. The car bucked a few times, coughed and started up, and I was turning to go when a man ran from a store hollering, "Police! Police! They're stealing my car!" I wanted to run but several men grabbed me and held me until the police came. They caught the thief two blocks away, and, luckily for me, the cop who had been drinking with Big John ran up. I told him what had happened; he believed me and let me go. They took the real thief to jail and I changed my mind about the south side and went to a movie instead.

I stayed on at the Southland until the end of January, hating each day. It was a harsh and ugly time, and I earmarked every penny I saved for a coach ticket back to St. Paul, longing for the time when I could get into a tub of hot water and soak out the smell of the place.

One morning I awoke to a commotion down on the second floor. And when I moved to the staircase to look down, a man ran up and past me toward my room. Several policemen were running about brandishing their guns. They had subdued two men, who lay handcuffed on the floor, and were searching for the one who had run past me. The men, I found out later, had been involved in a holdup. Big John was with the police, helping to search the cages, and after a few seconds they stormed up toward me.

"Anybody come up this way, boy?" I pointed in the direction the man had gone, realizing that he was hiding either in the toilet or in my room. The outer door was locked and the other cages were occupied so he couldn't have escaped. They found him under my bed, pulled him out, beat him and dragged him downstairs.

Three days later I found a pistol beneath my bed. The holdup man had obviously left it there. I knew I should have turned it in immediately; my conscience and better judgment told me so. But there was something appealing about having a gun in this place; it could be a protection against the place itself. And the longer I held on to the pistol, the harder it was to part with it. Each night, after the lights were dimmed, I took it out and fondled it, admiring its shape and power.

The trouble came one Saturday when I went to collect my pay from Big John. As on every Saturday he was drunk and boasting of his sexual prowess. Mike was there and a couple of drunks were stretched out on the floor, their backs propped against the wall. Big John was puffing about, his belly shaking up and down. Deep belligerent lines coursed from his sullen mouth to his chin. I sensed trouble the moment I asked for my wages.

"Git outa here, you black bastard! Don't you see I'm busy!" he shouted, doubling his fist as if he would hit me.

Everything blurred and my body shook with rage. I looked around for something to hit him with in case I had to fight. He was too big to take on otherwise. There was nothing but his battered typewriter and frayed ledger in which he kept records. A half-filled whiskey bottle was in his left hand, and he looked as if he might hit me with it. I knew I should have backed away but my temper was out of control and I foolishly challenged him. "Give me my money, you lousy dog! I'm quitting!" He charged me like a bull, pummeled my face and body, slammed me into the wall and kneed me to the floor. Pain streaked through my groin but I managed to slide from beneath his kicking and scramble out the door.

"You black son-of-a-bitch, you won't git a cent now! Turn in your lock and git the hell out of here before I kill you!"

"Kill you kill you kill you"—the thought burned into my mind all the way up the stairs. My lip was cut, my nose bled and my groin felt as if it were on fire. I ran cold water over my wrists, arms and head; and though the bleeding stopped my anger continued to rise. I had saved sixteen dollars that was in a money belt I had sewn together. When I lifted the mattress to retrieve it, I saw the gun. I buckled the belt around my waist and shoved the gun into my overcoat pocket. Then I walked determinedly down the stairs.

Mike was at the outer desk when I reached the office. "You'd better get out fast," he warned me; "he's half crazy. Come back tomorrow—he'll forget all about it."

I pulled out the pistol and pointed it at him from a low angle. "I won't come back tomorrow and I won't forget what he did to me in there. Now you go in there and get my money out of his drawer—and make it snappy," I ordered. My anger had carried me too far but I couldn't stop now. Mike started to raise his hands but I told him to keep them down. "This ain't a holdup. I just want what's coming to me." He turned quietly and went through the curtain, with me following close behind. Big John was seated now and he began shaking when he saw the gun pointing at his heart. I didn't know whether he shook from rage or from fear. And I didn't want to shoot, but the choice lay with him—if he charged me I would pull the trigger. I had made up my mind, knowing it would be fatal if he overpowered me again. In his mood he wouldn't have hesitated to kill me.

"Give me that gun, boy," he growled, "or I'll take it away from you."

"You try, and see what happens." The two drunks lay unmoving on the floor as if nothing unusual were happening. "Go ahead, Mike. Get my money out of that drawer." He looked appealingly to Big John, who grudgingly nodded his consent, and Mike, in his nervousness, gave me an extra dollar. I put it in my pocket and Big John sat smoldering, his hand inching toward the whiskey bottle on his desk. But I snatched it from his reach, emptied the contents into a glass and splashed it into his eyes—blinding him momentarily. He tried to rise but I knocked him sideways with the butt of the pistol. He tried to get up again but I swung viciously, catching him on the temple, and he collapsed in a heap on the floor. I ran from the building and kept running toward the Union Station, expecting any minute to hear a police siren; but none sounded. Halfway across the river bridge I slowed down and looked in all directions. No one was watching and I pitched the gun sideways into the water, then hurried on to the station. Inside I pulled the coat up around my neck to hide the bloody shirt and went to the washroom.

"Gordon?" The voice was frightening, familiar and friendly, and I turned toward it, filled with apprehension.

"Uncle Pete," I said in a half cry.

"My God, boy, what's happened to you?" He was dressed in a Pullman porter's uniform, ready to make his run back to St. Paul and on to Seattle. "What's all that blood doing on your shirt like that?" He had recognized me and followed me to the washroom.

"I've got to get out of here. I'm in some serious trouble."
My uncle, suddenly involved in a peril of his sister's
youngest child, reacted swiftly. "Button up and come with
me. You can tell me the rest later." He took me up to his
Pullman car, put me into an empty compartment and went
out to receive his passengers. It was like an eternity before
the conductor hollered, "All aboard." Then at last the train
was rolling. And a feeling of safety grew with every click
of the train's wheels as I relaxed in the comfort of the plush
compartment. Momentarily my mind reached back through
the trauma of Lysol, sweat, filth, cursing, drunkenness,
savagery and perversion, and I welcomed the distance between me and the Hotel Southland. There was a knock at
the door and, thinking it was my uncle, I opened it. It was
the conductor and he was smiling. "Don't worry," he said;
"everything's okay. Your uncle went to get food for you.
Just take it easy—everything's okay."

"You're lucky to be alive," Uncle Pete said after I had
eaten and spilled out my story. He made down a bed for
me and I washed, changed and crawled into the clean
softness of it, thinking that I would like to lie there forever.
Tonight there would be no inhuman voices coming from
the corridor, and there would be no ominous morning to
awaken to. In minutes I was deep in a dreamless sleep.

NINE

MY UNCLE got me up about an hour out of St. Paul the next morning and fed me ham, eggs and fried potatoes. He admitted he was a little ashamed for not having inquired of me since Momma's death. I had almost forgotten his being at the funeral until he mentioned Charlie, my mother's younger brother, whom he had bawled out for getting drunk before the burial. "Charlie's got bad blood," he said as he pushed the berth back into the ceiling. "I hope you don't take after him. Every time I see him he's liquored up. I don't know what's going to become of him. Nothing good, I suspect."

I didn't answer. It didn't make any difference to me that Charlie drank. Back in Kansas he was always smiling and telling funny jokes. His whiskey seemed to brew good cheer and he made me think of Christmas. Uncle Pete, on the other hand, always seemed heavy with gloom.

"Do you ever see him—your Uncle Charlie?"

"Once in a while, on the street or someplace."

"You're probably better off for that," he mumbled.

He fed me with fresh fruit, milk and advice: "Get yourself a job and stay out of Chicago. It's too big for you. And get back in school as fast as you can. I'm going on through to Seattle but you come to see me when I get back."

"Yessir," I said, sopping my plate. I didn't know how to thank him and suspected he didn't want me to try. He gave me twenty-five dollars before I got off and I promised to enroll in school the following week, and to stay out of Chicago. I was richer, rested and well fed. So, in a way, my return was more triumphant than my departure. My face and groin were sore but I was proud for having given Big John his lumps. He would be feeling worse than I. And it struck me that he might be seriously hurt—or dead. And I would be a fugitive, hunted like any other criminal: Negro. Medium height. Scar along left side of nose. Dark brown complexion. One hundred sixty-five pounds. Armed and dangerous. Wanted for robbery and assault—or perhaps murder. In the cold light of the description and charges, all the proper signs were there. I might be caught, hauled back to Chicago, convicted and jailed. The thought terrified me as I hurried from the station.

I cut through an alley and walked toward some ragged men warming at a fire they had built in an oil drum. Their begrimed and mummied faces belonged to the corridors of the Hotel Southland. Their hands stretched over the flames and their feet, wrapped in rags and gunny sacks, stomped and pawed at the snow. I passed them cautiously, my hand closed tightly about the silver in my pocket. The mere jingle of it, I felt, was enough to set them upon me.

My sister Cora embraced me with tears. Two nights before, she admitted later, she had dreamed I was being swept away in a river of blood and that she had caught my hand; she had tried to hold on but I had slipped away and drowned. Now she insisted that I live with her and this made me happy, for I loved her. I never explained the cuts and bruises on my face. There was no sense in my exciting her. It was all behind me, I hoped. After three days I got a job cleaning a small drugstore and I kept my promise and enrolled in school, even though it was the middle of February. The school was a mile and a half from the house, and the drugstore was a mile and a half beyond the school. I got up at five, walked the three miles, cleaned the floor, basement and windows and got to class by eight. I liked the owner. He was a kind, intelligent man with a name I never learned to pronounce—something like Hodop Keshishian. Most of his family lived in some far-distant and foreign place I had never heard of; and he had photographs of them dressed in strange clothes. Their faces were dark and healthy looking and smiled against alien backgrounds.

I had not written Sally while I was away, but I had telephoned her after reaching my sister's. Our courtship, it seemed, was still alive; and I went to her house in Minneapolis the next night. We talked lovers' talk on the living room divan and sneaked our embraces—despite the diabolical coughing of her father at the top of the dark stairway. We finally outfoxed him by moving out of his range. Then we grasped each other and continued to talk in an ordinary manner about ordinary things.

"Oh, you haven't seen this painting before, have you?" (Grasp.)

"No, I don't think I have." (Hug.)

"Mom's had it a long time." (Hug and kiss.)

And so it went until old Joe Alvis cleared his throat instead of coughing; which meant that it was time for me to go. It was a rather chaotic reunion but a glorious one and I returned to St. Paul happier than I had been for many nights.

Living with Cora was a joy despite the hard winter.

Marcella, her teen-aged daughter, had Momma's fire. Maurice, her eleven-year-old son, was slow like Poppa. Cora was a good, easygoing woman who worked hard to keep her children in food and clothing, but she was plagued with bills and generous to a fault. I ate much more than I contributed, and she was a soft touch for charming down-and-outers like Uncle Charlie and Larry Hickman, a three-hundred-pound sometime band leader, whose belly flopped up and down when he walked. Hick, a balding man with round dancing eyes, swapped humor and long-winded tales for food, hypnotizing everyone into inactivity as he talked, ate and refilled his plate. My sister, finally wise to his ways, offered up an amusing prayer at the supper table one night. Our heads were bowed and Hick was eying a chicken leg. "Dear Lord," my sister began, "make us thankful for what we are about to receive—and allow us to fill our plates before Hick fills our heart with lies. This we ask for our stomach's sake. Amen." We fell into uproarious laughter. Maurice and I dropped to the floor, tears streaming from our eyes. It was Marcella who got us back to the table. "You nuts had better come and eat. Hick is already on his second plate."

Hick had a marked talent for outwitting bill collectors. One tracked him to our house one day and Hick, watching from behind the curtains, picked up the telephone and instructed me to let him in. "Yes, two thousand dollars. The figure was right," Hick was saying when the man entered the parlor, "and I got the check this morning. What? I returned it because you didn't sign it. Aw, that's all right. Just sign it and send it right back. It's okay. Don't worry about it. Goodbye." He turned from the phone, grunting as he raised his weight from the chair to face the bill collector. "And what can the old maestro do for you, kind brother?" he asked innocently.

"I'm from Barker's Finance Company and—"

"Oh yes, the furniture bill. Well—" and he went on explaining the conversation he had just finished on the telephone.

"Yes, I heard," the man had to admit, not knowing that the telephone had been cut off for months. A few nights later, at supper, the lights snapped off, and we knew that the bill hadn't been paid. "Don't worry about it, sister," Hick said, still chewing. "We'll have brighter lights than ever in a few minutes." He took a ladder from the basement and ordered us to turn off the power switch; then he went outside. He returned after about twenty minutes. "Let there be light—without pay," he said. "Push on the switch!" And there was light—without pay—for nearly three months. Through some ingenious and illegal method, he had attached the dead line to a live circuit.

We also stole heat. When the coal trucks stopped for the signal lights or deliveries in our vicinity, we always managed to streak off with half a gunny sack without being caught. Maurice and I would also roam the streets and alleys for scraps of wood to stoke the furnace. Old man Jopson lived a few doors away. He was drunk most of the time, but he had a very tempting wood fence in back of his place. He met my sister on the street one day. "Cora," he complained, "do you know that I looked out back the other morning and there ain't even a stick left of my fence. I'm expectin' my outhouse to go next. Good Lord, what's this thievin' world comin' to, anyway?"

"That's a shame, Mr. Jopson. That's a shame," my sister said sympathetically. Now she knew who had supplied the last week's heat. And old Jopson didn't realize that two boards were already missing from his outhouse.

It was natural that we hoped for an early spring. But winter was deep in the earth and unwilling to be hurried.

So spring would sneak in a bit at a time, breathe upon the cold and then retreat. It gnawed at the snow, dwindling it with rain and sun, but the cold wind never slept. It roamed the nights, repairing the damage that had been done during the day. And off we would go again in search of another wooden fence or coal truck. It was good when finally the icicles fell and melted into the earth and the smoke left our breath and the frozen Mississippi moved again.

By now the land was stricken with poverty. Every newspaper and magazine I read showed photographs of men queued up at breadlines and employment halls seeking food and work. And this poverty attacked my family wherever it caught us. Yet hunger, I learned, was less frightening in the summer. I could walk slower and give more freely of what energy I had. And it was easier when the moon shone and the stars twinkled over the warm evenings, and love was close at hand.

July brought such evenings and also my first quarrel with Sally. It happened over some minor thing, but it kept us apart for months. And during those hours I worried and worked at a composition that spoke my feelings. The song was called "No Love"; and I wrote it at an upright piano my sister inherited with the house. And now that I had started writing songs again, I worked at it late into the nights and on weekends; music was the one thing that kept me hopeful. A peculiar experience had kindled my love for it long before Casamala decided that I should become a composer.

I was seven at the time. The Kansas day was hot and I was hunting June bugs in our cornfield when I heard a murmuring in the cornstalks. The murmuring grew into music, and I stood there, my mouth full of mulberries, puzzled, looking up at the slow-drifting clouds to see if they were the music's source. The violins, horns and drums were as true to me as the sunlight, and I had a feeling that the music was trapped inside my head, that it would be there even if I had no ears. I covered them with my hands, and the sounds were still there and they continued until all the clouds moved away and there was nothing but pale sky. Then it was gone as mysteriously as it had come, and I ran toward the house a little frightened, a little joyful, eager to tell my experience. But no one was around and I scooted up on the piano stool and started banging our old Kimball upright—trying to reproduce the sounds I had heard. The noise reached my father in another part of the field and he dropped his hoe and rushed to the house. He opened the door and watched me with astonishment; I was screaming as loud as I could.

"Have you gone batty, boy?"

I jumped down and started telling my story, but he only looked at me, at the mulberry stains around my mouth, and shook his head. "I declare, if you don't quit fondin' yourself on those mulberries, you're goin' to be swearin' you saw the devil. Now stop that bangin' and git to your chores."

Perhaps I never forgave my father's reactions to those delirious moments, for never again did we talk about things bordering on fantasy—not even a bedtime story. On that day, however (and to the woe of my good father), I began to play the piano. Several years later, Earl McCray, a music professor at the white school, offered me free music lessons. I was assigned a trombone and placed in our junior high school orchestra. But by now I was accustomed to playing by ear, and the slow process of learning to read music seemed unnecessary. I indulged in trickery. Each Saturday morning, before my appointment with Mr. McCray, my sister fingered my lesson on the piano and I memorized it, then I went off to astonish the professor with my "sight reading." He recommended me as soloist at the graduation concert. And everyone said that I played "The Rosary" with great feeling that night. Only my sister knew I couldn't read a note.

This was long past. But now at nineteen, five years later, I regretted the tricks I had played upon the professor. I had never learned to read or write music, though I was determined to compose; it seemed the one way to avoid a less-than-ordinary existence. I worked out a notation system of my own by referring to the piano keys as numbers instead of notes—a process that proved more complicated than the conventional way.

The next consideration was a publisher; it was disheartening to discover that all the important ones were in Chicago or farther east. And there were warnings against dishonest publishers who stole songs; but this didn't bother me. It would have been flattering, I thought, to have composed something worthy of a professional's theft. The difficulty would be to get someone to transpose my numbers to notes and then have the final work accepted. But I knew I couldn't depend on music alone. That first winter had taught me that I would have to fight with everything that came to hand. Learning, I knew, would be the most effective weapon against the coming years. So once again I seized upon books. After school I searched the local library shelves for authors who might help me in different ways. I pushed my mind into the foreign worlds of Thomas Mann, Dostoevski, James Joyce and others whom I had never read before. I tried stone sculpture, short story writing, poetry and, when I could hustle the material, painting. I did everything I could to protect myself against another such winter. Somewhere in between I played basketball for the Diplomats and my high school as well.

A collapse was inevitable, and it came during a basketball

game in October, 1931. I had dribbled past two guards and arched the ball perfectly, knowing it would swish through the hoop. But a blackness suddenly covered the court and the ball disappeared into it like a balloon into a cloud, and I felt myself falling. The coach had my teammates carry me to the locker room, where I was examined by the school nurse. Her only comment was that I looked awful hungry and thin to be playing such a strenuous game. But at home later that evening a doctor whom my sister called said I was on the verge of a physical breakdown. I had wasted from 165 pounds to 124 in less than three months. If I was to regain my health, he said, I would have to leave school for the remainder of the year and rest.

So at twenty I found myself an invalid. There was no chance of graduating with my class. I was already too far behind. In fact, I knew that I would never go back to school. For the next five months I sat in the dark of my room rejecting time, light and reason. I never heard from Sally during that time, but my sister helped me through the long convalescence and tried to get me to read, to write, to do anything that would divert my eyes from the blank wall opposite my bed. I finally opened a book one rainy afternoon. And gradually I began to read, think and hope again. One thing was clear. I couldn't escape my fate by trying to outrun it. I would have to take my time from now on, and grow in the light of my own particular experience—and accept the slowness of things that were meant to be slow. Spring was back again, but I was afraid to look upon its coming with any pleasure. It had deceived me once too often.

TEN

BY APRIL I had regained my weight and strength. And before long I was hanging out at Jim's pool hall again, for it was a good place to get back into the stream of things. Arguments were always going; they flared, blossomed and faded by the dozens. Some of them were senseless, some were heated, some were comical. Two friends of mine, Bud Kelly and a boy we called "Mice Titty," argued one night about which of the two was the lightest-complexioned. Tee Vernon finally squashed the dispute by declaring Mice Titty the fairest. But he ended by saying that "both of them look like they were born in an inkwell."

"It's all right," Bud countered. "The blacker the berry the sweeter the juice!"

"Then you oughta have honey between your toes!" Mice Titty hollered back.

During another argument, one man claimed that Glen Gray, the band leader, had a mustache. The other denied it. My interest was casual until one of the men, a waiter at the Hotel St. Paul, boasted that he should know since he "rubbed shoulders with Gray every night." He was lying of course about the shoulder rubbing, but he did see the orchestra leader regularly; anyone working there had the same opportunity. I wondered why I hadn't thought of this before. Many of the best orchestras played at the large Twin City hotels; if only I could get one of them to broadcast my songs. The thought grew and I hurried home, sorted out several of my compositions and set my alarm clock for six o'clock. And by seven-thirty the next morning I was at the Hotel St. Paul servants' entrance, the songs tucked in my pocket, applying for a waiter's job.

The time keeper, an old gray-haired man, looked me over and asked me to wait around until he saw the day's work schedule. And for the next four hours I paced the corridor, looking expectantly at him now and then. At eleven-thirty, he motioned for me.

"Are you an experienced waiter?"

"Yessir. Yessir." (I had never waited on table in my life.)

"You ever work here before?"

"Not yet, no, sir."

"Where have you worked?"

"The Minnesota Club, the Lowry, the—"

"Okay, okay. There's a Rotary luncheon today, nothing steady. You want to work it?"

"Is that where the orchestra plays?"

"Orchestra? What's the orchestra got to do with it?" he asked.

"Oh nothing, nothing. Just thought I'd ask." My heart thumped like a drum.

"Well, do you want it or not?" he snapped.

"Yessir, I'll take it." I stepped up to his table and signed in.

The banquet captain changed my status from waiter to bus boy the instant he saw me pick up a tray. And as I trudged back and forth between the kitchen and the banquet hall, under the weight of the trays of drinks, I could hear the music coming from the main dining room. It was frustrating to have Glen Gray so close and not to be able to talk with him. But the driving captain kept his eye on me, pointing to tray after tray. And only once, when the dining room door swung open, did I glimpse the tall, debonair orchestra leader directing his orchestra. And I noticed then that he did have a mustache.

Much later, the Rotarians were enjoying coffee, puffing cigars and asking silly questions of a mind reader they had hired for entertainment. I hung around, clearing dirty dishes from the tables—and listening to the questions and answers.

"Who's going to be the most famous in this room?" someone asked.

"Good question," the mind reader said. He then covered his eyes and turned his back to the audience. There was snickering as he supposedly searched the future. Whomever he chose was in for a good razzing. The laughter was already building.

"Gentlemen." There was a momentary quiet. "There is a boy in the back of this room in a white uniform" (every eye in the room turned on me). "He will be more widely acclaimed than any—"

That was enough. Bedlam broke loose. "Boy! Boy! Come up here!" It was the mind reader's voice screaming over the others. "Bring him up, somebody!"

Two men started toward me, but I grabbed a tray of dishes, and, fleeing the banquet hall, I tripped and threw the dishes in all directions. But I got to my feet and kept going until I reached the dressing room.

In spite of that fiasco, I was hired three days later as a regular bus boy, and assigned to the main dining room.

Glen Gray left soon after, without my having had a

chance to speak to him. But Kay Kyser, Bert Lown, Jack Teagarden and others, who came later, didn't get off so easy. Each of them suffered through my inexhaustible efforts—and they encouraged me. But none of them acted as though Tin Pan Alley was overlooking a great talent.

Late that summer, I was offered the head bus boy job at the Hotel Lowry, by the maître d'hôtel, a former wrestler whose name was Gleason. I took it. And for nearly three hours each day, after the luncheon crowd left, I had the main dining room and the huge grand piano all to myself. Once the tables were set for the evening, I played away before an imagined audience—using the light control switches for color combinations that added to the mood. On one such afternoon I was playing and singing "No Love" when I felt someone was behind me. Embarrassed, I stopped, turned and looked into the shadows. It was Larry Duncan, the orchestra leader who was currently engaged by the hotel.

"Is that your music?" he asked.

"Yes."

"Go ahead. Play it again."

I played it again and he listened attentively. When I finished he asked me if I would like to have it orchestrated.

"I sure would," I said, and it was probably the understatement of my lifetime. The orchestra's arranger spent the rest of that afternoon with me, taking the piece down as I played it. And, as I watched him work, I hoped that my afternoons of fantasy were coming to an end.

This happened on a Wednesday. During dinner on the following Friday night, Larry motioned me toward the bandstand. "We're broadcasting 'No Love' on the network show tomorrow night—with your permission, of course," he said.

I got Sally on the telephone and, without knowing whether she cared or not, I excitedly spilled out the good news. "I composed it for you—don't forget to listen." Her voice didn't reveal the slightest interest. She said, very casually, that she would listen—but, I found out later, she spent the next two hours telephoning all her friends. And I spent the rest of that evening and the next day drifting about in a trance.

On the night of the broadcast, Abby, the drummer, congratulated me and showed a group of waiters and myself the program. Fate had arranged things. There was my name among those of Irving Berlin, Duke Ellington, Cole Porter and Jerome Kern. Now, in spite of my imagining the worst—a broken microphone, a broken promise, a canceled broadcast—it was going to happen. I knew that Gleason kept a death watch on unfilled water glasses, so I went about filling them to the brim. I wanted to hear every word, every note, without being disturbed.

When at last the moment came, people continued to eat, drink and talk, as if they were unaware of the miracle taking place. I wanted to shout, to command everyone to listen, to ascend with me—far above ordinary things. But they kept on eating, drinking, laughing and talking. And, just before the vocalist approached the microphone, I took refuge near the bandstand where I could hear him sing my lyrics. But now, at such a moment, a drunk started rapping his glass with a spoon. He wanted more water. I ignored him. He rapped louder and I hated him for it.

"What is it, sir?" A shiver went up my back. It was Gleason's voice.

"Water! Water! Tell that damned boy our party wants water!"

Such was my lot, I thought, and I turned toward the

table only to have Gleason wave me away. He was filling the glasses and proudly explaining that the music the orchestra was playing was mine. The drunk whispered the news to his party, and his party whispered the news to the next table, and soon everyone in the entire dining room was looking toward me. When the orchestra finished a burst of applause filled the air. I smiled nervously, picked up a tray of dirty dishes and left the room amidst the ovation. Then, slipping into an empty room, I telephoned Sally. "Yes, I listened," she said, "and it was beautiful. Would you like to come over sometime, maybe tonight?"

"As soon as I can get out of here," I answered. The sky was overcast and it was chilly when I boarded the streetcar; but I couldn't accept such a night. There were stars and a moon instead, and a ridiculous hint of spring in the fall air. My heart, in its joy, would have it no other way.

Every morning after that I woke up expecting some new honor to touch my life, but each day was about the same as the one before it. Larry continued to play "No Love" two or three times each week—and always I would stop as if I were turned to stone and listen. For a few quick minutes I would be lifted above the waiters, the diners, the hot kitchens and surly cooks. Then just as quickly—after the song had ended—I was straining under a huge tray of dishes. I led two lives, and there was no easy balance between them. The extremes left me frustrated and morose.

Nevertheless trouble was furthest from my mind as I waited for a streetcar one evening after work. It was late, so I decided to telephone Sally and tell her that I was on my way. Approaching the hotel drugstore, I noticed three white men passing out handbills and pamphlets, and as I neared them I sensed trouble. It came quickly.

"Here, boy," one said, shoving a pamphlet into my hand, "tell your mammy and pappy to vote like this thing says."

"Go to hell," I countered, throwing the pamphlet to the ground. A sharp kick answered against my ribs, but I was prepared. Adjusting my ring, which was set with a crystal, I doubled my fist and swung at the one nearest to me. He fell to the street, his face cut from his eye to his ear. The second one ducked my blow, but I caught the largest of the three with a hard right. He fell backward toward a plate-glass window, and he grabbed me about the neck and pulled me with him. We both crashed through the window, but my neck, body and arms caught most of the glass. His friends pulled him out and they ran, forcing their way through a crowd of spectators who had gathered during the commotion. By the time I was carried into the drugstore, I was bleeding badly and the second finger on my right hand hung half severed from its joint. The drugstore employees covered my wounds with wet towels and someone called the police. Meanwhile, Gleason had happened into the drugstore. And, as luck decreed it, so had three of my friends. Gleason marshaled them, and off they ran to capture my assailants. The wisest thing I did, a doctor told me later, was to tape my finger back into its joint. Eventually the police took the three white men to jail—and I was imprisoned, along with them, as a "material witness." The three of them were locked up in a cell next to mine; only bars separated us from one another. I asked for a doctor; but by two in the morning none had come. At three o'clock the lights were turned out and I curled up on my cot and tried to sleep.

Imprisoned there in the foul dark, I felt like a caged and injured animal. The other three, having slept off their drunk, had begun to mutter obscenities: "You black son-of-a-bitch—we'll kill you the next time—goddamn dirty nigger—black bastard—wait till we git you on the street again." Now one of them was urinating through the bars onto my floor. I watched from the shadows, my mind racing and searching for some way to retaliate. But there was nothing, not even a glass to throw. I could only observe their depravity with disgust. It was hard to regard them as human beings; they seemed only a shadowy white mass—one so unbearable that even to hate it seemed futile.

I closed my eyes, still hoping that sleep might separate me from the experience. And in my despair I forced my thoughts from their ugliness and into my mother's grave. Then things were easier. The mere thought of her eased the tensions and the boiling inside me.

"You 'sleep, tarbaby?"

I didn't answer.

"Maybe the bastard's dead. Heh, we pissed on your floor!"

The odor bore him out, but I lay still, my mind's eye deep inside the grave. The image of my mother, slim brown hands crossed, face sharp and immobile, demanded in its repose that I remember her teachings.

"Wake up! Wake up, you black son-of-a-bitch!"

I thought of returning their filth, but I remained still and at last they fell quiet.

Some things about my mother had escaped me during the trials of these past three years, but now, in the silence of this prison, my thoughts were riveted to everything I remembered her saying or doing. I recalled how she once persuaded a judge to let her pass sentence on three boys who had stolen from us. Her decision: prayer meeting twice a week, church and Sunday school for six months— with no absences tolerated. "I'd rather have gone to jail," one of the boys told me jokingly, after he had served his sentence.

My mother was a small, wiry, straight-laced woman of reddish brown skin. Her sharp-boned face had the high cheeks and slanted eyes of the Cherokee. A pink scar, which looked like a faded strawberry, marked her left temple. This mark, I was told, had been inflicted by a lightning bolt during a storm. Her black hair, mixed as long as I could remember with gray, was always combed straight back to the nape of her longish neck; and I always thought her delicate ears looked like browned wax. Truth-fulness was one of her dominant traits; so I resented the gap between her front teeth after my third-grade teacher once scolded a boy, who had a similar defect, for lying. "Show me somebody with teeth like that and I'll show you a liar!" she had shouted. Righteous and stern, my mother applied the braided switch with authority. And when she became angry, everyone walked softly. A woman of religion, her habits were inflexible, and everyone attended church and Sunday school—as well as prayer meeting on Wednesday nights. No excuse short of sickness let you off.

She seemed to be in continuous motion as she whisked about, her gingham skirts sweeping the dusty roads. Even in the final hours of the day her restlessness showed as she rocked back and forth darning socks, mending overalls, murmuring prayers and humming hymns.

I lay there, my thoughts intermingling her goodness with the vileness of those in the next cell. My anger began to rise again—and suddenly out of control, I got up, lifted my cot and slammed it against the bars. The three barely stirred.

Only a flat grunt came from one of them. They were asleep and I looked in at them, wondering if they were capable of dreaming. Then, righting the cot, I lay back down. In my rage I had only hurt my finger and it was beginning to bleed again. Some time later the lights went on and a policeman unlocked the cell, shook the three men awake and told them they were free. "What about me?" I asked, as he started away.

"You just take it easy, friend," he grumbled, "you've caused enough trouble for one night."

"But my finger is half off and it's bleeding again," I protested.

"Ain't no doctor around this time of morning."

"How about a hospital then?"

"You just take it easy like I told you." He flipped the light switch, went out and slammed the outer door shut. And I lay back and tried to reason things out. Why, I wondered, were the police releasing them and holding me?

There was nothing to do but wait. And in the long interim I did a lot of thinking about the white man, and about his brutality—realizing that it was nudging me into a hatred of him. I lay aching until dawn, reassembling all the scalding experiences one by one. And I was overwhelmed by the many injustices already fastened to my memory. I had sort of limped through the early years, accepting as normal a scar for a scar. Now I felt a permanent anger after each clash. And I was becoming more sensitive to any situation that revealed a white man's attitude toward me. I never feared him or stood in awe of his achievements. "If a white boy can do it, so can you," Momma used to say, "so don't ever give me your color as a cause for failing." She made everything seem possible, even during the bleakest years, by feeding my young mind with all the things one could do in spite of the color of one's skin. Painstakingly, she was building a confidence and integrity in me.

But the injuries I received the night before kept gathering all the misfortune and futility I had known since childhood. They had, in a way, become symbolic of failure, making all the efforts of the last years meaningless. I was suffering with the others now—those imprisoned in slave ships from Africa hundreds of years before, those strung up by their necks in hatred-filled Delta bottoms, those gunned to death for "looking the wrong way" at some Southern white lady, those bent, gnarled and burned to black crispness under the white-hot sun, in the white man's field, so that the white man might live a white man's life, on a white man's land.

Dawn finally broke. And when they released me several hours later, undoctored and unfed, it was raining. The same bloody towels were wrapped about my neck, arms and hands. I stood in the doorway of the jail for several moments gulping in the air. Then I walked slowly in the downpour, letting the rain beat life back into my body. People huddling in the doorways observed me curiously, unaware of the bitterness inside me, where, only a short time before, there had been hope and joy. Ten new scars, inflicted by white men, ached beneath those towels. And my life, held now in a body of trouble and hurt, was ready to explode with hatred and revenge.

After a doctor had dressed my wounds and stitched my finger into place, I holed up again in my room at Cora's. And, as the cuts gradually closed, they seemed to seal in the experience. And the bitterness, trapped inside me, began poisoning all the senses that governed my thinking.

In my distress I forgot my music; I even forgot that it had been broadcast. I slipped back into days and nights of brooding; and composing no longer enraptured me; fate was playing games again—and it was winning. My sister, concerned about my unhappiness, kept a close watch over me, inquired of my needs and tried to make things pleasant. But I didn't talk much to anyone. I was too busy encouraging the suffering and pampering the hate that had taken over my heart. I eventually emerged from the room, quietly but dangerously violent—resolved to gain vengeance upon any white who crossed me the wrong way.

ELEVEN

WHEN I returned to work two weeks later, Gleason said that Larry was anxious to see me. But by now I had lost all my grand illusions. I had been dreaming instead of facing the truth, I said to myself as I knocked on his door. But the orchestra leader's first words shocked me. "We close here Saturday night and I'd like to take you along with the band," he said.

"Are you serious?" I answered with a false calm.

"You've got two days to think it over. Let me know as soon as you can."

I stood for a moment watching him dress for the evening's performance. Then, smothering my anxiety with indifference, I said that I would like to go along.

"Okay. The orchestra bus leaves from in front of the hotel at four on Sunday morning. We open at the Hotel Muehlebach in Kansas City Monday night."

"I'll be there at four." My voice was resolute but I left him quickly to hide my feelings. I hadn't asked or even wondered about my salary or position. It didn't matter. To be traveling with a famous orchestra, to compose, to have my music played were enough.

Packing the same night, I tried thinking of a goodbye

that would leave both Sally and me hopeful. Nothing I thought of seemed to be right. And during our last walk, the night before I left, I made several childish beginnings that all ended in a stutter. We were on the verge of parting when the right way came to me. "I'm leaving with Larry's orchestra early tomorrow morning," I said firmly, "and I'm going to make enough money to come back and marry you."

"Are you proposing?" she asked.

"I think so. If I am, do you accept?"

She answered with a kiss and hug and we took another walk. "I think Pa will raise cain," she said as we approached the house again.

"Then I won't bother to ask him," I replied. I was charged with hope when I boarded the bus the next morning. Things did look promising.

It soon became clear that Larry's musicians were not the most contented group on the road. "The fellows have been griping for days," Abby, the drummer, confided to me one night in Kansas City.

"What's the trouble?" I asked.

"Money, orchestral arrangements, restaurant food and being away from their families for so long. Some of them just don't like Larry any more. They think he's lost interest in the band."

"Has he?"

"It's hard to say. Musicians are always beefing about something, no matter what outfit they're with. What's he paying for your act?"

"Nothing so far. We haven't talked money yet."

"What are you waiting for? Get it settled tonight," Abby warned.

My act, as Abby called it, took place, sometimes, between dance sets. I wheeled a small piano to the center of the floor and played and sang "No Love"—maybe to the accompaniment of the band, maybe without it. And I accepted as many requests from the audience as my limited repertoire would allow. It was an uncertain situation. Sometimes I performed, sometimes I didn't. Larry's moods, which varied from day to day, determined my appearance—or nonappearance.

He seemed strangely detached from the orchestra. He traveled in his own car, dined alone and seldom attended rehearsals. Sometimes he would appear seconds before the broadcast, his face a mask of indifference, and raise his slender hand for the theme.

"The Mutual Network takes great pleasure in bringing you, from Kansas City's Hotel Muehlebach, Larry Duncan and his band of a thousand melodies," the announcer would dramatically announce to the air waves. And Larry, an icy smile edging his lips, would turn and acknowledge the applause. Once, when he was late for a broadcast, the arranger hustled me before the band. It was meant as an affront to Larry, to show that the lowest member of the band could do what he did. But when he finally rushed in and saw me conducting he smiled and signaled for me to continue, then left. The intended insult had backfired and only I had exulted in the little drama. After that he conducted with such apparent lack of interest it was hard to tell whether he led the orchestra or whether he just followed it. In any case, he always scooted out before I could talk about money with him. And what funds I got were drawn, with great effort, out of the band manager, who claimed to be broke most of the time. I might have pressed Larry, but I could never understand why he had taken me along in the first place. I had nothing apparent to offer him, and I was afraid he might discover it. Maybe he thought the presence of a Negro would inspire a new beat—or a new look. I didn't know. In retrospect I feel he must have acted on some whimsical impulse. Nevertheless, we both drifted along in this nebulous relationship, that confused the order of definite things like payday, rent, laundry and food. Actually he was playing it blind and I was following him; and by accepting the situation I had to accept the insecurity that came with it.

A fine orchestra was falling apart. Yet its failures didn't affect me then. I was caught in the spell of its music and the dramatic events and people that surrounded that music. Nearly every day I saw or heard something that delighted me. It was an exciting time; and I drank in the splendor of those nights and the jargon of those chosen characters, who drank heavily, ate well and made merry in spite of the breadlines mushrooming across the land. Sometimes it was hard to believe that I was a part of this, but the sight of a bus boy, struggling through the crowds with a trayload of dishes, always brought reality to the moment.

Tired at last of the bourgeois high jinks at the Muehlebach, Abby and several of us went off to hear Bennie Moten's great band, which was playing at the Paseo Ballroom. And this was my first substantial experience with real jazz. How different and wonderful were the sounds that came from their instruments. These black musicians played with a oneness that racked our souls. "Man," Abby would moan, "I'd play in a band like that for nothing."

Without realizing it, I was looked upon as a celebrity by the men in Bennie's band, because I was working at the Muehlebach—a place where no Negro had played before —but mainly because I had acquired the distinction of playing with a white orchestra. As questionable as this distinction was, it served a purpose. For Bennie, friendly man that he was, invited several of us to sit in with his band one Sunday afternoon. I wisely refused; but Abby got his wish when he and the trumpet player took to the stand. Abby drummed in ecstasy all afternoon; and from that moment on he acted as though he were indebted to me. "What a band!" he would shout sometimes. "I just can't get over it!"

Sally sent me a newspaper article from the Minneapolis *Spokesman* she had clipped. I read: "Local boy makes good with white band—will travel eastern circuit with it." And it went on to speak of my "success" in glowing terms. For a few moments I cheated and accepted the article as the truth. Then, embarrassed, I ate the lie, and tore the clipping to shreds so that no one in the band might see it. "Success"! It would be impossible now to go back without it.

We left the Muehlebach sometime during February and worked our way to Chicago playing one-nighters. Larry became even more vague. The band manager became more broke. And my quandary deepened. But I hung on. It was a matter of vanity now. A penniless success was far easier to take, I thought, than the humiliation waiting for me on every corner back in St. Paul. Abby was puzzled by my obstinacy, but he admired my spirit. "You got brass in your balls," he would say, shaking his head. "I'd a given up a long time ago." He could have understood if he had known how much the thought of failure repelled me. I was locked in a bitter struggle with pride. And I was in love. This alone, I felt, made one invincible.

At Cleveland, Ohio, several evenings later, Larry read a telegram from his agent that brought the entire orchestra to a standing cheer. "You open in New York at Hotel

Park Central on the night of March 3rd," it read. I didn't adapt very well to the excitement at first. This meant home to the rest of the musicians, but I only saw many miles and a big lonesome city. But I had become devoted to chance: maybe this was triumph beckoning. So, as the joy spread throughout the night, I slowly began to share in it. We celebrated well into the next evening. Then, tired from drink, we settled in our seats for the long trip east.

TWELVE

AFTER EVERYONE had gone to sleep I sat by the driver and watched the highway streak into our headlamps. I thought about New York as I had always imagined it—a canyon of tall buildings and bright lights, theaters and cabarets with names of famous people on every marquee; Broadway, a valley of brilliance teeming with thousands of city people. I thought of Harlem and scores of Negroes moving to the music of Duke Ellington, Chick Webb and Cab Calloway; of the Cotton Club, Small's Paradise and the Savoy Ballroom, where the floor, I once heard a radio announcer say, shook to the rhythm of happy black feet.

The driver was grumbling about the poorly marked highway when I finally went to sleep. But, as the miles fell away, my subconscious kept the city before me. And now and then I sprang awake, only to see our lights cutting the same rural darkness. New York was still far away. It was dawn when he shook me awake. "We're in the city, fellow," he said. "It's the Lower East Side—raining so hard though you can't see much." I sat up and wiped the moisture from the window and stared at the long rows of tenements; they looked gloomy and misshapen in the downpour. Depression stabbed at my stomach and doubts popped into my head. As we drove on I tried to shake off the tension that was mounting inside me; but a wave of insecurity persisted, and I suddenly felt lonely, in spite of the men snoring all around me.

Broadway was gray, wet and almost empty of people. We traveled along it all the way up to Fifty-sixth Street, then turned right and pulled up in front of the Park Central Hotel.

"We're here!" the driver shouted.

Things went wrong quickly. When I started through the front door the doorman called me aside and told me I would have to use the servants' entrance.

"I'm not a servant. I'm a member of the band," I explained.

"Makes no difference; you're colored. You can't go in the front way. Those are house orders." I became angry. Nothing like this had happened at the Muehlebach in Kansas City, where I had expected it. We stood glaring at each other for a moment; and, since I wasn't sure of how Larry would take this kind of trouble, I backed down. And even if I had won the victory would have been slight, for the orchestra, I learned an hour later, was disbanding immediately. No reasons were given, and I never saw Larry again.

Abby and I had coffee in a drugstore. We were troubled and silent while we drank. Finally he said, "I feel sorry for you. At least I've got a family here and I'd like to take you home with me, but—"

"It's okay," I said. "I've always wanted to live in Harlem." He smiled, knowing this was the only part of the city where I could live. We finished, then he slapped my back reassuringly and paid the bill. "You'll be all right. Just be very careful up there," he warned me.

"Oh sure, I'll be okay," I agreed. But my faith was already shaken by his warning. He asked me if I had any money and I said I had a couple of bucks. He didn't have much either, but he handed me five dollars. "This ain't a lot but it'll tide you over. You'll get something quick. Don't worry." Then he walked me to an uptown subway entrance and stood watching as I lugged my suitcase down the stairs.

"Where should I get off?" I shouted up to him from the bottom of the stairway.

"Take the A train!" he shouted back. "Get off about 125th Street—145th—any place along there!" That was the last time I saw Abby.

I dropped a nickel in the slot, pushed through the turnstile and moved into the crowd. I inched around nervously, trying to hide my greenness. The A train roared in, and as it screeched to a halt the crowd surged forward, carrying me with it. The door slammed shut on my bag, then sprang open again, and a man in a blue uniform shoved me into the car. The train lurched forward and we began to rumble through the underground toward Harlem.

I suspect that I chose 145th Street because it was the larger number. Coming up with the crowd, I turned to watch the train pull away, then continued up the stairs to the street. The rain had stopped, but sullen clouds still hung low over the buildings. But a certain excitement accompanied my first step onto the sidewalk. This was Harlem, and I was a part of it—its people, its songs and words. Then I started roaming through the sea of black faces, and they were not as I had expected them to be; they seemed troubled and melancholy. And walking along I found that, in spite of my color, I was a stranger here. This wasn't Kansas or Minnesota where people with dark skins usually nodded to one another. It was like being cast upon an island with kinfolk who had suddenly become alien.

I walked up St. Nicholas Avenue and saw a sign that said

ROOMS. It hung at a slant between gray lace curtains and
the glass. It was a stone building and, though there were
garbage cans lined up in front of it, I thought it looked
clean, so I went up the steps and knocked on the door and
waited; when no one answered I knocked harder.

"Who is it?" The guttural voice came from behind the
door.

In my very best Minnesota manner I said that I was
looking for a room. Then the door opened and a fat, gray-
haired woman looked out at me. Her eyes were deeply set;
her jaws worked up and down as though she were chewing. She looked me up and down as if she were determining
my ability to pay, and as she looked my pants never had
felt baggier, my shirt more rumpled, nor had my heels ever
felt more rundown.

"Where you from, boy, and what's your name?" she
asked in one breath.

I gave her my name, and told her I was from Minnesota.

"Up north?" she questioned cautiously.

"Yes, mam," I answered, wondering whether this
worked for me or against me. She might have more sympathy for a Southern colored boy, I thought. Maybe I
should have given her a Southern state.

When she mumbled that she only had a five-dollar-a-
week room left, I saw that she was toothless and only
chewed on her gums. And I was thinking that I only had
seven dollars. Past experience told me she would want a
week in advance.

"Well, you want it or not?"

"Yes, mam. I'll take it. That's just fine."

She looked me up and down again before allowing me in.
Then finally she said, "It's on the top floor and you have to
pay a week in advance and I don't like a lot of strange

people coming in here all the time and my name is Mrs. Haskins and this is a house of the Lord."

I stepped in saying that I didn't know any strange people since I had just gotten in town and that I was very glad to meet her. For good measure, I added that I had been brought up in a very Christian-like home.

I smelled garlicky cooking as we crossed the hall to the stairway. Then children's voices came from the next floor; and higher up muffled jazz drifted down through the spiral staircase. Mrs. Haskins started up and the boards creaked under her weight. "You pay your rent or out you go, and I don't tolerate young girls coming in and out all the time 'cause this is a house of the Lord."

"Yes, mam."

She looked up and grunted as the children's voices grew louder; and now there was the odor of wet-diapered babies. She stopped at the second landing, plodded to an open door and stopped. "These kids make too much noise, Jessie," she said to a woman who was ironing with a naked baby in her arms.

"All children make noise," the woman with the baby said. She looked tired and she spoke without looking up. Six of her other children sat on a bed that sagged to the floor. It was a small, wretched room. Aside from the bed there was only a card table covered with dirty dishes, a stool and a crude gas burner on which something was boiling that smelled like cabbage. Dirty clothes hung from the walls and lay about the room in disorder. At the sight of their landlady, the children wilted into a heap. Wide-eyed and fearful, they looked up at her as though she had come to pass sentence upon them.

"You heard from the police yet, Jessie?"

"Nothing yet."

All of them were dirty. The youngest on the bed picked running sores on his arms and legs. His head was splotched with them as well. A girl of about five had a wall eye that seemed to hold a constant tear. She was naked and of lighter skin than the others. The oldest, who looked about seven, was a sloe-eyed, asthmatic-looking boy. He sat hunched, his long legs doubled beneath his chin, watching the women as they talked. The other three chestnut-brown ones could almost have been triplets.

"It's been about a week now. You sure you ain't heard something?"

"I'd say so if I had. Think I'd lie about it?"

"I'm worried about my rent money. It's been a month since I had a dime."

"Joe'll pay you soon as he comes—always has."

"When he comes," the landlady repeated mockingly. She motioned for me and we started up the next flight. "Remember, pay your rent on time; no gambling, drinking or lotsa noise. This is the house of the Lord."

"Yes, mam. I understand." The jazz was louder now, sounding like a full band inside the room.

"Cut that thing down, Charlie! Cut that thing down, boy! Are you deaf? Cut it down, I say!"

"Okay! Okay!" Charlie hollered back. The music softened.

She took me to a room that was uglier than Jessie's. It was small, dirty and held a strong odor, like stale cabbage and iodine. There was a window, but one of the panes was broken, and a rag filled the opening. A linoleum, cracked from time and wear, covered parts of the floor, and the bed looked as if it had slept hundreds of bodies. The mattress was lumpy, stained and torn, but Mrs. Haskins quickly covered it with a sheet—one that had been washed but not ironed. A washbasin sloped from one of the corners, and when I gave the spigot a full twist only a rusty trickle of water came out, and it was cold. She pointed to a toilet at the end of the hall. The seat was cracked and the wooden handle on the flushing chain was cracked. "Keep it clean for the rest of the roomers—and remember this is the house of the Lord." She took my five dollars, threw me an old blanket she took from a closet and left. If, at that moment, someone had offered me a ride back to Fort Scott or St. Paul, I would have taken it.

I unpacked and lay across the bed to rest for a moment. But hours had passed before I woke to a gnawing inside the wall near my head. It was dark and I got to my knees, listening to the rat's teeth cutting the wood, trying to remember where I was. Charlie's jazz was going again; and now I remembered. I smacked the wall with my fist. The gnawing stopped for a few moments, then it started again and kept up all night. I finally went to sleep again, clutching a shoe, just in case he tunneled through the wall. Welts and spots covered my body when I awoke the next morning. Bedbugs had feasted on me. The sheet was spotted where I had smashed them during the night. Nevertheless I felt a lot better when the sunlight shone through the dirt on the window. At least the rain had stopped.

The problem of hunting for a job hit me when I touched the street. The sun was higher now, the sky clear, and far in the distance I could see Manhattan's skyscrapers rising from the tenements like rows of carved stone. I bought a newspaper at the corner, and on the front page there was a photograph of Franklin Delano Roosevelt. His chin was up, his smile was confident, and his hat brim was raised to the same angle as his arm as he waved victoriously. It was March 4, 1933, the day of his inauguration. I walked east on 145th Street to Lenox Avenue; and when I turned the corner there was a stand where one could get a hot dog and root beer for seven cents. I ate two portions while checking the want ads. Someone needed a plumber's helper; the Park Central Hotel needed waiters and dishwashers, but they wanted white waiters and dishwashers and the plumber wanted a white helper. The ads said so.

Harlem was fully alive now, but a chill still hung in the air, and the stoops were filling with Negroes, who stood warming in the sun. I walked slowly down the avenue observing them. They were gathered in groups, their eyes sullen against the morning light. Their mood seemed as ugly as their clothing and they looked as if all promise had died inside them.

The sidewalks were filling too, carrying a steady stream of slow-moving people in both directions, and soon I was lost in the stream, closed in by Ethel's Beauty Shoppe and Joe's Burgers and a funeral home and the Church of God in Christ and the church of good hope and small's paradise and a funeral parlor and the harlem bar and harlem lunch and harlem barbers and saturday night caskets between the black and tan bar and ebony lounge and pilgrims' baptist *shine mister?* and honking taxis doorway johnnies eying miss mighty stockings miss fine gams miss good bread all big-breasted and hip-swinging *black bastards who do they think I am?* and the sign of the believer and the sirens and hospital meat wagons FATS WALLER RECORDS COME IN AND LISTEN and undertaking establishment and funeral home *shine mister?* and butcher shops chitterlings collard greens hog maws crackling bread and the sharpie flipping the quarter georgie raft–style and the shiloh baptist and etha mae's beautee shoppe and carl's hot dogs root beer seven cents *give me some skin daddy-o* and the apollo the harlem master tailors *jew him down baby jew him down* mount zion funeral home and herbs for healing *shine mister?* ofay cops on every corner *looking mean daddy-o looking mean* herbs bibles candles pictures of black jesus marty's pawn shop and jock's place *thievin bastards police! Police! Police!* SADIE'S BALL GOWNS HALF PRICE DOLLAR DOWN DOLLAR A WEEK *the duke's latest hit come in listen the mooche come on in brother it don't cost you nothing* and the african methodist episcopal church and chick webb at the savoy *What a friend we have in Jesus! Halt halt halt or I'll shoot* and POLICE BRUTALITY CONTINUES IN HARLEM! BOY MURDERED! NEGRO GROUPS SET FOR PROTEST! *Get your paper here read all about it brother read all about it* ads ads ads white waiter wanted ads ads ads white plumber needed ads ads ads white nurse wanted ads ads white bartender needed *Can you use me for any kind of work mister any kind sweeping dishwashing window washing waiter cook any kind mister any kind? And to you, my friends throughout the land, as your president let me assert my firm belief that the only thing we have to fear is fear itself—nameless, unreasoning, unjustified terror . . . we are stricken by no plague of locusts. Plenty is at our doorstep. Shine mister shine?* HARLEM SOCIALITES TO ENTERTAIN AT THE SAVOY BALLROOM THIS WEEKEND DRESS FORMAL ads ads ads negro maid that can cook sew clean and care for two-month-old baby. *Get your amsterdam news your pittsburgh courier your chicago defender here read your black papers get the truth.* HARLEM SOCIALITE CAUGHT IN LOVE TRIANGLE POLICE BRUTALITY ON THE RISE WAKE UP HARLEM *Shine mister?* MASS RALLY AT 125TH STREET TONIGHT COME ONE COME ALL HELP BURY POLICE BRUTALITY HIGH RENT BAD HOUSING STARVATION *But the cotton club's in harlem so why can't a black man go there? So the moon is cheese daddy-o and*

why can't you eat it? MASS RALLY COME ONE COME ALL
HELP BURY MISTER OFAY TONIGHT AT SEVEN *Come in close
brothers let me tell you like it is here in harlem let 'em in
brothers make way for my people all my black friends who
have come to bury the white devil now I'm going to tell
you something that nobody else has had the guts to tell you
in front of these gun-toting cops standing all around you
no no no I ain't scared of none of 'em no matter how big
their guns are come closer come closer git around me so
you can hear something that's going to help you the white
man's day is coming to an end and we my friends are going
to push that day along we're gonna run 'em out of harlem
as sure as the african is gonna run 'em out of africa mark
my word I'm sick of our children being shot down in the
streets like dogs by these pasty-face bullies with guns that
they make you buy with your own tax money yes brother
I said your tax money listen did you hear what I said you
pay for those guns with your own tax money for those
ofay bandits to shoot your own children down in cold
blood how long are you going to let it go on brother how
long before you stop praying to god for help and help your
selfs he ain't caring nothing about you he's white just like
the cops you oughta know that by now so why are you
running to these dog-ass churches every night and falling
on your knees giving money to a white god who is murdering your children and the same time you are praying to him
for mercy and help wake up brothers brothers wake up
move in closer let my friends in closer gather around me
and hear the truth like it's never been told before mister
ofay is all worried now talking about a depression hell man
we have been depressed for over three hundred years and
they are still depressing us beating us robbing us in these
filthy rat-gnawed buggy smelly funky firetraps that they*

charge us more for than they ever charged the whites before they left all this crap behind for us black people o my brothers and sisters I ask you how long are we going to put up with this before we arch our backs and run the jews and all the rest of these white bastards off our doorsteps how long children how long will you allow these ofay bandits to suck your life's blood like leeches where are your so-called black leaders tell me where are they I'll tell you where they are they are out in mister ofay's kitchen begging him for a crust of mangy bread and mister ofay says here nigger now I'm giving you some bread so you keep all the rest of those niggers up in spooksville quiet yassuh mister ofay yassuh mister ofay I tell you my friends you and me are going to have to solve our own problems with our own black hands 'cause our leaders pardon my expression ain't shit no sir they ain't shit now you take walter white he's supposed to be goin' down south passin' for white so he can find out what the white man is planning to do to us negroes hell man who does he think he's foolin' he is white and he's taking your black money and goin' down south to see his relatives and gitting drunk and layin up with the rest of those crackers and laughing like hell cause you bunch of stupid niggers yeh that's what he calls you stupid black niggers give him money to help you o my children wake up wake up can't you see what the white man is doin for you can't you see yeh mister ofay said in the papers not so long ago that we had to war against a scarcity of money food and unemployment hell man he oughta make us his generals because we got more experience at fightin' those things than anybody on earth right right right right tell me I'm right brothers and move in closer now there's only one way to fight this battle that's with money and guns the same weapons mister ofay uses

*against you but first we're gonna need money o yes we
gotta have money cause mister ofay ain't got nothin' but
money so we have got to fight fire with fire blood with
blood so I'm gonna ask all you brothers and sisters to step
up and help me start the ball rollin' 'cause we've got to
have lots of things if we are gonna bring mister ofay to his
miserable cotton-pickin' knees yeh you heard me he should
have been pickin' all that cotton your pappy and your
mammy has been pickin' tell me I'm right that's right yell it
out hell ain't nobody gonna hurt you now it's too many of
us here tonight let my brothers in closer let my brothers
and sisters put something in this can so I can come back this
weekend and keep telling you some more truth like you
never heard before right right I'm tellin' you like it is now
let those good people come in with their money to help me
advance the cause thank you brother thank you sister
thank you thank you thank you they talk about communist
to hell with communist thank you brother thank you sister
hell all we want is something to eat and a decent place to
sleep and some good schools to educate our children hell
brothers and sisters that's all we want right tell me I'm right
ain't nobody going to hurt you say I'm right there's too
many of us tonight they're scared when we're all together
like this thank you thank you brother thank you sister no
we don't want their women we got pretty women of our
own just look around you brothers at those choice brown-
skins at your sides hell their women are like bloodless pups
in comparison tell me I'm right thank you pretty little heart
let 'em in closer closer don't leave I've got plenty more to
tell. . . .*

It was nearly eleven o'clock that night before I started
back to Mrs. Haskins' place; and I was tired, nervous and

disturbed by the raging speech. The big, heavy-fisted man had worked the crowd to a fever. Crouching like an animal beside the limp American flag, he would leap as though he would sail right out into the crowd; and the white cops had stood around in twos and threes, listening but not listening, their voices muffled, their faces grim and turned from the man who berated them. Walking back down Seventh Avenue, I tried making sense of what I had heard. His audience knew what he was talking about. They were the shattered examples. And their "amens," "tell 'em, brother," "right, right, right" proved that.

The accusation against Walter White shocked me. It couldn't be true. But I could vouch for the rats and bugs and brutalities of the whites. And I too had found myself agreeing with what he said. I had become part of the crowd and hollered "right" with them. Had they suddenly turned against the cops, I would have turned with them; and this frightened me now, for I knew that all this was really beyond my understanding. But if he intended to buy weapons why was he telling the policemen? The thing about Jews puzzled me too. Ben Myers, the tailor who had made our Easter suits in St. Paul, was the only Jew I had known. He lived in our neighborhood, and he and his wife were good people.

I cut over to Lenox Avenue. The streets were in full swing now. There was more happiness in the air. Tambourines and gospel music, soft laughter and talking mixed with the noisy traffic. Chick Webb's name was on the Savoy Ballroom's marquee and his music spilled through the open windows to the street below; and boys and girls were lindy-hopping on the sidewalk to its brassy sound. I watched fascinated for a while. Any couple would have been a hit at Minneapolis' Orpheum Theater.

Somebody was obviously right about the Cotton Club. I stood watching its entrance for over an hour, and the only Negro I saw go inside was a doorman—who ran into the lobby to help a drunken white man to his feet.

I stopped at Mac's for another hot dog and root beer on the way home. A boy about my age was at the counter that night and he said, "Good evening, brother," in a very friendly way. His face was an Indian brown, and he was stocky and of medium height. When he smiled, big dimples dented both cheeks, and his teeth were unusually white and even. After watching me gulp down the hot dog, he smiled and said, "I hope you won't think I'm being too personal, but you seem awfully hungry."

"You're right. I'm hungry—and broke," I answered.

He looked around. Mac, his boss, was in the rear counting money. "Have a round on the house," he said, shoving me another helping. "I was as broke as you before I got this job last month." We shook hands and he said his name was Bill Hunter. He worked nights and slept days, and I came by the stand several times that week and filled up. Bill was very intelligent and he knew Harlem. And he told me more about the "ghetto," as he called it, than I could have learned in months on my own. "The main thing is not to let it eat you up, brother," he would say after discussing it.

But that first night I had walked home with "mister ofay" deep in my mind. He was the enemy now, the lord of this filthy ghetto, the cause of Harlem's terrible underside. And Harlem was a prison, owned and operated by mister ofay, and exploited by him. Its inmates were all guilty of the same crime: they had been born black.

Each day there were the long walks in search of work, as far down as Forty-second Street sometimes. And I would return weary and desperate, my face and manner showing the strain of the fruitless journey. A long skinny man with bulging eyes sat on the stoop one Saturday evening when I got back. He looked as though he belonged to the place, and when he spoke I sat down beside him and we shook hands. His skin was damp and felt like leather. I gave my name and he introduced himself as Charlie, saying he lived up on the third floor.

"You must be the one with the jazz records," I said, observing his wide-brimmed hat and flowing zoot suit.

"Yeh, I got a big stack when I used to work in Sam's record store on 125th Street." We sat watching the weekend revelers pass and now and then he would look in my direction, as if he were studying me. "You a stranger here?" he asked, taking out a cigarette from his shirt pocket.

"In a way."

He lit the cigarette and inhaled it deeply, then breathed heavily, like someone sleeping; then he inhaled again, letting the smoke stay inside several seconds. When he exhaled, an odor like burned cornsilk struck my nose. "Want a drag?" he asked, pushing the cigarette toward my mouth. I seldom smoked but I accepted his offer, more as an act of friendliness than anything else. "Man," he said drowsily, "you waste the charge, blowing it out quick like that. Suck it in and git the glow—like this."

Now I knew. It was marijuana. And, slightly embarrassed by my squareness, I made a bolder effort the second time by pretending to get the glow—but it still tasted like cornsilk, and there wasn't any sensation. I coughed and looked about, hoping now that we were not being watched. Then fear shot through my body; a squad car had stopped in front of us. When a policeman got out Charlie casually stuck the butt beneath his heel and ground it out. My heart pounded. "Oh God," I said to myself, for now the policeman was approaching our stoop. He looked at us, not nearly as closely as I imagined, and went on to the door and knocked. Charlie didn't even look back, but I sat rigid, sweating and frightened. Mrs. Haskins must have been expecting him, for he entered the house without saying a word.

"Goddamned ofay cops always snooping around," Charlie muttered under his breath. I didn't answer. The other policeman at the wheel was eying us, and a red light from the dashboard sent a shadow of his nose up to his forehead, making his face a crude mask.

Suddenly the door behind us opened, and there was crying. We turned to see the policeman and Jessie, the mother of the small children I had seen the first day. She was sobbing and asking Mrs. Haskins to mind the children until she got back. The policeman opened the door for her, and she stumbled into the back seat. As they drove away Mrs. Haskins waddled to the edge of the stoop to watch.

"What's up? They still looking for her old man?" Charlie asked.

"They found him." Her tone was flat and caustic.

"Where?"

"Floating in the East River. They're taking her to identify his body." She turned to go back into the house. "What are you doing down here child?" The little girl with the wall eye was standing, frightened and naked, in the doorway. "Where they taking my momma?" she was asking.

"She'll be back soon. Come on now, let's go back upstairs."

We sat quietly for a few moments, and then Charlie said, "Well, that cat's gone to glory or some place with forty bucks of mine."

"Did you lend him money?"

"He bought some gage off me on time, forty bucks worth. Now all that fine stuff is at the bottom of that stinking East River," he said dolefully.

"What's gage?" I asked.

"Weed, man, like you just had." My dumbness earned the next question. "Hell, man, where're you from anyway?" he asked.

I spent the next half hour telling Charlie how I got to New York and how badly I needed a job. He listened without interrupting and at one point he lit up another "stick" and shoved it toward me. I puffed generously this time and captured a little bit of the glow. When we had finished, he got up and stretched. He was well over six feet tall, and the high-crowned hat he wore made him look even taller. He invited me upstairs to listen to records; and he did have a stack of them, by Duke Ellington, Don Redman, Claude Hopkins, Chick Webb, Fats Waller and Fletcher Henderson. Several times Mrs. Haskins hollered up to him: "Turn that thing down!" But not until after she had banged on the door and threatened to throw him out did Charlie soften the music. "I like my sounds loud so that it's inside me and all around me," he said.

I had gone to bed very late, but Charlie rapped on my door early the next morning and announced himself in a sleepy voice. He still wore the big hat and the zoot suit and looked as if he had never gone to bed.

"How'd you like to make a little bread this morning?" he asked with a yawn.

"Bread?"

"Yeh."

"Money, you mean?"

"Yeh, man, bread, loot, anything you wanta call it."

"How?" I asked, knowing I had only sixty cents left.

"Nothin' to it," he said. "Come by my place after you git dressed."

I was green, but I knew that Charlie was what my dad called "bad blood," that he was trouble. I remembered Abby's warning, "Just be careful up there!" but I threw it off with the first growl of hunger and started dressing. I'd seen Charlie's type before. He was very slick; I would have to watch him.

I had a shoe in my hand when I spotted a big rat loping toward a hole in the corner. I hurled the shoe and upended him before he escaped. But when I reached for the shoe to finish him off, he leaped for my hand. I jumped back, but not until he had bitten my toe and scurried under the bed. I blocked the hole with my suitcase, pulled the other shoe off and waited. When he didn't budge I frightened him into the clearing by slinging a pillow beneath the bed. This time I hit him squarely with both shoes, and I kept pounding him with the heels until he was a bloody pulp. It was as if I was releasing all the vengeance that had been stored within me for months. And since Mrs. Haskins had scoffed at my complaints about the presence of rats, I wrapped him in newspaper, went down and dropped him beside her door. Then I went back up the stairs to see Charlie.

"What the hell was all that racket a while ago?"

"Just killed a big rat," I said. I pulled off my shoe and sock so that he could see the bite.

Charlie laughed. "Hell, man, you're lucky. They ganged old lady Haskins' tomcat one day and chewed him to pieces." He pulled a cork from a bottle of corn whiskey. "Here, pour some of this on it. It'll kill the poison." I did as he instructed and let out a howl when the raw alcohol burned into the wound.

"That'll kill you or cure you," he said, laughing again.

"What's the work you've got for me?"

His eyes were very bloodshot. He closed them and rubbed the lids, then he looked at me curiously. And in the morning light I noticed that his lips were scorched from the heat of too many reefers. A regular cigarette now hung from his mouth and its smoke, curling over his hawk face, emphasized his blackness. His suit, looking as if dirt and grease had been pressed into it, had the same smell as the house. Charlie motioned me into a chair, then stretched out on his bed, which was broken and too short for his body. He was a rather funny sight, lying there, his pointed-toe yellow shoes hanging over the bed's end.

"Fact is, I'm mighty tired. Too much work. I need help." He pointed to a neat pile of small, newspaper-wrapped packages on the floor. "All you gotta do is deliver some of those for me every day and pick up some envelopes for me. Simple as that. Okay? You get a buck for every trip you make."

It seemed mysterious; and Charlie made it more so by not telling me what was in the packages. Evidently he intended this to be his private affair. I knew he wasn't peddling religious objects; I wasn't totally ignorant of his game. I simply didn't ask questions. I accepted his offer, and he immediately wrote out the names and addresses for my first deliveries.

A few minutes later, on the third floor of a building less than a block away, I knocked at door 3-B.

"What you want?" a voice growled from the other side.

"I've got a package for Shorty." My answer was in a tone that said I was hip, that I was in the know. "I'm from Charlie," I added nonchalantly.

The door opened slightly, and a dark giant of a man looked out evilly at me.

"You Shorty?" I asked haltingly.

"That's right." He yanked the package from me, shoved a dirty sealed envelope into my hand and slammed the door shut. The other package went to a man named Red who lived in a basement on 135th Street between Seventh and Eighth avenues—a few doors down from the 135th Street Police Precinct. Red seemed to be waiting for me and opened up at my first knock. Red was black, small and as hairless as a billiard ball; probably I had made a mistake.

"You're Red?"

"Yeh. What you want?"

"I'm from Charlie."

"Got the package?"

"You sure you're Red?"

"Yeh, man. Give it here." He too handed me a soiled envelope. "Tell Charlie I'm a deuce short. I'll even on the next buy. Okay?"

"Okay," I said rather negatively as though Charlie might not like his being a deuce short, even though I hadn't figured what the term meant in this particular case. "Okay," I repeated, "I'll tell him." What in hell is going on, I wondered. Shorty turns out to be a giant, and Red is as black as the ace of spades.

It so happened that Charlie wasn't very happy about his being a deuce short—"Son-of-a-bitch already owes me two bucks from the last buy"—but he liked my speed and accuracy. "There'll be three more this afternoon," he told me.

By the end of the week, I had made over thirty dollars. My rent was paid, my stomach was full and a little extra "bread" was stashed under my mattress for safekeeping. Things looked better. The following Friday I bought a pair of shoes, not too unlike Charlie's, and made a down payment on a suit at the London Tailors, a 135th Street shop that specialized in the "Harlem Drape."

I hadn't seen Bill in over two weeks. "I've been worried about you," he told me later that evening. "Oh, I've been doing pretty good," I said, showing him the new shoes.

"What have you been working at?"

"Oh, helping a guy with packages."

"Packages? What kind of packages, brother?"

Either Bill suspected something, or I was getting the least bit shaky about my new situation, or maybe it was the way I had said "packages." In any case, he was quiet for about a half hour, waiting now and then on a customer. Finally, he said: "Brother, you seem a little nervous about something. Everything all right?"

I was about to lie and say that everything was all right, but there was a sudden need to unburden myself of the secret and, feeling that Bill could be trusted, I told him exactly what I had been doing.

His usual smile was replaced by surprise, then dismay. "Brother," he said, "that's fire, the worst kind. They'll throw the book at you. And your luck could run out tomorrow. Forget that you ever saw that guy."

His manner and concern brought home the seriousness of what I had done, and I lay awake for hours that night worrying about the possible consequences, damning myself for having become so involved. And, despite my ingenious attempts, I couldn't justify my wrong through either need or hunger. What, I wondered, had happened to my sense of right and wrong? My mother's religious teaching? I no longer prayed or thought seriously of the God I had been trained to pray to. Yet I remembered saying "Oh God" when the cop came toward Charlie and me on the stoop that night. Was it, I wondered, that I really believed in

God, or was it a reaction to all the prayer meetings I had been hauled off to when I was a child? This calling on God at the moment I needed him was nothing new. I had done it countless times. Now I felt a little guilty about it.

Before I went to sleep I rather selfishly concluded that it was the church that was at fault, not I. The contradictions, borne by the people who called themselves Christians, had killed my faith. It was God, whom I had always assumed to be white, who gave us such a strange birth. It was He who molded us of black clay, breathed life into us, then willed us such trouble. I thought of all the black people in Alabama, Georgia, Mississippi and their sister states, whose prayers had gone unanswered for hundreds of years. If heaven was to be judged through its disciples on earth, then there would be separate pews for black and white angels. Wasn't my mother, devout as she was in life, buried on the black side of the cemetery, across the dusty road from the manicured green of the departed whites? And I wondered if the God she had served for a lifetime had given her a just reward in death. I doubted it. Still, after such a noble try at self-absolution, I went to sleep knowing that my actions, and my character, lay in my own hands. My conscience would not allow me to condemn God, the church or the evil of others for what I had brought upon myself.

I ducked Charlie for the next three days and went looking for a job again. But on the fourth morning he knocked on my door and walked in. "What's the matter, daddy? I've been looking all over for you. There's a lot of stuff to be delivered," he complained.

"I've been awful sick, Charlie, going to the doctor every day."

"Well, hurry up and kick him, man. I've got plenty for you to do." I told him I would contact him when I got better. As he started out the door I thought of the money his packages could bring me. Nearly all I had earned was spent for the new suit. "Charlie," I said as he was closing the door.

"Yeh?"

"Nothing. Nothing," I said. "I'll see you when I get better."

Bill was off that Saturday night, so we decided to go to the Savoy Ballroom. I picked up my suit that evening and hurried home. There was a letter from Sally asking about my work and my plans. I thought for a few minutes before sitting down to answer; and I weighed the virtue of truth against the embarrassment of failure. I finally wrote that everything was going well for me, that I wasn't with the band any more, but she was not to worry for I was forming one of my own. It wouldn't be long, I promised, before I would come back to marry her.

I had just sealed the letter and was licking the stamp when my door burst open and two cops with drawn pistols crashed into my room. Startled, I jumped up from the bed only to be knocked down again. Then one of them started punching me about my face and neck. "Okay, you black bastard, where's the stuff? We know it's here! Where is it?"

"What stuff? What stuff?"

"You know what stuff, you son-of-a-bitch!" Now he was bumping my head against the wall, while the other cop was pulling all my clothes from the closet and looking beneath the mattress with a flashlight.

"That ain't Charlie! That ain't Charlie! His room's down the hall!" Mrs. Haskins had come to my rescue. The beating stopped abruptly; the cop dropped me on the floor and they plunged down the hall toward Charlie's room.

"This is the house of the Lord," Mrs. Haskins kept mumbling as she stood in the door shaking her head and wringing her hands. But Charlie was gone. Evidently someone had tipped him off. His luck hadn't run out yet. The cops bulled about his empty room, kicking boxes and newspapers, which they knew Charlie used for storing and packing. As they left, I stood sullenly in the doorway, expecting some sort of apology; but they stomped past without even noticing me. I glanced over the banister as they went down. Red was standing in the shadows, handcuffed to a waterpipe. His face was puffed, and it looked as if they had beaten him. They unsnapped the bracelets and pulled him down the stairs behind them, and now I realized it must have been he who had tried to lead them to Charlie. I was thankful he had not spotted me.

"This is the house of the Lord! I won't stand for such goings-on around here!" The old lady's voice fell on deaf ears, for now the cops were punching Red's ribs with their billies. "Where'd he go, you bastard? Tell us or we'll break your goddamned neck!"

My new suit lay on the floor, wrinkled and searched. I picked it up and pushed the pockets back into place, then I wet a towel and bathed my wounds. The letter I had written lay crumpled on the bed; I smoothed it out and went down to the mailbox. I hesitated for a moment, then dropped it in, regretting my action by the time it hit the bottom. But then it was too late. I didn't go to the Savoy that night or even see Bill. I was too upset to see him or anyone else.

A light sprinkle of rain fell over Harlem the following morning, but I awoke early, dressed and for some reason I hardly understood decided to go to church. I went to one on St. Nicholas Avenue near 138th Street. The people were dressed differently from those who had attended our church back in Fort Scott, but the sermon, prayers and hymns were about the same. And, when the preacher called for sinners, I got an impulse to rejoin the church. But on the way up to the pulpit I began feeling that my emotions were playing pranks on me; so I turned back, grabbed my hat and hurried out the door. And behind me I could hear the choir singing, "What a friend we have in Jesus."

I wandered aimlessly in the drizzle for nearly an hour. Then I bought a Negro newspaper and read about a white mob taking a Negro boy from a deputy sheriff in Opelousas, Louisiana. They had castrated and lynched him for an "alleged" attack on a white woman.

I imagined the horror of his final moments. The extraordinarily awful moments when a terror-filled heart is famished of all hope, yet prays to a God who is either absent or unlistening; when the lips, bloodied and bruised, ask for a mercy which will not come. And eventually the torso would swing gently in the hot breeze, dripping blood into the dust.

White people were making it easy for me to hate white people. I was still sore from the cop's blows and I remembered past lynchings and the earlier assaults in Bemidji and St. Paul. The image of all whites was suddenly an image to despise. And it was an image that had started as far back as I could remember. I was only twelve when a cousin of mine, a fair girl with light reddish hair, came to spend the summer at our house. One day she and I ran, hand in hand, toward the white section of town to meet my mother, who worked there as a domestic. Then unexpectedly, three white boys, ranging from twelve to fifteen, blocked our path. I gripped my cousin's hand, and we tried going around them, but they spread out across the walk before us.

"Where you going with that nigger, blondie?" one of them asked.

We had stopped. The youngest boy eased behind me and dropped to his knees, and one of the others shoved me backward. Pain shot through my head as it bumped the sidewalk, but I could hear my cousin screaming as she ran for help. Then one of them spat in my face and kicked my neck from behind. I jumped up and started swinging, but they beat me down again. The next time I hit the ground, I grabbed a foot and upended its owner, then, scrambling up, I tried to run. A fist sent me down again, but then I realized someone was helping me. Another white boy whom I knew had come to my aid. Then suddenly he was down beside me, hit on the head with a stick. The three boys ran off. "How did it all start?" my rescuer asked as we walked along nursing our bruises. I told him.

"The dunces," he said. "Hell, I knowed she was a nigger all the time."

THIRTEEN

I HAD been at Mrs. Haskins' for about a month when she finally showed the intolerance she held for penniless roomers. One morning after I had returned from job hunting, she met me downstairs with my bag, which she had packed; then, screaming disgust, she ushered me out the door. It was a very noisy eviction and several people stopped to watch, but I hurried past them, avoiding their eyes, and went to the hot dog stand. Bill wasn't there but Mac said that I could leave my bag until I found another room.

Walking through Central Park I decided I was fed up with poverty, hunger and New York. I had tried everything I knew, and failed. I began to think about hopping a freight back to Kansas or Minnesota—or any place besides this hopeless city. A winter here would either send me to jail or to my grave, I thought. It was no place for a country boy to try his luck; not with so many jobless and unfriendly people. I would try another day. If things didn't work out I would either start hitchhiking or ride the rails.

It was a long walk through the park and I came out on Fifty-ninth Street, hungry and tired. There was a delicatessen with big jars of pickles in the windows. I spent a nickel on one and fifteen cents on bologna and crackers; then I was completely broke.

I went back to the edge of the park and sat beneath a tree to eat. The meat tasted good between the brittle crackers and I would take a bite of the pickle after each sandwich. And I ate very slowly, not knowing when I would eat again. I meant to save a little for later on, but I was so hungry I devoured everything I had bought.

The same doorman was puffing under a load of baggage when I passed the Park Central Hotel a half hour later. And the offensive expression on his face brought back the wet morning when he had ordered me toward the servants' entrance. I hadn't thought about him since that day. But now I was angry at him again. And there was a strong urge to trip him up. The picture of him sprawled on the sidewalk among the bags was delightful and clear. Moving over to Broadway, I wondered about Abby, Larry and the others. And I thought that no matter where they were they couldn't be any worse off than I.

I tried restaurants, grocery stores, theaters, barbershops, pool halls, shoe-shine stands, amusement galleries, dance halls, garages, bookstores and churches. I even asked about a cleaning job at a police station near Times Square. But it was always, "Sorry, boy"—"Can't pay the help I got"—"Nothing here"—"Sorry, we don't hire colored people."

I stood on the corner of Forty-eighth Street and Broadway and watched the late sun slide down toward the horizon; and its warm orange coloring slanted deep shadows on the buildings along the street. It looked lovely and I thought that I would like to paint what I saw or write about it. But it would all be gray soon and the sky would be dark and I would be homeless and hungry again. It was a frightening thought, and I tried to put it out of my mind.

But a finger of panic had touched me and I had to keep telling myself that I wasn't going to starve. I would rob and steal before I died on the streets.

A lamp light flicked on in one of the third-story windows across Broadway. It made an amber glow behind white lettering that read, W. C. HANDY PUBLISHING COMPANY. It seemed ironic for me to be standing there afraid of the coming evening when, just a few strides away, was the office of the composer of the famous "St. Louis Blues." He of all people should understand my situation. My songs were pretty good; I should have gone to him before. So, after I got up enough courage, I went up to his office and knocked on the door.

"Come in!" someone hollered.

I opened the door and went in. There was a middle-aged brown-skinned man sitting at a roll-top desk. He was portly and his face was chubby and pleasant. He was alone and looked up from some papers to greet me. "What can I do for you?" he asked.

"Are you Mr. Handy, the famous composer?"

"No, I'm his brother Charles. What do you want to see him about?"

"I'm a composer."

Charles Handy smiled slightly and leaned back in his chair. "You have a song you want published?"

"Yessir. I've got several of them."

"Where are they?"

"Well, sir. I don't have them with me, but I can play them on a piano for you."

"First tell me your name. All good composers have names." And I spoke my name haltingly, as though it had caught up with me for the first time and I was acknowledging it with some misgiving.

"Okay," he said, pointing at an upright in the corner, "sit down and play them for me." A rather bad audition followed. I was nervous and excited and made a number of mistakes. Once I stopped altogether but he said, "Go on, go on." And I finished knowing it was the worst I had ever played. "Tell me a little about yourself," he said without commenting on my audition.

I started off cautiously, telling him about my experience with Larry's orchestra and how it had folded and left me stranded. He asked me if I had friends in New York and how I had managed to live and eat without a job. And I told him about Bill, but not about Charlie or Mrs. Haskins.

"Seems you've had a pretty tough time. How many composers do you think there are in this city?"

"I couldn't guess," I said honestly.

"And no one else could either," he said rather sadly. "They're a dime a dozen. Some good ones too, but they can't get the breaks. There are more of them on breadlines than there are in offices." He laid the odds before me rather frankly. And he told me of his brother's struggle and he named other famous ones who hadn't found the going easy. When he had finished we both sat quiet for a few moments. The lights had begun to come on over Broadway, and the chances of my name's ever appearing beneath them seemed dimmer than ever. Finally I got up, thanked him for listening, then started to go.

"Hold on," he said, reaching for his hat. "You can ride uptown with me if you like."

He took me to his brother's home in Harlem that evening. And there were fried chicken, mashed potatoes, biscuits and hot apple dumplings. W. C. Handy and his wife, his daughters, Lucille, Catherine, Elizabeth, and Wyatt, his son, made up a family that was a lot like my own had been years before. And, as I ate, talked and laughed with them, I kept remembering. I spent two days there until Catherine found me a room with another good family, the Pearsons.

Three other boys roomed there also; and Mom Pearson fed us when we were broke, mended our clothes and looked after us as if we were her own. Then Bill got me a job working with him at the hot dog stand. Things were now beginning to look up and I started composing again. But two weeks later Bill and I arrived to find the place locked. Bill went off to telephone the boss. He returned ten minutes later, his face enveloped in gloom.

"What's up?" I asked, sensing the worst.

"Old Mac is dead."

"Dead? Dead from what?"

"His wife thinks it was poison liquor. A friend of his is dead, and another one is dying."

We walked aimlessly down Lenox Avenue with less than ten dollars between us. Bill bought a sympathy card for Mac's widow, then we wandered over to the 135th Street YMCA. There in the lobby was a sign urging young men between eighteen and twenty-five to enlist in the Civilian Conservation Corps. Bill was the first to comment. "Brother," he said wryly, "I think it's about time we looked into that."

On the 18th of April, Bill and I, along with hundreds of other boys from Harlem, passed our physicals and joined the CCC. We were instructed to meet at a designated place in lower Manhattan the following morning, where buses would transport us to Camp Dix, New Jersey.

We were lucky to meet those buses the next morning. Perhaps we were lucky to be alive. It was Bill's good looks that got us into trouble. Celebrating our last night in Harlem, we wandered into a speakeasy and Bill, after three drinks, was getting a bit unruly. The owner, a huge man called Big Joe, stood at the end of the bar eying Bill. But also eying Bill from a table at our left was Big Joe's pretty brown-skinned woman, Lil. I felt trouble and tried to get Bill to leave, but he was far too involved in the flirtation. After two more drinks, he became completely unmanageable. The bartender tried to quiet him, and he took a swing at the bartender and fell flat on his face. The next thing I knew, we were getting the bum's rush by four of Big Joe's boys. We landed on our behinds outside the place.

At least we were out of trouble, I thought; the problem now was to get him home. I shoved and pulled him for about three blocks; then, as I steadied him at the curbing, a black sedan stopped in front of us.

It was Lil, beckoning for us to get in. "Come on. I'll give you a lift home," she said. I helped Bill into the front seat beside her and got in the back. She asked me where I wanted to be dropped, but I refused to leave until Bill was safely home. She didn't like this, but I wouldn't get out; so she drove around for about thirty minutes, stopping finally at a building up in the Bronx. She got out and opened the door for Bill. "He'll be out in a jiffy," Lil said. "You can wait down here."

By this time I was tired and content to wait, but Bill fell at the door, and Lil hollered for me to help her get him up the stairs. After we had got him into her flat, Lil, fearing she might need more help, told me I could wait in an adjoining room. Time went by, and I fell asleep. About three o'clock in the morning I jumped awake to a banging on the door, then a man's voice. "Lil, this is Joe! Open up this damn door—else I'll blow the lock off!"

This was no time to question the existence of God. I called upon him silently, fervently, as I jerked the window shades up in search of a quick exit. Lil was asking help from the same quarter as she tried, unsuccessfully, to arouse Bill and get him into his clothes. "Oh, my God—my God," she moaned. "Help me get him dressed."

"Is there a back way out?" I asked, gathering up Bill's belongings. She just stood shaking in fear, saying, "No—no—no."

Meanwhile Joe was banging the door with the butt of his pistol. "Open up, goddamnit! This is the last time I'm telling you!"

"Open it," I said, "or he'll come in shooting and kill us all." My mind raced. Would he really kill for this woman? Was she worth it to him? Would he shoot Bill, lying there groaning in his nakedness? Would the fact that I was clothed save me? Would he murder all three of us?

"To hell with the big bastard," Bill was mumbling, "I'll take care of him. . . . Let me at him." How fortunate for him to be so sublimely unconscious at such a moment, I thought. If it does happen, he wouldn't know what hit him.

Big Joe didn't shoot the lock off. Instead, he threw the weight of his body against the door several times, and the locks began to give. Then, behind a mighty thrust of his foot, he came crashing through, pistol in hand, like an enraged bull. He took one look at Bill and me, whirled and knocked Lil all the way across the room.

"Now Mr. Joe," I began, "let's talk this thing over. . . . We . . ." I couldn't say another word. Joe stood looking at us, the pistol pointing in our direction, as though we were unreal. I can't say whether the next thing Bill did saved us or not, but at least it broke the impasse. He staggered up to swing at Joe (and this was probably as incredible to Joe as it was to me), but before the angry man could react I knocked Bill down, then started pulling him out the door. Joe stood watching us dumbfounded. When I finally got Bill to the door, Joe threw his clothes out and gave me a boot in my rear, sending me sprawling over Bill in the hallway. By this time, everyone in the building had awakened. I could feel them peeping at us from behind their doors as I dragged Bill down the stairs. But they didn't matter; the important thing was that we were out, and safe. If I could help it, they would never see me in that building again. Finally, with the supreme effort that comes to one during such emergencies, I got Bill down to the street, dressed him, hailed a taxi and took him home.

By five o'clock that morning, we had crammed our few personal belongings into one bag. I left a note thanking the Pearsons, and we took a subway to meet our bus. When we arrived at the rendezvous point, it was raining and everyone, except a few stragglers, had boarded. We showed our papers to the driver and made our way down the aisle, observing the other recruits as we went. Worn, beaten, hungry, the lot of us smelled and looked like hard times. We didn't know what fate held for us. We were just looking for something the streets of Harlem had denied us.

After we were seated, Bill shook his head wearily and summed up the situation. "Brother, it looks like death row at Sing Sing. God help us all." He smiled weakly, slumped into his hangover and fell asleep. By the time our convoy rumbled away, the rain was falling steadily; and, it seemed, the very order of things was mocking my failure. My exit was proving as dismal as my arrival had been. As I watched the skyscrapers fade in the distance, I hoped I would go back one day and try again. Somewhere beneath the fog that covered the city there was, I felt, a niche for me. Perhaps I hadn't tried hard enough or given myself enough time.

Bill's head bobbing upon my shoulder recalled our predicament of a few hours before. Now it all seemed unreal. We had faced death over a senseless flirtation. In a way, it had been a test of my friendship for Bill. But I realized I had stayed with him because I was trapped with him. I wondered what I would have done had there been a chance of my escaping alone. And I hoped neither of us would ever have to prove our loyalty under such a condition again.

FOURTEEN

IT WAS still raining when we reached Camp Dix later that morning; acres of mud and rain-soaked tents stretched out before us. After we got off the bus a big tough-looking Negro came forward and snapped us to attention. Then, as we shuffled about trying to form a line, he stood, arms akimbo, legs spread in arrogant authority, scowling down upon us as though we were poisonous insects. Behind him, dressed in army surplus, their boots dramatically anchored in the slush, were a sullen group of six Negroes who had also struck commanding poses.

"I'm Michigan Jones, your section leader, and this is Jack Brewer, your sub-section leader—and Tate, Rufus, Fats, Marcus and Brown here are my assistants! I give orders and they see that they are carried out!" the big man barked. "Everybody understand that?" It was quiet for a moment. The sound of the rain pelting the mud grew sharper. Suddenly I was sorry I had come. "Okay, don't forget it! Left face!" he shouted. Our ranks turned in every possible direction and Michigan, a sadistic grin on his face, turned his back to us and addressed his colleagues: "What a dumb bunch of bastards we got this time." All of them sanctioned his remark with grim headshaking and Michigan faced us again, pointing his finger east (which meant to our right) and barked, "Left face!" Those of us who faced left were ignored; those who mistakenly followed his finger were called a bunch of "fart heads." Other men were watching from the tents now and enjoying the show that Michigan and his "assistants" put on with each bus load of new recruits. Finally the line was pointed in one direction and we were marched off to the supply barracks. There we received dungarees, floppy work hats, army shoes, socks, underwear and raincoats. At the end of a long counter, we were given mess kits—oblong pans with covers that held a metal knife, fork, spoon and drinking cup.

"There's something awful wrong here, brother," Bill said as we changed into our new clothes. "Something smells—and we've got to do something about it." I didn't answer him but I knew what he meant. He had suddenly come alive and I could sense that he was already making plans far beyond my thinking. He learned quickly that only four men were assigned to each tent, so he went over and made hasty friendships with two recruits who had sat behind us on the bus.

"Those two brothers over there are going to bunk with us," he whispered. "They've got more brains than the rest and we're going to need all the help we can get." I was amazed. We hadn't been in camp an hour and he was already plotting the downfall of Michigan and his gang.

"Do they know what you're up to?" I asked.

"They will soon enough, brother."

"What're their names?"

"The light brown one is Hubie Carter. The big black one is Leon Williams." I started to speak again but Bill beat me to it. "Take it easy—Brother Michigan and his boys seem to be taking a very special interest in us."

Now Michigan spoke. "Where're you two from?"

"New York City, Brother Jones. And where are you from?" Bill asked.

"I'm asking the questions. You give the answers—and you can stop that brother shit." He spat on the floor and walked away.

"Looks like we're on his list already," I said.

Bill chuckled. "Don't let it bother you, brother. It's a dumb fox who shows his nose to the hunter."

Next we were marched from the barracks and lined up in front of the headquarters tent. There the commanding officer and our forester—the only white men attached to our company—would inspect us. The rain had slacked off and we stood awkwardly erect, waiting. The captain stepped out first. He was a big man with pink cheeks and sleepy eyes; and he was dressed in full army regalia. Jones and his men snapped to attention and saluted smartly. Our line attempted the same courtesy, but the results were discouraging. The forester, a youngish blond man wearing puttees and leather boots, stepped out beside the officer.

"I'm Captain Harry M. Littleton, your commanding officer, and this is Mr. Robert Cummings, your forester. We welcome you to the 235th Company of the Civilian Conservation Corps," he said. And he went on welcoming us in clipped army language for about ten minutes, including meanwhile the rules we were to live by. He ended by demanding that our company be the best disciplined in the entire Corps—and that every one of us help to make it so.

After the captain and Cummings left, Tate strutted to the head of the line and gave an order: "All right, all you black bastards heard what the man said about discipline. Don't forget it! And don't forget that we're running this show! Break ranks and get some chow!"

Bill, Hubie Carter and I withdrew from the others and as we walked slowly toward the chow line I saw a slight smile playing on Bill's face, the reason for which escaped me. The entire situation seemed unbearable and I was already tired of being called a black bastard every five minutes—even if the name callers were blacker than I. His smile broadened when I asked him what he thought of the two white men. And he didn't answer immediately. Then the dimple in his cheek deepened even more and he said, with an easy laugh, "Brother, those two white men are mighty unhappy."

This was more than I had been able to observe and I challenged his remark. "Something's bothering them—and I think I know what it is," he said. We waited for his reasons but he didn't give them. "A little luck and patience is all we need," he said as we got on the end of the chow line.

Through camp scuttlebutt we soon found out that Michigan Jones had been picked for leadership by the captain because of his ruggedness and intelligence, and Littleton used him effectively as a liaison between himself and the undisciplined company he had inherited. But Jones had surrounded himself with slick gamblers who had cleaned out the camp before we arrived. Studs Brown, a prison alumnus and ex-fighter with bulging muscles and a nasty temper, was the gang's strong-arm man. They ruled the camp and could not be opposed or rejected without trouble.

But Bill Hunter's charm spread through the camp like a disease. By the second day he had more than doubled our acquaintances. And on the third night our tent was filled with recruits, boisterously sharing one another's jokes and experiences. Some, having been at camp for several weeks, had already acquired rather unusual nicknames. Shim Sham, a tall pigeon-toed hypochondriac who wore rubbers and carried an umbrella on sunny days, was being cheered as he did the dance that he had been named for. Slops, a humorous glutton, was noisily defending his rights for thirds on the chow line. Geechi, from South Carolina, a bullish, incoherent fieldhand, was stomping wildly and singing in an odd accent of the South and the West Indies. And there were Pussy Cat, River Frank, Spats, Hope, Moose Jaw and a host of others, all talking at the top of their voices. No one was surprised when Michigan stuck his head through our tent flap and ordered us to "Break it up!" Michigan was surprised, however, when for the first time nobody obeyed him. The noise continued as if he had never spoken.

"Did you bastards hear me? I said break it up!" he bellowed.

"Why you call us men bawsterds all de time? You go crawp in your boot!" big Geechi shot back. Now the place roared with laughter.

Bill's strategy was working. In him the harassed recruits had found themselves a rallying point, and Michigan, sensing this immediately, stood glowering at Bill and me.

"Come on in and join the fun," Bill said smiling.

"The real fun ain't started yet," Michigan countered. "You two report for latrine duty tomorrow morning after chow." He dropped the flap and left. And the party went on.

"Latrine duty can be pretty nasty work," I complained to Bill as we sat finishing breakfast.

"Don't get upset, brother. Our friend Michigan is playing right into my hands." Bill seemed confident, and instead of reporting to the latrines after chow we went, at his insistence, straight to the captain's tent and asked to speak with him. The orderly ushered us in and instructed us to sit down. Littleton was talking on the telephone, and after he finished he shuffled a few papers, lit a cigar, then turned to us.

"What can I do for you fellows?" he asked gruffly.

Bill began with an extreme degree of tact and polish. "Sir, we hate to bother you but we feel that we have been maliciously assigned to a very unpleasant duty—which we feel we don't deserve."

"What's this duty that is so unpleasant?"

"The latrines, sir."

"The latrines?"

"Yessir."

"Who are you? What're your names?"

"Hunter—William C. Hunter, sir, and this is Gordon Parks."

Littleton gave us an extremely close look before going on. "Well now, who ordered this duty—and why?"

"Mr. Jones, sir. I can't say exactly why, other than he seemed particularly annoyed because we took it upon ourselves to entertain a few of the recruits in our tent last evening—some who, I might add, were very low in spirit."

The captain began drumming the table with his fingers. We were nervously quiet. Then he relit his cigar. "How long have you two been in camp, Hunter?"

"This is the fourth day, sir. And I would like to say that Parks and I enjoyed your welcoming speech." What a liar, I thought, but I was sure by now that we wouldn't have to face latrine duty.

The captain's face lit up. "Well—thank you, Hunter."

"You're welcome, sir."

"You say 'low in spirit'; do you find that to be the general feeling around here?"

"If you don't mind my being frank, sir, I would say yes."

"What's your background? Where did you come from?"

"Parks here is from Minnesota and I'm from New York City."

"And your schooling?"

"Columbia, sir."

"Columbia. Good school." He fidgeted for a moment and turned sideways in his chair. "Now, sir," Bill cut in, "please don't think we feel that such a duty is beneath us. It's just that we hoped to be of more advanced service to you and Mr. Cummings."

Littleton got up and started walking back and forth. "Yes, I see what you mean, Hunter. I see what you mean." He sat back down. "You two come back after lunch. I want to speak to Cummings about this." We got up to leave. "After lunch, remember."

"Thank you, sir," Bill said airily as we started out. Then he turned back to the captain. "I beg your pardon, sir, but are we to report to the latrines, or is that order to be reconsidered?"

"Er, oh yes, by all means," my heart fluttered for a second, "the order will be reconsidered. I'll speak to Jones personally."

"Thank you, sir. Thank you very much." And we walked erect, lively and in step as we left the tent, feeling that the captain might still be watching us. After we were around the corner, Bill slapped me on the back. "That's the luck I was talking about, brother. All we need now is the patience."

"That was a real grease job, Brother Bill," I said happily, "but you laid it on kinda thick about the welcoming speech."

"It was either that or clean those stinking latrines. A tankful of French perfume wouldn't help us after a day on that job."

Bill was right, we found out that afternoon when we reported back to the captain's quarters. He and the forester were indeed unhappy about several things—company morale, the lack of discipline, gambling and the growing animosity toward Michigan's gang. Both men quickly sensed Bill's potential, and they immediately suggested that he become camp leader. And their joy in finding such intelligence amongst the impoverished Negroes turned to embarrassment when Cummings—intending to compliment —said that Bill's mannerisms and speech were more white than colored.

"Negroes and whites use the same English books at Columbia," Bill had answered politely.

But taking over Michigan's job wasn't going to be easy. Bill turned to me. "What do you think, brother? You would be my foreman if I were to take the job." The consequences seemed perilous. Neither the captain nor the forester could give us any help; our only hope lay in the support of the disgruntled recruits. "Maybe we should go outside and talk it over," I suggested, although I knew there was no turning back now. Everyone agreed to this and Bill and I went outside the captain's tent to discuss the situation. We didn't do much talking. "Are you with me?" Bill asked. And I answered, "All the way." Then we went back to tell the captain that we would accept, only to find him in a quandary. He couldn't think of a way to "diplomatically" demote Michigan Jones and Jack Brewer. So, in a matter of seconds, our company became perhaps the only one in the vast Corps with two sets of leaders. And this wouldn't help matters any.

Now, instead of the thirty dollars a month allotted to recruits, Bill would get forty-five and I would get thirty-six. This was reason enough for celebration. Slops, we heard, was running a little bootleg business, so we looked him up and bought a couple of bottles of liquor—on time. I awoke the next morning terribly sick and gave up all my dinner to the latrine which I had escaped the day before. By noon my right side ached and my body was wet with perspiration. I was getting worse and Bill finally insisted that I be taken to a hospital. On the way I passed out; and in less than two hours I had been anesthetized and wheeled off to an operating room.

Morning had come. And Bill stood above me smiling. "Take it easy—take it easy," he was saying.

"Where am I? What happened?"

"You're at Camp Dix hospital—minus an appendix. And everything's going to be all right."

There were eight of us in the ward altogether with ailments such as colds, diarrhea and poison ivy; but one man had a broken back; another had a crushed shoulder; and then there was a recruit with an incurable blood disease that sometimes twisted him in great pain; and one young victim of a dynamite blast lay supine, with his body, head and eyes heavily bandaged—uncertain as to whether he would see again. My bed was next to his and I remember him as Philip. All, except me, were white, though I can't say what Philip looked like because I never saw that much of him. They always took him away to change the bandages—and it was then that we, in deference to his cries, grew quiet.

Yet, in spite of such serious casualties, our ward was remarkably free of despair. In fact, we raised so much hell Miss Clarke, the harassed day nurse, called our ward "the inferno." She was a plump, good-natured woman whose bossiness earned her the title of "Madame Simon Legree." Everyone but Philip was kidded about his particular ailment —especially the diarrhea victim. Each time he struck out for the lavatory, half the ward shouted, "Enemy sighted!" Then the other half would shout, "Bombs away!" Sometimes the poor guy made it; sometimes he didn't. And we made nickel and dime bets on him as though he were a racehorse.

Then one day Poison Ivy raised the ante. "I'll bet a dollar he don't even make it to the door on his next run," he said. Broken Back and Bad Blood took him on—and lost. That evening they both accused Poison Ivy of slipping castor oil into Diarrhea's tea. An argument developed and after that Madame Legree prohibited all betting.

Philip didn't talk much. He seemed to be shut up in his darkness; and this was easy to understand. I was surprised when, after everyone was asleep one night, he called my name.

"Gordon," he said softly, "are you sleeping?"

"Nope. Are you okay?" I asked, thinking he might be in pain.

"I just wanted to ask you about somethin'—if you don't mind."

"Go ahead."

"Do you believe in God and religion and that kinda thing?"

I was puzzled. I remembered asking my mother something similar once when I was a child, and I had started to repeat her answer; but I wasn't sure now that her answer had been the right one. "Do you?" I asked, somewhat in self-defense.

"Naw, not me. Ma was the churchgoer in our family, always singin' and shoutin', but it never got her nowheres."

"Are your parents living?"

"I guess so. Least, I hope so. I ain't heard hide nor hair of any of 'em since I left 'em on a highway outside of Lebanon, Oklahoma. That's about two months ago."

"Where are they now?"

"Somewheres between Oklahoma and Californ'a I guess —lookin' for work. Pa was what they called a sod buster and our land dried up one day and we woke up one mornin' with nothin' but a bacon rind and dust in our shack. Pa owed a lot of people and they took the land and knocked our shack down with a tractor. Pa stood there lookin' for a minute, then he spit in the dust and loaded Ma and my brothers and sisters in his old jalopy and took off down the road." He stopped for a moment, then went on, "Somethin' come over me about three miles down the road when I saw a train track and I got out and told them goodbye. I rode boxcars all the way out here and landed in this CCC outfit."

He was quiet then for a few moments. "Why'd you ask me about God and religion?"

"I don't know. I guess I'm worried about seein' again. I never thought about prayin' and such till I got messed up like this. Maybe I'm crazy or somethin'. I don't know."

"I don't know either, Philip. I can't say I believe in God and religion the same way my parents did—but I feel like there's something bigger than all of us out there. And sometimes I pray to that."

"Oh, so you prayed before?"

"Yep. When we were kids we prayed every night before we went to sleep."

"What did you pray for anyhow?"

"Oh, for lots of things, but mostly I asked the Lord to help Momma and Poppa and all my brothers and sisters and my sweetheart—if I had one."

"Did you always get what you prayed for?"

"Not all the time but sometimes I did."

There was another long silence and I thought that he had gone to sleep. But after about fifteen minutes he said, "Could you pray a little for me tonight?"

"Why I've been praying for you every night—and when they take you to change your bandages."

He was surprised. "Why didn't you tell me?" he asked.

"I didn't tell my brothers and sisters when I prayed for them," I answered. "Who are you, something special?" I hoped he would laugh. And he did.

And I prayed for him that night. I asked—whoever I prayed to—to let him see again. And I prayed that he wouldn't hate what he saw when they finally removed the bandages.

At Philip's request the two of us went to church together that following Sunday morning. He was placed on a small mobile bed and I wheeled him into the hospital chapel. It was hard to tell how the minister's words affected him, for afterward he only lay quiet; and I assumed he was sleeping. But the ward was unusually peaceful that afternoon so I took advantage of the mood and wrote Sally of all that had happened to me, saying finally that my "promotion" would hasten our marriage. And I arbitrarily set the date as October 15, which was nearly seven months away.

Our company was fully rostered and at work when I returned to camp ten days later. Its first assignment was in a forest several miles to the north. Each morning after breakfast we piled onto flat-bed trucks with our axes and rode to work singing—our voices startling the animals and birds of the quiet woods. There were two groups; one, headed by Bill, went ahead blazing all undesirable trees; another group, headed by Michigan, trailed closely and felled the trees we had marked. And it was a good feeling to be deep in the pine-scented forest hearing the melodic Harlem voices shouting: "Timber! Timber!" and the great trees cracking, slashing, then booming to the earth. During extremely foul weather, we stayed in camp and crowded together in the recreation hall; and there the talented ones sang and danced, lifting the gloom that comes with such weather. And I, being the only piano player, was kept busy accompanying them.

At first Michigan's gang never took part; they preferred gambling. But soon there was no one for them to gamble with, for evenings and weekends the men flocked to the recreation Bill set up for them. Other than music there were checkers, chess, books and magazines he gathered through donations from the surrounding towns and villages. And there were organized boxing, wrestling and track meets, for which modest prizes were given. He assigned Hubie Carter and Leon Williams to encourage discussion groups. And he got Cummings to explain, to those who were interested, the mysteries of the forest, and to tell the genuses of certain trees. In a few weeks some of us went about spouting terms like *Quercus stellata, Pinus strobus, Acer macrophyllum.* It seemed that every move Bill Hunter made was intended to lift the spirit of that desolate camp. Then, after he had everything set up as he wished, he executed the real stroke of genius.

"Brother Jones," he said to Michigan one day, "I need your help. We would feel honored if you would hand out the prizes to the winners of the track meet this weekend."

Obviously here was a chance for Michigan to shine. "I'll think it over," he said gruffly. That weekend he was there—handing out the prizes as if he had made them with his own hands. And, after that, his entire gang became friendlier.

But for a while the marriage became more deadly than the separation had been. A simple conversation between Studs and Leon Williams ended with Williams lying unconscious from a brutal uppercut thrown by Studs. And Tate became enraged and called me a dirty son-of-a-bitch when I beat him in a checkers game. I ignored him at first but then he "put me in the dozens," or, to put it simply, he cursed me in the name of my mother. For this, unless you were a coward, you fought. Everyone gathered around and we started to square off, but Bill, thinking rightly that this might end in a free-for-all, suggested that the two of us remain in camp the next day and fight it out. We both agreed; and we were to use nothing but our fists.

Stripped to the waist, we faced each other in the quiet of the deserted camp the next morning. Only the pleasant chirping of birds came from around us. We didn't speak. Then, as I raised my fist, Tate snatched a sharpened messkit knife from his back pocket; and I stood there—speechless with fright—defenseless against his glistening weapon. There was no point in running just to get it in the back— no point in denouncing his treachery, or even asking for mercy. He crouched and I backed away and now he was set to spring.

"Tate! Drop that knife!" It was Bill. He had jumped from behind a tent and held a pickaxe ready to strike. "Drop it, brother! I mean what I say!" Tate stiffened and dropped the knife at his feet. "Kick it away from you, brother!" Bill was closer now. He circled, kicked the knife away and motioned to me. "Okay, brother. It's even now. Go get him."

I raised my fists again but Tate dropped his arms and refused to fight. I looked at him for a second, ready to strike. But his viciousness of a few moments before was replaced by timidity.

"Fight!" I screamed, freeing my own fear at last. "Fight!"

He remained silent and shaking. And more, I feel, for the cowardice he displayed than for my anger against him, I banged a hard left to his belly. He doubled up and I knocked him to the earth. And he lay there, refusing to get up.

"That's enough, brother." Bill was by my side, restraining me.

We turned away. I put on my shirt and we went toward the woods to join the others. "What brought you back?" I asked him.

"He's a knife man. He never intended to fight you fair. And you'd be surprised who told me—just as we were leaving camp."

"Who?" I asked.

"Tate's good friend Studs Brown." No one was ever told how the fight came out. And Tate and I got along very well after that.

Fats was the next and last of Michigan's gang to cause trouble. He put a snake, a nonpoisonous one he had caught in the forest, under Joe Riley's blankets. Now Joe Riley was a very quiet boy who seldom said much to anyone. When he got into bed and felt the snake curling around his leg, he could tell by the look on Fats's face who had put it there. So Joe reached down calmly and took the snake by the head; then he got up and went across to Fats and began to beat him in the face with it. It took several men to stop him. Joe Riley didn't report for roll call three days later. And when Bill went to investigate he found Joe Riley dead—from natural causes, the autopsy said.

Our company was saddened by Joe Riley's death and Bill collected money for flowers and wrote a fitting eulogy that he read before they took the coffin away. But bad luck struck again the following week when one of our flat-bed trucks sideswiped another. Sam Thompson's legs had been hanging over the side of our truck, and were crushed. He was remarkably tough, hanging on to consciousness all the way to the hospital, not once complaining—asking only for a cigarette now and then.

"Everything's going to be all right, Brother Sam. You'll be up and around before long," Bill was saying as they prepared him for the operating room.

And Sam laughed. "You ain't foolin' me none, Bill. I saw what was left same as you did."

"Does it hurt, Sam?" I asked.

"There ain't enough left to hurt," he replied.

Down the corridor I could see my old ward; and I thought about Philip and the others. And while Bill kept vigil outside the operating room, I went to visit. There were mostly new patients in the room now. But I recognized Broken Back sitting up in a wheelchair. We exchanged greetings warmly and I asked about Philip.

"That's him looking out the window over there," he said.

I walked over to Philip. "Remember me?" I asked, taking his hand with one finger missing, noticing that he looked much better than I had expected.

"I know your voice."

"I'm Gordon. I was in the bed next to yours."

He looked at me strangely for several seconds and his

scarred face creased into a smile. "Well, I'll be damned," he said, "old Philip never thought he'd ever see you."

"Same for me," I answered. We were at a loss for words for a second or two. Then Philip said, "I hope you don't mind it but I'm about to say somethin' awful silly."

"Go ahead."

"Well, I swear, I thought you was white."

"And I swear," I answered, "sometimes I thought maybe you were colored." We stood there laughing like hell. He told me that his parents had been located and that the government was bringing his mother to see him. He seemed happier than I could have been had I been in his shoes; but then I had never been denied, even momentarily, the sight of the sky, trees and green earth.

"They took both of Sam's legs," Bill told me as we left the hospital. And, as we rode back to the camp in silence, my mind kept going back to the severed limbs. How and where did they discard them? I wondered. Were they crumpled together in some garbage can, buried or burned in some special furnace? The last seemed plausible but still I wasn't sure. "What do you think they'll do with his legs?" I finally asked Bill.

He sighed heavily. "Who knows, brother? They'll probably wind up on some skeleton in a medical school." That night he went to every man in the company and collected money toward Sam's new legs. It was nearly one o'clock before he walked wearily into the tent and dumped the bag of coins on his bed. "Not a single man refused to give something," he said. "There are some good Joes in this outfit. It's just that so many of them never had a chance."

He was right. Many of them had spent parts of their lives in orphanages, reformatories and prisons. Names like

Clinton, Dannemora, Wallkill and Elmira were bandied about as though they were rival high schools. And often, as you became closer to these men, they would entrust to you the bitterest secrets of their experience.

One day, I was lazying on the banks of Chenango River with a boy we called Spots. Twice during our talk he had referred to his mother as "that old bitch." Each time it was a jolt but I tried to accept it casually. Then, unable to resist, I asked him how he could speak of his own mother like that.

"She was a bitch. Whata you mean mother?" he asked heatedly. I waited, then he went on. "You ever hear of anybody calling herself a mother who'd sleep in her kid's bed with three or four different cats a week? You ever hear of a mother tellin' her kid one guy was his old man then forget and finger another cat? She steals a bicycle for me one Christmas, then when the cops catch me with it she tells them *I* stole it—and beats me in front of them so it looks like she's on the ups. Mother—hell. I did three months for some junk she lifted from Blum's store on 125th Street."

"I'm sorry. It's none of my business. I shouldn't have asked."

"You might as well hear the rest—then you might dig what I mean." I protested mildly but he went on. "Well, I was goin' with a little chick in our block on 119th Street. The chick and I both are about sixteen at the time. I come home early off my job one day cause I got a killin' tooth-ache and I go upstairs and guess who's in bed with my little chick?"

The two of us got to our feet. We walked along the river, then cut through the forest of silent trees. I was thinking about my childhood, of how very little there was for me to regret.

The battle-scarred Studs told me how the cops had picked him up, beaten him and tried to force him to confess to a murder he hadn't committed. "I spent about three months in jail; and when they caught the cat who did it they patted me on the head and told me how sorry they was." These were the memories that thrashed in the darkness of these young men's souls.

Over two million of us eventually joined the Corps. We planted millions of trees, fought the Dutch elm disease, built fishponds, fed wildlife, cleared tremendous areas of beach and camping ground; and forty-seven recruits lost their lives fighting forest fires. We were earning our keep. But when July came the depression still choked the country, and I knew that it would still be around when our time was up in October. There would probably be even less for us to go back to by then. Although most of the bonus marchers had been taken into the Corps, the employment offices, park benches and hobo villages would still be full. On the 18th of August Bill posted a captain's bulletin that lifted our spirits. President Roosevelt, it read, had extended the camps for another six months.

Our wedding was set for October 15; and despite this new extension, I made up my mind to go through with it. I had saved nearly two hundred dollars and Bill had lent me another hundred. In late June our company had moved to winter barracks at Chenango Forks, New York. Since Binghamton was nearby, I would bring my bride there—so that she would be near my company. Knowing that I would have to save money, I started hitchhiking to Minneapolis on the morning of the eleventh.

I got rides with trucks for a long way. Then, in Ohio, a traveling salesman gave me a lift. He had a few stops to make but he was going all the way to Chicago. He sold rubber heels for orthopedic shoes and he carried his wares in the back seat under a tarpaulin. We were making good time, and I was talking about marrying. Then suddenly there were four policemen with shotguns and rifles on the road ahead of us, signaling us to stop. Both of us got nervous when they poked their guns into the car and demanded that we pull back the tarpaulin; and the policemen seemed awfuly relieved when they saw the boxes of rubber heels. They waved us on without an explanation. And in Lima, a small town further down the road, we found out who they were looking for. Three men, posing as police, had killed a sheriff, broken into a jail and escaped with John Dillinger, a bank robber and killer, billed the most notorious public enemy of the thirties.

I took a day coach from Chicago to Minneapolis. And there, among a few close friends and relatives, we said our vows to my brother Jack, who had just been ordained a minister. And while this took place, Joe Alvis, Sally's father, sat in the kitchen in his overalls, grumbling and cleaning a mess of catfish. We were too happy to be angry with him; so we went to say goodbye before taking the train back to Binghamton. The old man's face was like a stone when we approached. I put out my hand, but he wouldn't shake it.

"I'm sorry you didn't come to the wedding," I said.

"You didn't ask me for her so why should I be a part of givin' her to the likes of you?" My bride tugged at my arm and we turned to go. "Young man." His voice had softened.

"Yessir."

"You got her. Now be sure you take good care of her."

"I promise I will."

"And when you git out East, or wherever you're headin', hand her your britches when you git up in the mornin' and tell her to put 'em on. When she refuses, you put 'em on. And be sure you wear 'em from then on."

"I'll remember that," I said.

"Don't you ever forget it. Now go catch your train. I hafta fry this fish for your ma's supper." We shook hands and he wished us luck. Then we hurried through a shower of rice and good wishes. We took a day coach as far as Chicago; but that night the obtrusive presence of mankind forced us into the comfort of a lower berth.

We stayed at Chenango Forks until March, 1934. When we moved on to another campsite near Philadelphia, I got Sally a room in the city with a family named America. It was a comfortable home and they were good people. There were Mrs. America, the prudent mother, Richard and Howard, her two grown sons, and Mabel, a daughter about Sally's age. Their library was filled with good books and albums of Bach, Schumann, Beethoven, Chopin and Brahms, and there was home-cooked food. Now I contentedly spent my weekends and furloughs there; and it seemed that the old feeling of poverty, despair and loneliness would never return.

Richard, the older brother, was a walking encyclopedia. He was interesting, and I liked and respected him. But like forty-five million other Americans, he tuned in each week to hear Detroit's "Radio Priest," Father Charles E. Coughlin, a man that neither Mabel, his sister, nor I could stand. Coughlin, a rabid, right-wing isolationist, sermonized more

on politics than he did on religion. What's more, his sermons became more anti-Semitic as each Sunday went by.

"Richard, why do you listen to that stupid old man?"
Mabel would ask. Her brother seldom answered. He would
just sit there, the pipe smoke curling up through his mustache, and listen. Then, likely as not, he would criticize
most of what Coughlin had said. "Yes, Richard, but you'll
be right there next Sunday taking in every word he spits
out," Mabel would say.

"I want to hear all sides before I make up my mind about
anything," he would answer, closing the argument with the
finality of his tone.

"He's just curious, Mabel," I would say in her brother's
defense.

"Curious? He's just damned pigheaded," she would
reply.

I never tired of talking to Richard. He was imaginative
and insatiable in his quest for facts and figures. "Roosevelt," he would say with positiveness, "was sworn in at
exactly 1:08 on March 4, 1933"; or "Seven Negroes were
lynched between February 1 and September 25, in 1930,
three in Georgia, two in Texas, one in Oklahoma and one
in South Carolina." Or, about boxing—"No, you're
wrong. It was Max Schmeling who knocked out Stribling.
He did it in Cleveland on July 3, 1931. I'll bet on that." And
it was not well to bet against him. He was always disgust-
ingly right—whether the conversation was about Chopin,
turtle soup or baseball. Through all this Mother America
went about eternally tidying up the place, cooking and
telling Sally everything she felt a young bride should
know. She failed her somewhere along the line, because we
had decided against children—for at least two years. But

that spring, just before the CCC disbanded, I came home to find my wife gently rocking away and knitting from a ball of pink yarn. On the floor beside her was a book Mrs. America had given her. It bore the simple title *Your First Child*.

The final days of the CCC were filled with uncertainty and a confusing kind of melancholy. We were breaking friendships that had been welded through kindness, good times, bloodshed and even death. Scarcely a year before, we had entered camp hungry and in despair. Now, with full stomachs and hard bodies, we looked like the company Captain Littleon had demanded we be on that first dismal morning. Michigan's entire gang had been won over by Bill Hunter's guts and charm. It was good now, and it was strange, to see him and Michigan sitting and laughing together.

But our disbanding would have no bearing on what we would face within the next forty-eight hours. The same rat-infested tenements, the jobless day, the crime-filled night, the same jails, park benches and injustices would be waiting for us again. On the June morning we were mustered out, the men went around slapping backs like graduates who had just gotten their degrees. But the gestures fell like those of men attempting to slap out the fear they knew to be in each other's bodies.

I would miss these men, especially Bill Hunter. Through him I had seen how courage, compassion and intelligence can emancipate man from evil. Bill's standards were high, inflexible and as closely wed as virtue and morality. He was unmanageable after a few drinks of whiskey, but his main weakness, if one could call it that, seemed to be his unselfishness. Not once, for as long as I knew him, did he do anything for himself that matched the good he did for so many others.

I had decided to try my luck in New York, but he talked me out of it. "You've got a family coming, brother. Go back to Minnesota. It's bound to be easier there," he said. And he came to the train to see us off. And as the train pulled out, he walked, then ran waving beside it until we began to outdistance him. Then he was out of sight. And he was gone.

FIFTEEN

IT WAS a lovely July day when we came back to Minneapolis. The trees were heavy with leaves; lawns were green and the colors in the flowers were intense and fresh. Mary and David, Sally's sister and brother, met us at the train. The four of us were feeling good as we drove to my father-in-law's house for, obsessed now with the idea of becoming a grandfather, Joe Alvis had fully relented and demanded that we live with him.

I accepted the change with pleasure. It was almost impossible now to remember his surliness on our wedding day. Joe hit me on the back and called me "son" and went out and caught another big mess of catfish to celebrate our homecoming. But Mom Alvis put them aside for breakfast and fried three chickens instead. David slipped in two bottles of cold wine, which we drank upstairs, since Joe's and Ida's religion would not tolerate such a thing. I had suddenly become more than the outlaw who had stolen Joe's daughter, and he sat until after midnight asking me questions about our experiences out East.

David waited on table at the Curtis Hotel and that week he got me a job there. I would start as a bus boy and become a waiter with the first opening, he told me. It was good to be working and to have the feeling of love and coming parenthood. But at times, especially when I heard Dick Long's orchestra during the dinner hour, the old urge to write music would come rushing back. And I knew that it wouldn't be enough even if I were made headwaiter. "Take your time," I would say to myself. "You've got a responsibility. Stick with what you've got." And I took my time and got to be a waiter and saved for the hospital bill, the crib, the diapers and blue knit suits. I was sure it was going to be a boy.

Before long I was trying to write music again. Between meals I worked at new songs and lyrics on the big Steinway; its tone made me sound better than I really was. When big bands like Duke Ellington, Benny Goodman or Cab Calloway were booked into the Minneapolis Orpheum, I went to as many shows as I could. I would listen, go back and write music; go back, listen, come back and write some more. Ellington was my favorite and I bought every recording of his I could find. I was making more money as a waiter now, but my spirit was growing more restless, and I liked it that way.

Finally I went to Dick Long with a couple of my songs. He was a friendly, heavily built man with sleepy eyes and blond hair. He led the orchestra with his violin, which didn't help his orchestra much. But his was the best of the local bands, and the Twin City radio station broadcast his music several times a week. "These are very good," he said the next day about my songs. I was very happy about this, and when he promised to orchestrate them my spirits lifted even higher. That next week he broadcast "No Love" and another tune called "Night Blossom."

This accomplishment only got me into an embarrassingly funny situation. The hotel's waiters planned a dance to raise money for their union. Brutus Cassius, a young waiter and former football player whose looks fitted his name, was put in charge of preparations. It was Brutus who came up with the fatal idea. "We'll hold it at the Coliseum. And since Parks here has just got all the publicity over the radio, we'll get a big union band and let him direct it." Frankly, I was frightened, but Brutus had a way of having his way. "The ayes have it," he said without even counting the vote. The next week posters went up all over the Twin Cities: "Come One! Come All! To the Big Waiters' Ball! Featuring Gordon Parks and His New *Casa Loma Band*—Direct from New York City!"

Brutus was an operator. He jived an advance from the treasury and outfitted me in an expensive white suit with a ridiculous wrap-around belt. Then he bought himself a white Palm Beach suit, black tie and white pointed-toe shoes. "Why not," he asked Ragland, the treasurer. "Ain't I going to be the master of ceremonies?"

It poured the night of the ball. Rain came down for three hours straight, and the streets were flooded. The Coliseum was one of the largest ballrooms in the world; thousands could get into it. But by ten o'clock that night there were only nineteen of us in the cavernous place—sixteen white union musicians, Ragland, Brutus and myself. And all of us were worried about the same thing—money. Ragland took the easy way out. He got drunk. Brutus Cassius walked back and forth, rubbing his hands and peeping out at the pounding rain. And I stood nervously in front of the disgruntled musicians, with a long white baton. "Go on, Parks; try a number for luck," Brutus said, still fidgeting. When we swung into "A Tisket, A Tasket," I saw him duck out the door, and I knew he was gone for the night.

Then, with sixteen irate musicians at my heels, I went to the box office and asked Ragland for their pay.

Ragland rolled around; his eyes were half closed. "How much do we owe 'em?" he said drowsily.

"Three-ninety-two," I replied. The fee was $24.50 per man.

"Okay, my good fellow, here 'tis." And he pushed out four dollar bills and told us to keep the change.

While the musicians tore open the box office I ducked out and jumped in the car David had lent me. When I turned on the headlamps I saw Brutus's white suit duck behind a pillar. There was a huge puddle of water beside him and I hit it at full speed. Poor Brutus was drenched. "The failure was an act of God," he declared to the finance committee at the next meeting. No one could dispute him.

Though my debut as a conductor proved disastrous, things went well the rest of the summer. Sally and I often spent our weekends with my father and sisters in St. Paul. They too were doing better; and after a simple meal we would sit around the table and reminisce about the old days in Kansas. My sister Lillian told of our finding an empty cupboard when the two of us came home for lunch one day. When a hen cackled, we both raced for the egg. "Well," she exaggerated, "I outran him but he knocked me cold, took the egg, fried it and went back to school." This was all laughable now. And Poppa recalled my riding his best horse to death after I had seen Hoot Gibson in a Western movie. "Hadn't been for your momma," he said, "you'd a got an awful wallopin'." Everyone remembered my brother Clem's returning from overseas in his dashing officer's uniform and how I got jealous as he stood by the porch charming a group of young ladies one day. He was just bending to kiss a hand—French style—when I doused him with a bucket of bluing water from on top of the roof. It wasn't a very pretty picture of someone who was about to become a father. But it made good after-dinner talk.

Fall was beautiful but it worried me, for next would come winter. And, since winter had been so unkind to me in Minnesota, I hated to see its arrival once again. I watched its approach with a wary eye, admiring a few leaves that held stubbornly to a limb outside our bedroom. One morning when I woke, they were gone; and I knew that the sharp December wind had finally cut them away.

Our first son was born on the seventh of that month; and my wife named him after me. He was a robust baby who slept a lot, ate a lot and muddied up a lot of diapers. His grandfather immediately became his philosopher, his guardian, his doctor, his savior—and a general pain in the ass to everyone in the house. The hospital had set up a feeding schedule but he insisted my wife was starving the child to death. He wanted it fed every time it opened its mouth. He accused her of neglecting the baby if she didn't pick it up when it cried. He raved if it slept too much and demanded its temperature be taken practically every hour. To make matters worse, he kept the house at a blazing heat. "You want to give that child pneumonia?" he would shout when we complained.

By January "Butch," as I preferred calling our son, had developed a serious asthmatic condition. The doctors did everything they could; and Sally sat up nights with him throughout the long winter months, determined to keep her son alive. And I said to myself that I had not judged that winter too harshly. Its coming did have an ominous meaning. The stifling heat that Joe used to ward off its cold had nearly taken our son. Now the old man went around grumbling that we had conspired to kill the boy. I felt sorry for Joe, for inwardly he was remorseful, but he was much too obstinate to show it. At times he would shut himself up in his bedroom for hours and all of us knew he was praying fervently for his grandchild's recovery.

It was an unhappy winter but when spring finally came we breathed easier. And whenever we could we put Butch on a pallet and spent long hours with him in the sun and fresh air. By midsummer he was robust and healthy looking again. But the short-drawn breath was still there. The ailment had only given in temporarily to the new season; it would return to plague him again, and we knew it.

That summer I got an extra job playing the piano at a place called Carver's Inn, an old converted farmhouse located several miles out of the city. It served fried chicken, good barbecue and beer. Red, the drummer I had met at Pope's that first Christmas, came to work with me and we made good money there. It was an after-hours spot for musicians, single men, single ladies, men with wives and men with mistresses. The young, the old, the rich, the poor, the good and the bad—all came to Carver's. It was probably the most thoroughly integrated place in the whole Northwest. Ma Carver, a kind old lady who walked around in her bedroom slippers, was the owner. Her son Fred was the boss; the cooking was done by the old lady's daughters, and it was good. There was never any trouble there. The bouncers Fred hired saw to that. And that summer I made enough money playing requests for "No Love" and "Butterfly" to buy a Ford car and move my family to a small apartment. Joe fought our taking his grandson, but we compromised by moving only two blocks away.

I worked steadily at both jobs for two years, saving money against the severe winters and Butch's medical bills. But in spite of his recurring illness he had grown into a strong, handsome two-and-a-half-year-old by the summer of 1936; and, though I raised hell with his mother for entering him in a city-wide baby contest, it was I who walked around the big auditorium proudly showing the golden crown he won.

SIXTEEN

I WAS born restless. As a child I would saddle a horse and roam the woods and countryside until dark, imagining myself some sort of adventurer, dreaming up situations for myself as I rode along, dressed in blue jeans and a pair of satin boots I filched from my sister Cora's closet. One day I was William S. Hart in search of a kidnaped sweetheart. The next day I was Hoot Gibson tracking a dangerous outlaw, or Tom Mix escaping from a band of murderous Indians. And there were times when I rode along quietly, searching deep into the woods for that exceptional something that I always felt awaited me. I enjoyed the loneliness that came over me at such times, feeling it somehow set me apart from ordinary ways and lives of other people. It lulled me into dreams that could only be fulfilled far beyond the Kansas cornfields and prairies. Now, at twenty-three, I was feeling this restlessness again.

"I'm tired of these jobs and this town," I said suddenly to my wife one Sunday afternoon. "I want to try something else."

"I've known that for a long time," she answered. "What have you got in mind?"

"There's the railroad. They're hiring waiters now. I

could see other parts of the country and make money at the same time."

"It's okay by me. Just be sure you know what you're doing," she said.

I drove the Ford over to the Northern Pacific Commissary in St. Paul the following morning and applied for a job. A man named Wolters took my application and told me I would hear from him. He kept his word and on the twentieth of June I started my first continental run as a waiter, going first to Chicago, staying overnight, then to Seattle, Washington. I woke early the next day in Chicago and out of curiosity went over to Wabash Avenue and walked slowly past the Hotel Southland. The sun glistening on the window made it difficult for me to see inside, so I turned back, shaded my eyes and looked through the smoky glass. The place wasn't as full as it had been the day I fled from it. But there were a few drunks and bums sitting around the lobby. Mike wasn't at the outer desk either. Then I looked closer, thinking about Big John, wondering if he was still alive after the blow I had given him with the butt of the pistol. I was just about to leave when I saw him waddle out of his office and go toward the stairs. He looked as healthy and ornery as ever. It was a load off my mind; and I walked back to the station over the same route I had fled that evening, thanking my luck.

Those first days on the dining cars were exciting for me. Interesting people rode the trains, especially the Pullmans: mountain climbers, politicians, millionaires, Hollywood stars, gamblers, cattlemen. There were the added sights of the rugged Dakotas, Montana, Oregon and Washington. The summer crews usually consisted of six Negro waiters and a white steward. And there were two types of crews—those that shared unlawfully in the daily profits and those that didn't. And you went the way of the crew, or you got bumped the next trip. The stewards had different signals. One long, tall one used to rub his hands and say, "Have no fear, the coast is clear. The inspector's sleeping in the rear." And another one used to shout, "Profit-sharing day!" And you knew the take was on. You either got home honest and broke, or dishonest and loaded. It all depended on the type of crew you rode with.

The narrow kitchen, lined on each side with iceboxes, sinks, broilers and cooking ranges, took up about a quarter of the dining car. Four cooks labored there preparing the meals that we served during the six-day trip; and between the kitchen and the dining room was a four-by-four-foot pantry with an opening through which they shoved the food at us. Often, at the height of a meal, as many as six waiters jammed this tiny place—cursing, bumping and pushing to get at their orders. We didn't walk around; we moved each other about.

I learned to balance the heavy trays of food on one arm, and there was a feeling of accomplishment in leaning against the rocking motion of the train as it sped into the curves. It didn't occur to me that some of the aged waiters, after so many years of service, found this a painfully tiring business. Whereas we young men sort of floated between the long row of tables, the older ones went at a jarring half trot—their failing limbs rebelling against every step they took. But their cunning made up for their lack of speed, and you watched them closely, learning the subtle tricks of the trade. For instance, a good tip was never pocketed before your new passenger had a chance to gaze upon it for a while. This, of course, was meant to influence his generosity. A small tip was either plucked up quickly, or fattened by the waiter, for the same reason. You buttered the

Pullman porters up on the first day out, for they were sources of information. Who were the good tippers in their compartments? What time would they come to eat? A hot sandwich and a bottle of beer might very well induce the porter to advise his wealthy passengers to ask to be served at your station. Since the amount of a waiter's monthly income depended a lot on his tips, such knowledge was invaluable.

After serving each meal we ate, cleaned the silverware, glasses, pantry and salt and pepper shakers. Then we swept the car and mopped the hallways leading to it. We rested during the little time that remained. And the vilest epithets were silently bestowed upon any passenger who insisted on being served during rest periods. At night the cooks and waiters slept on crude metal bunks in the rear of a baggage car. We were usually hooked directly to the puffing, whistling locomotive, and the smoke poured into our quarters. The mucus we blew from our noses or coughed up each morning was always black with soot. Our dining-car steward was more fortunate. He was assigned a lower berth back in the Pullmans.

You got to know many characters on the road. My favorite one was a waiter named Charlie Quiggley. He was about six foot three, brown-skinned, with bushy gray eyebrows, and he stuttered. Between meals he wore a checkered linen cap, smoked a great curling meerschaum pipe and rocked about the car loading the young waiters with all his work. And you didn't give him "back chatter." He had an in with Mister Thompson, the superintendent. To get even with Charlie we used to fill his station with passengers from the coaches. They were low tippers, and Charlie called them snakes. One night a farmer, after eating a seventy-five-cent plate, asked Charlie for his bill. Charlie looked around to see if the steward was near. "One—one—one dol—dol—dollar and fifty cents," he whispered. "How much?" The farmer seemed hard of hearing. "One—one—one dollar, sir," Charlie said a little louder. "This here menu says—" "Lo—lo—look, mister, ju—just give me se—seventy-five cents and—git the hell out of here," Charlie said in exasperation. The farmer tipped him a nickel and stomped out. We looked straight ahead but we felt Charlie's eyes. There would be a lot of extra work for us the next day.

Another time, Mr. Horowitz, a frequent passenger on our run, got after Charlie for serving him coffee in a dirty cup. "It happens every time you wait on me, Charlie," he said pleasantly. "Now go get me a clean one." Charlie's station was filled, and he grabbed the coffee and rushed off to the pantry in a huff. But he only wiped the dirt off the original cup and returned it to the table.

Horowitz examined it carefully. "This a new cup you brought me, Charlie?" he asked.

"Why-why-why, sure it is," Charlie stammered indignantly. Then he stood gawking as Mr. Horowitz's spoon fished a silver dollar from the bottom of the cup.

And there was the tale that Charlie never denied involving Pretty Boy Floyd, the notorious bandit, who, it was said, held up the North Coast Limited. He had forced Charlie at gunpoint to collect jewels and wallets in his checkered cap from the wealthy passengers in the observation car. Everything went well until a tiny dowager refused to drop in her diamond necklace. "A grown man like you ought to be out working instead of robbing people," she admonished Floyd. And Floyd had pressed the gun harder into Charlie's ribs, telling him to take it from her neck, and she had slapped Charlie's fingers when he tried.

The gun pressed harder. "Li—listen, la—lady, put that thing in my ca—cap. This—this ma—man ain't bull shittin'." He was supposed to have been laid off for thirty days for that phrase.

Then, when Charlie was a Pullman porter, Inspector Hannibal had caught him sleeping on duty. Charlie woke to see the inspector's shoes shining beside him. "—and dear Lord, please bless Inspector Hannibal," he said, pretending to finish a prayer. Hannibal, flabbergasted, stormed out of the car shaking his head in disgust.

Charlie used to read a lot and one day I thumbed through a magazine he had left behind. There was a portfolio of photographs in it that I couldn't forget; they were of migrant workers. Dispossessed, beaten by dust, storms and floods, they roamed the highways in caravans of battered jalopies and wagons between Oklahoma and California scrounging for work. Some were so poor, the captions read, they traveled by foot, pushing their young in baby buggies and carts. And there were photographs of shanties with siding and roofs of cardboard boxes; the inside walls were dressed with newspapers. I thought back to Philip and wondered if I were staring at members of his family. And across two pages was a memorable picture of a father and his two small sons running to their shanty in a dust storm. The names of the photographers too stuck in my mind—Arthur Rothstein, Russell Lee, Carl Mydans, Walker Evans, Ben Shahn, John Vachon, Jack Delano, Dorothea Lange. They all worked for the Farm Security Administration, a government agency set up by Roosevelt to aid submarginal farmers. These stark images of men, women and children, caught in their confusion and poverty, saddened me. I asked Charlie to give me the magazine and I took it home and kept looking at those photographs and the names of the photographers for months.

The following months I read John Steinbeck's *In Dubious Battle* as well as Erskine Caldwell's and Margaret Bourke-White's *You Have Seen Their Faces*. And, for some reason I could not yet explain, I was becoming restless again. The railway or the money I made there wasn't enough any more. The extraordinary thing was, perhaps, coming closer.

Ida Alvis, with that remarkable inquisitiveness mothers-in-law have, sensed this restiveness. She concluded that it was threatening her daughter's security and trouble struck our little family full and hard. "Mom thinks you ought to stay on the road." "Mom thinks I ought to get some new clothes." "Mom thinks you're buying too many books." "Mom thinks you ought to give me a trip to Chicago to visit David. She thinks you've got enough money to afford it."

"Your mom is thinking too much for me nowadays. *I think* she had better keep her nose out of my business—and *I think* that you had better stop listening to what she thinks." We had the first big argument of our marriage and it cut a distance between us that grew wider each day. The Sunday picnics stopped; the moonlight rides by the lake stopped; the trips to the movies stopped. "Perhaps I was unfair," I would think sometimes when I would see her lying in troubled sleep, but I could not bring myself to wake her and tell her so. Now only Butch and I would go to the soda fountain on my days off to have the giant hot dogs and malted milks he loved so much. It soon became a lonely ritual for us. Then I tried to mend the breach by buying her a coat I couldn't afford. It was a pretty impractical one of black velvet trimmed with marten. When she tried it on all the salesladies fluttered around telling me how beautiful she looked. And I, bursting with pride and stuffed with their flattery, pulled out a hundred dollars—all the money I'd saved since our marriage. With a forced calm, I paid for it while Sally preened before the mirror. She didn't really need the coat and Joe condemned me roundly for wasting my money on what he called "a rag with skunk hair." I didn't mind. It was an expensive but honest attempt to rekindle the love I knew we had for each other; Joe, in his crude way, was only complaining that I had gone about it the wrong way. He was right. But Sally liked it, and that was most important to me.

SEVENTEEN

THERE WERE different ways to kill time during our stopovers. The older waiters usually slept, and the younger ones went out on the town. What tips they made between St. Paul and Chicago were usually left in the cheap bars, whorehouses and night spots on Chicago's south side. And they would return to the train sullen, depressed and over-eager for the "take." They tried coaxing me out with them, but I was too weighted with the unhappiness that lay over Sally and me. One night I did go out to a bar but then I drank too much and came back in even lower spirits. I killed time at the movies or, during the summer months, I bought picture magazines and read them as I walked along the lake shore. But mainly, during those days when Mussolini bombed Ethiopia, Franco overran Spain, and Hitler and Horohito armed against the world, I was concerned about saving our marriage.

Out of curiosity, one morning in December, 1937, I wandered into the Chicago Art Institute on Michigan Avenue. I had no intention of staying long, but awed suddenly by the beautiful paintings I spent several hours in this large and voiceless place. My reaction to these paintings was much the same as that I had toward the FSA photographs nearly five months before, and by now I was convinced of the power of a good picture. And I decided to visit the Institute whenever I came to Chicago.

That same afternoon I went to a movie and, during a newsreel, I saw Japanese war planes bomb the U.S.S. *Panay*. The photographer had stayed at his post, shooting the final belch of steam and smoke that rose when the ill-fated gunboat sank into the Yangtze River. The newspapers and radio reported the bombing; but the newsreel, through its grim directness, brought me face to face with the real horror of war. "It's the same thing the FSA photographers did with poverty," I thought as I sat watching. When the newsreel ended, a voice boomed over the theater intercom system, "And here he is, Norman Alley, the photographer who shot this remarkable film!" Alley stepped out on the stage in a white suit amid the cheers of the audience, bowed, and after it was quiet he talked about his experience. I was enthralled. He had no way of knowing it, but he had just changed my life. I sat through another show; and even before I left the theater I had made up my mind I was going to become a photographer.

The very first thing I did when we reached Seattle was to go camera hunting. But the high prices of the good ones came as a shock; and for a while I walked the streets, with seventeen dollars in my pockets, wondering how to raise more money quickly. I remembered what I had spent for Sally's coat and began to regret it. With that hundred dollars, and a little more, I could have bought a very professional-looking German camera one dealer showed me. I fondled it for nearly a half hour, asking all sorts of questions about its construction and how one operated it. Then, ashamed at having taken up so much of the man's time, I lied and said I would be back for it later that afternoon. But I had made up my mind to get a camera before leaving Seattle, and this determination brought me to Abe Cohen's pawnshop on a side street in the downtown area. There were probably better cameras in his shop but only one had that professional look which suited my taste, a Voigtlander Brilliant. I liked that name and when he told me it was only $12.50, I hurriedly pulled the money from my pocket. "I'll take it," I said without bothering to inspect the camera.

"You want film?" the pawnbroker asked.

I hadn't thought of this, but I answered, almost indignantly, "Why, of course. Give me three rolls."

"What kind?"

"The best you've got" was the only answer I could give him.

The pawnbroker smiled. Certainly he knew that I didn't even know how to load it. Neither did he for that matter; and we spent a half hour figuring out how the camera worked. He wished me good luck when I went out the door; and I walked on toward the waterfront, shooting buildings, people, signs and anything else that interested me, confident that those first pictures would be masterpieces.

It turned out to be a remarkable start. I went down to the wharfs and fell headfirst into Puget Sound, trying to shoot pictures of seagulls. Luckily, some firemen were nearby and I hung on to my camera, splashing about hollering for help until they fished me out with a long pole. But I lost no time in getting back to my new profession. Dripping wet and shivering I hurried to the dining car, dried out my camera, then changed into a clean shirt and my waiter's uniform. Later that day I went back to the pawnshop and bought two more rolls of film and a handbook on exposure, and I shot pictures until the sun went down. From that night on, after the other waiters had gone to bed, I sat up in the empty dining car, studying my camera and any magazine or paper that had a good photograph on its pages.

This new venture only caused Ida Alvis and me to argue all the more. And my bewildered wife, caught in the center of the barrage and torn between affection for her mother and allegiance to me, took refuge in another room or out of doors when Ida and I began our raging. During my long trips she was under constant fire to halt my spending.

Eastman Kodak developed the first roll of film—surprisingly, it had survived its bath in Puget Sound. And when I went for the prints one of the clerks complimented me on my first efforts. "Keep it up and we'll give you a show." I didn't take him seriously and he realized it. "I mean it," he said. "You've got a good eye."

"Are you kidding?"

"Nope, I'm not. I showed them to the manager this morning. He liked them too."

Still cautious, I thanked him, saying that I would hold him to his word. He kept it; and six weeks later Eastman gave me an exhibit in the window of their downtown Minneapolis store.

I lived in ecstasy for days after that, shooting skiers, clouds, women, children, old men, sand dunes, ocean fronts —anything that passed in front of my lens. John Boles, the famous Hollywood star, sat for me backstage at the Orpheum Theater. My wife began posing for me, and soon all the attractive young Twin City girls took their places before my camera. Though I wasn't paid for it, the St. Paul

Pioneer Press ran a feature on some photographs I had taken to them. And my mother-in-law's complaints quieted down.

Perhaps I would have become the best waiter-photographer on the North Coast Limited, had it not been for a Southern steward named Barnes. He gave Negro college boys and "young uppity nigras" who read books and studied a hard time. Many of them "bumped" themselves when they found out he was to be their steward. But I was blossoming in confidence when he took over our crew in the winter of 1938. "I'll read at night if I have to sit up in the locomotive," I told one of the waiters who warned me against him. Yet I got an uneasy feeling the first night out when he switched off the lights while I sat in the empty dining car reading.

"Beg your pardon," I said, "would you turn those lights back on? I'm reading." He gave me a sour look. "You studying to be the first nigra president of the United States?" Then he went off to bed, and I got up, turned on the lights and continued to read. But from then on nothing I did was right. Barnes wrote my orders out wrong, then blamed me if a passenger complained. He piled extra work on me. I mopped the hallways, polished silverware that didn't need polishing, cleaned and recleaned the pantry. If he thought that fatigue would stop my late reading, he was wrong. I called on every ounce of strength and patience to take the work and his goading. Each night after he switched out the lights, I got up and turned them on again.

He finally provoked me into violence a few hours before we arrived in St. Paul one evening. During dinner he intentionally pushed my arm, and I spilled four bowls of hot soup on a passenger and myself. My skin burning and the passenger cursing me, I forgot that it was winter, that I had a family and needed a job. I shoved Barnes into the pantry, snatched up a bread knife and held it against his throat. Two waiters rushed in and grabbed me. Barnes never uttered a word. He stood there shaking, then backed out of the pantry and into the dining car. And, ashamed to face the passengers again, I went up to the bunk car, changed my clothes, and lay across my bed until we reached St. Paul.

Our apartment was strangely quiet when I reached it late that night. I pushed the bedroom door open gently and looked in. Neither Sally nor Butch was there. I switched on the lights. A sheet of lined tablet paper lay on the bed. There was something foreboding about the way it lay folded on the blue silk bedspread. I glanced about the room quickly, seeing the bareness of the dresser, the absence of the ordinary things, like her bedroom slippers and bathrobe, or Butch's toys, that usually lay about the room. I somehow sensed what was written on that note but I couldn't bring myself to believe it. I finally picked it up. There was only one very short sentence. "We have gone to Chicago, Sally."

I stood in the middle of the room for several minutes lost in a forest of thoughts. I suspected her mother had something to do with this, and my first flush of anger was against her. I picked up the phone and called her number.

"Mrs. Alvis?"

"Yes."

"Where's Sally and the baby?"

"In Chicago—I suppose."

"I know that. I mean her address."

"Don't ask me. I don't know."

"When is she coming back?"

"I don't know that either."

"So you don't know where she's at or when she's coming back, huh?"

"That's what I said."

"Well, you can tell her for me that I want a divorce when she does get back." There was a silence on the other end of the line, then a click. I hung up the receiver and stood thinking again. Perhaps she'd gone to see her brother or maybe she's gone to see some guy. The last possibility was more acceptable to my mood. "What the hell," I said aloud. And I walked out of the house and into the night—in search of a woman.

On October third I was called into the commissary for a "hearing." Mr. Barnes was there and so was the entire crew who had witnessed the trouble. Thomson, the superintendent, knew Barnes and his hatreds but he contended that it was I who was on trial, not Barnes. And after the "hearing," where only one waiter, Bill Williams, condemned the steward's actions, Thomson said icily, "You're fired."

Wolters, the man who had hired me, telephoned the next day. "Thomson says you can have your job back if you apologize to Mr. Barnes." He sounded rather hopeful.

"Thanks," I said, "but I'd rather eat snowballs."

A month passed. She came to the apartment alone.

"Well, I see you're back," I said to her.

"That's right," she said.

"Where's Butch?"

"At Mom's."

"Well, I guess you want a divorce."

"It's okay by me."

"Okay, you can get it. I'll pay for it."

"On what grounds?" she asked.

"Make it adultery. Anything you like," I replied flippantly.

When the papers came from her lawyer, I noticed that she had followed my suggestion.

I signed them unwillingly and sent them back.

EIGHTEEN

MY WIFE and son went back to live with her parents and I moved to St. Paul and stayed again with my sister Cora. But I never stopped taking photographs, even though the pleasure I derived from it did not compensate for my loneliness. The thought of being away from my child, of the possibility of his someday having another father, burned me. And now that I had found what I considered to be my future, I blamed it for having robbed me of the two people I loved most. Each day I went out to hunt for a job, but I failed to find anything. And this bothered me because it meant that I had nothing to send toward my son's support.

Nearly two months passed before I went to see Butch. His mother and I exchanged a few words, not very pleasant ones, about my taking him for a walk. "He's not leaving this house with you. Not for one minute," she said. She was angry; I had not sent her any money for a month.

"I'm going to take him just for an hour," I insisted.

"I said no and I mean no," she answered, her voice rousing my father-in-law from his nap. I looked at Butch. "Come on, kid," I said, taking him by the hand. "We're going to the park." After all, he was my son; I would take

him if I liked. And during the brief tug-of-war that took
place Joe came down the stairs with a shotgun. He put
it within five inches of my head and ordered me out. I
could see that both barrels were cocked. I looked directly
into them for a moment, my heart foolishly daring him to
shoot. The shaking gun didn't frighten me—not before my
son.

"Pa, put that silly gun down," Sally said weakly. "I can
handle this." She slumped into a chair while the old man
kept the weapon at my temple. "Please go, Dad. Please go,"
Butch pleaded. I patted his shoulder and started out, then
looked back at her for a moment. Her anger was gone and
she sat sad, beautiful and withdrawn—as if she were never
to be looked on with pleasure again. "Something's wrong,"
I said to myself as I drove back to St. Paul. "She doesn't
seem too happy there." For some reason this pleased me.

A friend of Sally's had asked her to marry him, so I
heard; and he was there the only other time I went by to
see her that summer. I returned the "friend's" greeting
coldly, spent an hour on the porch with Butch and left. By
autumn I was still trying to find work. Then one day a man
named Harry Crump telephoned me. "I'm manager and
coach of the House of David basketball team," he explained. "I've seen you play several times and would like to
sign you up for the tour this season."

"But I haven't been on a court for a long time," I
explained.

"You've got a month to get in shape," he assured me.

"What's the pay?"

"There's a six-way split between the coach and the five
players. We are booked solid for three months. We come
back here for the Christmas holidays."

"And there are no substitutes?"

"Nope. It means more money for the players."

I had never expected to play basketball again, but after one month of training I found myself in some noisy arena every night, either in Minnesota, North Dakota or Iowa, trying to please an audience that damned us when we won—and damned us if we lost. A happy medium had to be reached. We had to make bad teams look good by keeping the score close, and beat the good teams decisively. We had five stars sewn to our jerseys; we had to live up to them or get booed off the floor—or run out of town. I was seven years older than the other four, and at twenty-six I was referred to as the "old man," and felt like one. The younger players had to give me strenuous rubdowns each night to keep me going; and I never got enough sleep. Jimmy Griffin was our center, Johnny Nelson and Byron Riff our forwards and Buddha Crowe and I were the guards. We had all been taught the art of "befuddling." And this is what the spectators came to see. Buddha was the expert, and a great athlete. The crowd howled when he spun the ball teasingly on his index finger before an embarrassed player. If the poor man went for the ball he might find it on top of his head—where Buddha had skillfully placed it. When we got too far ahead the crowd would become surly. Then we would have to fake an argument among our players, whereby two of us would stomp off the floor, leaving three men to play the other team. This worked sometimes but often the other team was so befuddled that we could hand them the ball and they still couldn't score. When that happened there was only one other out. We took the ball and scored for them by shooting into their basket. Our skill at befuddling was the only thing that kept us going. No team, without substitutes, could play such a hard game every night without resorting to trickery.

But our trickery on the floor could not compare with the trickery of Harry Crump at the box office. The arena could be packed to the rafters but seldom did we have more than enough to pay for our room each night and get a good steak. He charmed us with his thievishness. "After all," he would say when we complained, "I get a manager's share, a coach's share, and there is the wear and tear on my car—and the gas, oil and repairs." In the end one had the feeling that it was Harry who was being robbed.

There were two awesome snowstorms in the Northwest that winter. And we got stuck in the middle of both of them. But the one that nearly took all our lives caught us one night between two small towns in North Dakota. It blew up fast and heavy; and after a few miles we couldn't even see the highway. We stopped; and it was frightening. I had never seen it snow like this before. Harry was driving so he lent me his sheepskin mackinaw, and I got out and walked ahead so that he could keep his lights on me. We crept along for about five miles; then the car chugged to a stop. The drifts had become impassable. This wasn't my first storm and I knew its danger. It was hard not to show my concern to the younger men. Harry knew. I could tell by the irregularity of his breathing. Someone suggested that we try to push. So they all got out and pushed—only to have the old jalopy slide sideways and poop out in the middle of the road. Now our shoes were soaking wet and as the temperature dropped we sat huddled together in the car, our limbs stiffening from the cold. When daylight finally came we were practically buried. It was impossible to walk or drive through the deep drifts. So we sat there all morning in quiet panic, freezing and hoping for rescue. We had all but given up when we saw a cloud of snow coming at us. A huge plow was burrowing through the whiteness, throwing it high into the air. Luckily the driver saw us in time. The big blades clanked to a stop just a few inches from the side of our car. They pulled us out and got us started; and as we drove down the highway we could see cattle standing frozen in death.

Farm women were waiting with hot coffee and doughnuts at a general store when we reached the next town. It was a good sight; and it was a good feeling to be safe and to have the steaming hot liquid warming our insides. There were some, on that same road behind us, who would never arrive to eat and drink again. The plow didn't reach them in time.

We played in many strange places that winter but the strangest was a school for deaf and dumb Indians which had its court in a converted hayloft. One big Indian astounded us by standing at one end of the court and throwing the ball into the basket at the other end. This not only baffled Buddha, who was quite a show-off, but it cut into his gallery applause. During the last half of the game, he tried it, but the ball fell short and knocked the chief's squaw flat on her face. It was bad enough that they took our gate receipts to replace three of her front teeth; but after we got outside we found Harry's car with four flat tires. Two vindictive squaws had let the air out of them.

But we played some very good teams that year, the best being a group of All-Americans that were assembled to play us at Fargo, North Dakota. It was our last game. Harry had appointed me captain, simply because I was the oldest, and I thought we should play them the same way we did all the others. Buddha disagreed. "They'd murder us," he said; "we have to play good straight ball. These guys won't go for the befuddling crap."

"We're not five All-Americans," I protested. But Buddha was the star and our defense and offense were built around him. So we played "good straight ball," and at the end of the first half we were about twenty points behind and smarting from the boos. Buddha was so angry he wouldn't go back on the floor the second half. When the crowd saw only four of us come out, they, and the All-Americans, assumed we had dropped points purposely during the first half. The gallery got anxious and our opponents got increasingly nervous. Then we called the "football play." "Hike! One! Two! Three!" Riff squatted over the ball and passed it back to me like a football center. I drop-kicked it through the air and Jimmy, who had run down the floor, accidentally butted the ball into the basket with his head. The crowd went wild—and the All-Americans went to pieces. When Buddha heard the cheering he came out. Now he put on his act. And he never had a greater night. By the end of the game we were fifteen points ahead. And Harry Crump was so delighted he only took the manager's cut that night. The same night, tired and suddenly jobless again, we started the long drive back to St. Paul.

It came about in a most natural way. Sally came to a party with a new boy friend from Chicago. And I escorted a beautiful girl to the same party. Her name was Henrietta Bonaparte and she had large soulful eyes and honey-colored skin and she was a poem in her crimson velvet gown. Sally took one look and immediately lost both her earrings. She was nearly in tears over those earrings when she came to ask me to help her find them. Loyal to her sex, Henrietta suggested that I go. We were lucky. They had accidentally fallen into Sally's party bag.

And she thanked me and we danced several times and she said that Butch missed me and I said that I missed him and that I would come over that weekend and she said that would be fine and I went over and we went for a ride in the moonlight and the next week we got married—again.

We moved considerably farther from Joe Alvis' place this time. Our apartment was small, comfortable and furnished on credit. Butch was almost five now; and in the spring the three of us began with the picnics, lake rides and visits to the parks again. For some time I had been making a photographic collection of attractive girls, and Cecil Newman, the editor of the Minneapolis *Spokesman and Recorder*, began running them on the front page of his paper each week. There was no pay; I accepted the space for the pleasure of seeing my work published. It was good to see my name, in bold type, beneath the featured beauty each week; but I wasn't making money. So I told Cecil some sort of financial arrangement had to be made if we were to continue. His paper was in more financial trouble than I, but the two of us outtalked his wife, who resisted to the end, and raided her treasury for enough money to buy a press camera. Then Cecil appointed me official staff photographer—and circulation manager. My pay was a certain percentage of whatever amount of new circulation I could manage to get. Unfortunately I was a better photographer than circulation manager, so I tried to increase distribution by ignobly hinting to mothers that their *lovely* daughters might be photographed and put on the front page if they bought a subscription.

Cecil was a small, brown-skinned man of perpetual motion and tremendous spirit. I admired the way he kept the paper going from the cramped and disordered space he called his office. He wrote the editorials, sports, news and society columns, hustled ads and kept his numerous creditors at bay with fast talk and sincere promises. And he was an honest man. His confidence in himself and his paper was more than the average person would have dared dream. He didn't have much money to offer his few employees, but the titles he handed them were of Herculean stature. If you wanted to be a correspondent instead of a reporter that was your prerogative. If you wanted to be a *foreign* correspondent, then mail back a story on your trip abroad. You could be anything from copy boy up to assistant managing editor—as long as you could afford the title and live off the pay.

By September my commissions had become far less praiseworthy than my title. Winter, my bitter enemy, was coming; and so was another child, my wife informed me. So I began looking for a title that would have less prestige and more money attached to it. I had already made matters worse by going into debt for new photographic equipment to Harvey Goldstein, the dealer from whom we had bought the press camera. He had a blind faith in me, although he had no reason for such trust; I hadn't paid him a cent all summer. But he gave me everything I asked for, including plenty of helpful advice.

I was handed my new title on the 23rd of September. It was not to be compared with the one Cecil had bestowed upon me. In fact I loathed it so much I refused to admit its existence. When the Chicago Northwestern Railway hired me on a bar car as a *porter*, I decided then and there that I was an *assistant bartender*. It had more dignity and sounded much better, I thought. I was not altogether a liar. I did serve drinks after the bartender had made them; but my specific duty was that of a porter—a title which I prefer not to mention again. But, most importantly, I had a regular salary and a source for tips.

NINETEEN

THE "400" was a fast, modern train that ran daily between Minneapolis, St. Paul and Chicago. It was a good run for me because I was home every other night and in Chicago several days a week. There I photographed the skyscrapers and bridges, the boats moving up and down the canal. During the winter months I roamed the desolate areas along the river that cut through the heart of the city, photographing bums warming at bonfires, beggars wandering the windswept streets. All this recalled my first trip, by boxcar, to this cold, hard-boiled metropolis. Some days I would visit the Southside Community Art Center, learning from the graphic protests of Charles White, Ben Shahn, Isaac Soyer; the grim paintings of the jobless and oppressed by Max Weber and Alexander Brook; the merciless satires of William Gropper and Jack Levine. Their works, on exhibit there, had forsaken the pink ladies of Manet and Renoir, the bluish-green landscapes of Monet, hanging at the Art Institute several miles to the north on Michigan Avenue.

In purpose, and execution, the two kinds of expression tended to oppose each other. And, concerned about this, I confided in Mike Bannarn—a painter and sculptor who lived near us in Minneapolis. He sat drawing on the curved stem of his huge pipe, chipping away at a hunk of stone that afternoon. He didn't answer immediately, but his furrowed brow indicated that he was thinking of a way to abate my confusion. "Art," he finally said, "is born of man's intense feeling about things he loves, or perhaps the things he hates. A hell of a lot of things influence an artist." His rough hands, a chisel in one, a mallet in the other, spread apart in a wide, spontaneous gesture. "Some artists paint what they see while others paint what they feel. It depends on the man. Now Gropper hates corrupt men and he bops you over the head with their ugliness." Then, dropping his tools to the ground, he beat dust from his baggy trousers. "I get just as riled up over preserving the beauty of things as I do about destroying the ugliness of them." I took his words to heart and told myself that it could be the same in photography.

I worked hard at my double life, savoring with anticipation the day I could leave the railway forever. I would take it slower, learn my craft well and then strike out. I felt my wife would be with me all the way. My conscience demanded that I hurry before time and a bigger family trapped me. I read every book on art and photography I could afford. I talked to painters, writers and photographers whenever I discovered them on my car.

One day I saw the word *Life* in big red letters on a passenger's camera bag and discovered he was Bernard Hoffman, a photographer for that publication. We talked for a long time. "Come and work with us someday," he said when he got off in Chicago. And I laughed and promised him that I surely would. Then a few weeks later Bob Capa, the famous war photographer, came aboard, hoping to sleep the four hundred miles back to Chicago, only to be kept awake with my constant barrage of questions. And he said, "See you in Europe someday," when he stepped wearily off the car several hours later. The contact with these men transformed me into a dynamo.

Vogue was one of the magazines well-to-do passengers left on the train. I used to study the luxurious fashion photographs on its pages and the uncommon names of the photographers who took them—Steichen, Blumenfeld, Horst, Beaton, Hoyningen-Huene. How lucky they were, I thought. Day-dreaming once, I printed my name under a Steichen portrait of Katharine Cornell. And my imagination assured me that it looked quite natural there.

No one could accuse me of being unaggressive now. I went to every large department store in the Twin Cities asking for a chance to photograph their merchandise. The manager of John Thomas, a large women's store in Minneapolis, seemed astonished when I approached him. Looking at me curiously he said, "But our photography is all done out in New York." Then he turned from me without another word.

But I kept trying, coming finally to Frank Murphy's, the most fashionable store in St. Paul. Frank Murphy had all but walked me out the door when his wife, a handsome woman with a shock of black hair, spoke to her husband. "What does he want, Frank?"

He gestured hopelessly. "To photograph fashions."

She was waiting on a customer but she looked me over and said, "Well, maybe he can." Frank Murphy looked back at his wife as though she had lost her wits. "But, darling . . ."

"Wait for me, young man. I'll be with you in a minute," she said. And by now I was as bewildered as her husband. For, aggressive as I was, I wasn't prepared for such a triumph. "Wait around; she'll talk to you," Frank Murphy said helplessly.

After her customer left she turned to me. "Have you any samples of your work to show me?" she asked.

"No, I'm sorry."

"Why do you want to photograph fashion?"

"Because I know I can. That's all."

"Well, our clothes are photographed out east"—my spirits sank—"but I'm willing to give you a chance. I think it would be fun." She thought for a moment. "Can you be here tomorrow evening, right after we close? I'll have the models and dresses ready."

"Oh sure. Yes, mam, I'll be here right on the dot," I said anxiously.

"All right." She was turning to another customer. "We'll be here waiting for you."

The ease and quickness of her decision stunned me. If I went on my regular run I would be in Chicago the next evening. What's more, I suddenly realized I didn't even have lighting equipment or a camera suitable for fashion photography. But that evening I had Sally call the commissary and say that I was ill. Then I hurried to Harvey Goldstein and told him about my assignment; and he became as jittery as I, rushing about finding the necessary lamps, bulbs, films and camera. We were both exhausted late that night after he had assembled the equipment and showed me how to use it.

The dresses and models were beautiful. And Mrs. Murphy seemed just as excited as I was about the whole thing. She went around buttoning the girls into the lovely evening dresses she had selected. And Frank Murphy stood by, watching us with a quizzical and skeptical eye. The models had more enthusiasm than talent; but they too were helpful and held the long tiring poses I demanded of them. My lighting, inspired by the pictures I had so often studied in the pages of *Vogue*, wasn't at all bad. The biggest problem came when the models appeared on the ground glass upside-down. Harvey hadn't warned me about this. And I went through the four-hour sitting with the awful feeling that there was something cock-eyed about the lens or the camera. But I bluffed it through without anyone's being aware of my nervousness. And, when we were finished, Mrs. Murphy, obviously impressed with the way I had lighted and posed the models, asked me if I would like to continue shooting sports clothes at the country club the next day. I couldn't have been happier; and it must have shown on my face, for she bade me goodnight with a smile of deep satisfaction.

The big blow fell at exactly two o'clock the next morning when I developed the film. My wife was asleep when she heard the moaning and my head bumping against the kitchen wall. "What's the trouble?" she asked through the outer door.

"My life is ruined! Your life is ruined! The whole damned world is ruined!" I screamed, throwing open the room to her.

She stood, her hair up in curlers, bulky with our new child, looking at me in pity. "What's the trouble?"

I sat down dejectedly. "I've double-exposed every damned picture but one. After all that work—all that work. I can't face that woman tomorrow. I just can't face her."

"How'd it happen?" she asked.

"Those damned holders. I didn't turn the black side out after I exposed the film."

We were silent for what seemed like an age, sitting there

in the dim light of the kitchen. I had been given my big chance and had muffed it. "Goddamnit! Goddamnit! Goddamnit! Goddamnit!" I kept groaning. "Why the hell did this have to happen to me!"

"I'd blow up the good one, and show it to her," my wife suggested as she went off to bed. I sat for an hour before her suggestion sank in. Then I made a huge enlargement of the only good negative. It was elegantly framed and standing on an easel at the entrance to the country club when Mrs. Murphy arrived with the models the next afternoon. "My dear boy," she exclaimed, "it's absolutely beautiful. Where are the others? I just can't wait to see them."

I was tempted to lie. "But a woman like this deserves the truth—no matter what," I said to myself sadly. So I told the truth. "Forget it," she said cheerfully; "we've got more work to do." My heart lightened instantly. "But," she warned, "no more of those nasty double exposures." The next week my photographs were shown throughout her store and in all the front windows. And I must have walked up and down that street a hundred times that first night, feeling good every time someone stopped to look at one of them.

Marva Louis, the wife of the heavyweight champion of the world, Joe Louis, came to St. Paul while my photographs were still on display. And, as good luck would have it, someone took her by Murphy's to see them. And Marva, who was interested in fashion design, telephoned to compliment me before returning to Chicago. "This is Marva Louis," she said simply. "I saw your wonderful photographs at Frank Murphy's, and I think you are wasting your time here. Why don't you come to work in Chicago? I could get you a lot of work there."

I was overwhelmed, hardly knowing how to answer her.

"I've been thinking about that, Mrs. Louis. Should I call you when I do come?"

"By all means," she said; and she gave me her address and phone number, not realizing, I am sure, the great joy she had brought to me. In my excitement I forgot to thank her for calling. I'll have to do that when I get to Chicago, I thought, and I hurried to the kitchen to give the news to my wife. She was frying potatoes when I burst in upon her. "Soon as the baby's born, we're going to Chicago," I shouted. Then I told her about the invitation Marva had extended me. Sally only smiled as she kept turning the potatoes. "Don't you understand what this means?" I said indignantly. I was crushed by her calmness.

"You're just restless again," she answered.

"Call it restlessness or whatever you want, but we're going to Chicago. I've made up my mind to that."

"We'll see," she said softly. And she kept turning the potatoes while I moved excitedly from room to room, feeling as if the eyes of the entire world were suddenly on me.

Our daughter was born shortly after that on November 4, while I was on a run to Chicago. My wife had named her Antoinette Stephane by the time I reached the hospital; but after one look at that name on paper I overruled her. A mild fight ensued but we eventually compromised on Toni. And that was what it would be.

TWENTY

FOR THE rest of that winter, and the following spring and summer, all my thoughts were of moving to Chicago. Neither Sally nor I discussed it openly; her mother, we knew, would try to thwart my plan. Sally wasn't exactly enthusiastic about my giving up the railroad, and at times she allowed herself faint murmurings about the big chance we would be taking. But, knowing that I was fully determined, she finally decided to keep whatever doubts she had to herself. Her pessimism, however, was by no means groundless. I was spending almost everything, after food and rent, on new photographic equipment, preparing for the day when we would leave. I wouldn't have tolerated any objection to my spending. "How can I work without good equipment?" was to be my answer to any complaint. But the complaints never came.

An accidental meeting one day in Chicago with David Ross, the curator at the Southside Art Center, led to my abrupt departure from the Twin Cities that fall. It turned out, during our conversation in the gallery, that his wife Verlita and mine had struck up a friendship when Sally had visited Chicago before our divorce. We went to a bar and got slightly potted on his favorite drink—rum and Coke.

Our friendship was almost instantaneous. I thought he had some awfully big ideas about things, but then he probably thought the same thing about me. We both sounded off under the power of the strong Jamaican rum, expanding our dreams far beyond our capabilities. David was fair-skinned, thin and dapper. His fingers were long and bony and he used them freely to press his points.

I told him about Marva Louis's suggestion and my preparations for moving.

"Well, what's keeping you?" he asked.

"A studio or some place to work from," I answered. I had never really considered this as a reason. But it came easily to my tongue; and it suddenly made sense. We parted with plans to see each other on my next run to Chicago. And I had already started across Michigan Avenue toward our rooming house when he caught up with me. "Damn," he said. "We've been yakking all night and I've just realized that we can do each other some good."

"Like what?"

"Well, we've got a fully equipped darkroom at the center, with nobody in it. We need a photographer and you need a place to work."

"Sounds great."

"We couldn't pay you anything but you wouldn't have to pay rent. We'd want you to photograph our activities now and then or an exhibit or things like that, and you could use one of the big rooms for your studio. How does it sound?"

"Sounds great," I repeated.

"It's a deal. Just let me know when you're coming. I'll start looking for an apartment for you." We pumped each other's hands happily and parted again. That night I lay awake till nearly dawn, trying to make the final decision, and two days later I gave the Chicago Northwestern notice. And, leaving the "400" on September 30, I swore never to ride it again except as a passenger.

The packing and storing of what little furniture we had were clandestine. My mother-in-law was suspicious but she didn't know about our plans until three days before we were ready to go. Instead of declaring outright war she took a just-you-wait-and-see attitude, predicting starvation for us before the winter was over.

Soon after, a letter came from David telling of a four-room furnished apartment someone had recommended. "I haven't seen it but it sounds pretty good and rents for $37.50 a month," he wrote.

"I'll take it. Arriving by car at ten Saturday morning," I wired back. But our battered Ford, filled to the corners with clothes, toys, sheets, blankets, developing trays, cameras and even my enlarger, suffered two flat tires and a boiled-over radiator. We finally chugged up to David's house at three o'clock that afternoon, hungry and weary. We rested and ate some fried fish and potatoes Verlita fixed for us. Then, anxious about our new home, we drove over to see it.

The dreary brownstone sat next to a vacant lot in a rundown neighborhood just outside the south side's black belt. Its ugly façade frowned down upon us when we got out of the car; and Sally, I noticed, was frowning back at it. The neighborhood, lying between the teeming black ghetto and the wealthy white residential section to the east, was in a sort of social limbo. An area where blacks were moving in and whites were moving out, it was a dwindling line of demarcation between the rich and the poor. The nondescript frame buildings surrounding ours had housed generations of Irish, Italians, Jews and Poles; and they had taken on the architectural whims of these early immigrants, most of whom had prospered and moved on. "Property for Sale" signs were all over the neighborhood.

A small, graying, brown-skinned man opened the door when I knocked. He said, in a high squeaky voice, that his name was Mr. Reynolds, that he was the superintendent and that he had been waiting around for us all day. I apologized for being late and asked him to show us the place. "I'll show it to you," he said, "but somebody better stay with that car. Half your stuff'd be gone by the time you got back."

Butch volunteered, being deliriously happy to sit alone at the steering wheel. Toni was asleep but I threw her over my shoulder and carried her up the three flights through the gloomy hallway. It somehow reminded me of Mrs. Haskins' place in Harlem the first day I had gone there; nearly eight years had passed since then.

Mr. Reynolds took out a bunch of keys and started opening the door. "Need strong locks 'round here. Well, here's the living room," he said making a quick gesture with his hand.

I glanced at the dirty green walls, the worn carpeting and the blistered ceiling. "Needs painting," I said, breaking the uncomfortable silence. I turned for a look at Sally. With Toni in her arms now, she stood in the doorway, unhappily observing the drab pieces of furniture.

Mr. Reynolds ignored my remark. "Here's the two bed-rooms," he squeaked, pointing in their direction.

Sally didn't move. "Come on," I said, "take a look." She hesitated for a moment, then came over and peeped into the dimly lit rooms. There was the same grease-splotched paper on all the walls, and its tawdry design, imitating the worst of the Victorian era, went well with the ornate brass beds and the credit-store dressers.

"The bathroom ain't much. Just a tub and a toilet stool.

Look it over if you want to." Sally passed it up. But one quick look confirmed his description. There was an old-fashioned bathtub with claw feet and a primitive-looking stool. "And here's the kitchen. Comes with a gas stove and icebox." And a lot of grease and bugs, I thought, watching him squash a big cockroach with his foot. It was a darksome, dingy place, but my family was tired and needed some place to sleep. I didn't dare ask Sally if she liked it. I just took $37.50 out of my pocket and paid the little man a month's rent. "It'll be fine," I assured her after he had gone; "just give me a week to fix it up and you won't know it."

"We'll see," she said; "we'll see."

The landlord gave in the next day and painted the place. Sally made new curtains for the windows; and with a few odds and ends we picked up at a second-hand store, our home began to brighten. So by the end of the first week we had settled into the big city existence rather easily.

I began work at the Art Center right away. It was on South Michigan Avenue, nearly three miles north of where we lived, and quartered in an old red brick mansion, bought with solicited funds and proceeds from community benefits. There were about thirty employees on the staff, most of them teachers paid by the Federal Works Administration. Peter Pollack, a bustling curly-haired man, was the director and David was the assistant director and curator. There were three floors where the partitions had been cut away to make larger rooms. And the entire place, a haven for striving painters, sculptors, dancers, writers and poets, was always alive with some sort of activity. My darkroom was located in the basement and it was complete with loading room, storage space and good working facilities; and, as had been planned, I used a large room on the third floor for my studio. A good deal of Peter's and David's time was spent assuaging the feelings of opinionated officers and trustees, all of whom had different ideas for running the place. A revolt of some type was always at hand. At first my position was questioned, but at a tumultuous board meeting David shouted, "We don't pay him a red cent. He's doing as much for us as we are for him!" And that crisis was abruptly ended.

I did a brisk business from the very start. With the help of some of the influential board members and Marva Louis, whom I telephoned, I began gathering a steady clientele through a word-of-mouth campaign. The champion's beautiful wife had invited me to lunch at their Michigan Avenue apartment one afternoon. Before sitting down to eat I was shown the large, mirrored and elegantly over-stuffed apartment from front to back. I gawked at closet after closet of dresses, drawers of gloves, a floor-to-ceiling rack filled with shoes of many patterns and colors—and there was one closet, nearly as large as my bedroom, where she kept her hats and coats. "You can use anything here you like for photographs," she said, "and I'll be delighted to pose for you." Over a nice but unfilling soufflé we talked of our hopes for the future. She was struck with the idea of being a designer, and it was easy to see where I fitted into her plans. I agreed to photograph her the follow-ing week. We flung ourselves into the effort with devotion. She was extremely photogenic and easy to work with. And clothes. My God, we had clothes; room after room of them.

Our exertions were rewarded with a page of photo-graphs in the Chicago *Sunday Tribune*, featuring Mrs. Louis and some of her new creations. And this brought me work from all over the city. At times I made as much as $150 a day.

Although I continued to photograph Marva, I did not meet Joe Louis for a long time. But shortly after he knocked out Arturo Godoy in June of 1940, Marva told me they had had a little spat, and asked me to escort her across town, where I was to leave her at a party. While I sat in the living room waiting for her, Joe came in, munching on an apple. He didn't speak. He just ambled his magnificent two hundred pounds over to Marva's door and leaned against the frame. "Where you goin', baby?" he asked, viciously destroying the big apple.

"Out!"

"Out where, baby?"

"That's my business!"

"Don't keep dressin', honey. You ain't goin' no place."

"That's what you think!"

Joe kept chewing and Marva kept dressing and I began looking for the nearest exit.

"Are you ready, Gordon?" she called out, trying to plump up her courage.

"Pardon?" was all I could say—very softly.

When she switched out the door, Joe's big twelve-inch forearms gently embraced her and he lifted her up toward the ceiling, where she kicked away like a child having a tantrum. I figured, while he had her up, that this was a highly propitious time to bid the Louises goodnight. And I did this with dignified haste, while Marva hollered in vain, "Wait for me, Gordon! Wait for me!" As I descended I thought back to the bodies of Braddock, Schmeling, and Tony Galento lying prostrate at Joe's feet. And I walked a little bit faster.

There were a number of talented young people who worked at the Center during those days, and one of the most promising was Charles White, a painter. He was mild-appearing, bespectacled, and blessed with humor, but his powerful, black figures pointed at the kind of photography that I knew I should be doing. We became close friends as the days went by. It was good to laugh and talk with him; and it was good to watch him strengthen an arm with a delicate brush stroke or give anguish to a face with mixtures of coloring. We had great hopes, Charlie and I, and we spent hours talking to each other about them. "I've tried to get a damned Julius Rosenwald fellowship a couple of times," he complained sadly one day, "but those granny dodgers won't give me one."

"What's a Julius Rosenwald fellowship?" I asked.

"It's a fund set up for exceptionally able spooks and white crackers," he explained. "You oughta try for one next year."

"Has a photographer ever gotten one?"

"Not that I know of. Fact is I know they haven't. But that's all the more reason you should try."

"Hell, man," Charlie said, "let's me and you get one of those hunchers in '42. What say?"

"I'm with you, buddy," I agreed. And we laughed and shook hands on it.

The Saturday morning I started poking around the south side with my camera, I knew that more than anything else I wanted to strike at the evil of poverty. And here it was, under my feet, all around and above me. I could point the camera in any direction and record it. My own brush with it was motive enough, yet this landscape of ash piles, garbage heaps, tired tenements and littered streets was worse than any I had seen. Everything looked wrecked and bombed out: this is what I would photograph and submit for the Rosenwald fellowship.

I hardly knew where to begin. So I walked along, pacing off this area where life and building alike had fallen into grave disrepair. Then I came to a vacant lot where a large black man stood with a shovel in his hand and a woman and two children at his side. They were silent, looking as if they were at a graveside. A little girl, holding on to her mother's dress, was crying. I lifted my camera and shot the strange scene. As they made their way toward a tenement house I followed them. And, passing the fresh grave, I saw a board stuck into the ashy earth. There was a crude crayon drawing of a dog on it. Beneath the drawing, printed also with crayon, and in a child's hand, were the words BUCKY, OUR FRIEND.

I was photographing this pathetic eulogy when the man looked back to me. "What you doin' there, fella?" he asked.

"Would the kids like a picture of the grave?"

They all looked at me strangely. "Yes, Poppa," the weeping girl said.

"What you chargin' for it?" the father asked.

"Nothing. Nothing at all. I'd just like for them to have it—if they want it."

"Yes, Poppa," the child repeated.

"How do we get it?" He seemed suspicious of me.

"Just give me your address and name and I'll send it to you."

"That's all? We don't have to send you nothin'?"

"No, sir, not a thing," I said. "Have you got a pencil and paper?"

"In the house. We've got one in the house," the child said eagerly.

"Come on," the father said. I followed them over the lot to their building. We passed a sign on a large brick wall:

FIRST CLASS UNDERTAKER—HOME OF JENKINS FUNERAL
SYSTEM ASSOCIATION—DON'T LET DEATH EMBARRASS YOUR
LOVED ONES—JOIN TODAY—PREMIUMS AS LOW AS 10¢ PER
WEEK.

I climbed a rickety stairway behind them to their third-
floor room. The man invited me in, and after sizing me up
properly he asked me to sit down. The chair he offered was
held together with baling wire. His wife sat on a stool and
he stood up. "I thought you was some kind of inspector
or somethin'," he said after we talked for a while. "They're
always snoopin' round mindin' other people's business stead
of cleanin' up this stinkin' place." And when I told him
what I was trying to do with my camera he pointed at his
miserable quarters. "You won't find much worse'n this. Go
ahead, take all the pictures you want. Just don't try to sell
us none cause we're busted."

I started slowly, shooting first the one mattress where all
of them slept on the floor. There was a small, round table
covered with cracked oilcloth, and a greasy edition of
Cinderella lay on it next to a stack of unwashed dishes. A
wall shelf, covered with a piece of torn, dusty lace, held a
framed picture of Christ and a Bible. There were a gas
burner and a washtub with a chunk of ice in it, which
served as their refrigerator; a fruit crate sat in the corner,
filled with dirty clothes, and there was a sink, propped up
with two broom handles. All the clothes the family owned
hung above their heads on a rope that stretched across the
room—overalls, gingham dresses, socks and underwear.
Most of the plaster had fallen from the walls and the
rotting laths showed through.

"This here is what they call a one-room kitchenette," the
father went on. "Only about eight white families lived in

this whole building once. When they cut out, the landlords chopped it up into the kinda holes you see I'm livin' in here. Now, there's more'n eight families on one floor alone. Gas and light free, they say. Well, we got two burners, and one of them works, and that one light bulb hangin' up there."

I broke in to ask him how much rent he paid.

"Seven bucks a week—when I can scrape it up. I got laid off from the slaughterhouse about six months ago. I get a odd job now and then. Most of the time I don't get nothin'."

"Do all of you sleep on this one mattress?"

"That ain't nothin', brother. There's a poor fella livin' down the hall what's got six children and their place ain't no bigger'n this. There was eight of 'em till two of the younguns got drafted in the army a month or so ago."

"Where's your toilet and bathroom?"

"Take him down the hall and show him, Lil. Show him good." Lil, his wife, nodded toward me and I followed her down a dark corridor, where she opened a door and pointed in. There was an old bathtub with most of the enamel broken off and a filthy toilet. The seat to it had rotted and fallen apart, lying in a heap of other decaying boards and fallen plaster. The foul air was unbearable. "Would you wash your child in that mess?" she asked. I didn't answer. I knew she didn't expect me to. I just took a picture of it; and we went back to her husband and children.

"Well, how'd you like it? It's a dog, huh?" I nodded, and he went on, "Eight families use it, brother. See that baseball bat over there in the corner? Well, my boy there don't play ball with it. We kill rats with it. There's three times more rats in here than there is Negroes. Got so my wife and me have to sleep in shifts to keep 'em from gnawin' up the kids."

"You lived here—in Chicago—all your life?" I asked, having nothing else to say.

"Naw, I freighted in here from Georgia 'bout eight years ago. Met my wife and started raisin' these kids 'bout three years later."

I looked at the children. They sat wide-eyed on the mattress. The girl was about five, and she held her three-year-old brother's hand tightly. They watched their father as he talked.

"They're growin' children, good ones, but what's livin' like this gonna do to them down the line?"

Having seen some of the restless, beaten black boys and girls on the corners and in the taverns and poolrooms, I knew.

"Already," he rambled on, "we've got to watch that somethin' bad don't happen to our girl there in these dark hallways. It's a shame, ain't it, brother? Yessir, it's a shame," he said, answering his own question.

I wrote down their address and promised to send them some of the pictures. I wanted to ask about the dog they had buried, but not before the children. I finally mentioned it to the father when he walked me outside. "He was the kids' pet. Nobody better not touch them while he was around, not even me. We got him to fight rats and keep guard round here. But my wife, she puts out some rat poison the other night and Bucky gets hold of it. And that's all of him."

This was only the beginning of weekend after weekend of tramping through the dismal acres of the south side, photographing depressed black people and the shacks and brick tenements that entombed them. I got to know number runners and their hangouts. I sneaked pictures of men, and boys, gambling in the hallways. I saw two young black boys dying from each other's knife wounds on Forty-seventh and South Park one afternoon. I watched a Negro cop known as two-gun-Pete beat a Negro youth senseless with the butt of his pistol one night—just because he didn't move off the corner fast enough. And one night two white cops stopped me, for speeding, they said. One got out and pulled forth his ticket book, saying he hated to see me go to court. "If you want to act right, well . . . " I knew what that meant, so I started fishing for some money, just as the other cop walked up.

"Go back. Stay with the car," the one cop said to the other.

"Everything's okay. I'll wait," the other one said. They began to argue; then they went off into the darkness fussing with each other, obviously over the suggested "bribe." The other cop didn't want to get the short end. They stood there so long, hollering at each other, they forgot me; and finally I drove off.

And there were the churches, big ones, little and middle-sized ones scattered among the taverns, butcher shops and mortuaries. On Sunday mornings I turned my camera on those ardently religious folks as they went, in their Sunday best, to the store-front Bethels, God in Christs, African Methodists and Pilgrim Baptists that they kept going with pennies, nickels and dimes. "Religion is all we got left," an old missionary woman told me one day. I had asked her to pose for me, and she stood, a little white bonnet perched on top of her head, a Bible under her arm, looking into my camera. The lenses of her steel-rimmed glasses were like mirrors; focusing sharply on them, I caught a reflection of the desolation that surrounded us.

Being proud of that particular picture, I showed it to a society matron whom I photographed in her north-side penthouse the next afternoon. She held up the picture in her jeweled white hands and observed it carefully. "A darling old lady," she purred, "an awful lot like the mammy we had as children," and in the same breath, "Oh, I do want so much for you to make me beautiful!" And, with deceit and guile, I told her what she wanted to hear, "You *are* beautiful." She shrieked with delight when I took her the finished photographs that Friday. And, with the handsome fee she paid me, I bought more film to expose in that frightful ghetto once again.

When the cold shock of that winter knifed in from the big lake, the south side became desperate, and death stalked the side streets and dark alleyways. The robberies and slayings increased and I walked the area with caution, aware of the danger in every block. There were always a lot of funerals during the winter months and I photographed these sad rituals, catching when I could the despair on the faces of the mourners. The preachers' voices were always caressing to the families of the deceased, even when the deceased had died taking someone else's life. But sometimes, caught up in the emotion of their words, the preachers lost all feeling of time and the dead beneath their makeshift pulpits; and they lashed out with fury at the sin and corruption that hemmed them in. And, swaying with passion, they lifted the mourners into uncontrolled weeping, dancing and shouting; the floors shook, the coffin shook and it seemed that the one they had come to bury was forgotten. Once I followed a coffin to the baggage car.

On the pine box it was shipped in was penciled the name Joshua Collins. He was going back to Natchez, Mississippi, where his life had started in a sharecropper's shack. "He wanted to be put away down there," his sister told me as the train pulled out, "I don't know why. I don't want to ever see that place again. We had such a hard time gettin' out."

I worked hard the rest of that year and most of the next. The Art Center promised me a show in the early fall of 1941; this, Pollack and Ross thought, would give the Rosenwald people a chance to see my work at its very best. Charlie White worked hard too, and at times we got together and talked about our chances. Meanwhile we set out to bag sponsors, as required by the fellowship fund. My list eventually included Alain Locke, the first Negro Rhodes scholar; Horace Cayton, the writer; Pollack and Ross. I spent most of August printing the things I had shot. For an amateur, I had a well-rounded selection to choose from—the south-side series, landscapes, seascapes, fashions I had shot at Frank Murphy's and some of the wealthy ladies who sat for me in Chicago.

Fall came quicker than usual, it seemed; but by working day and night I was able to meet the deadline. David hung the show, and we spent the final hours changing or readjusting the order of the pictures for what he called "impact." By the time Sally and I arrived, the gallery was already filling. And, if attendance had anything to do with it, the show was a success. It seemed that half of Chicago was there. The elite, dressed in their furs and finery, rubbed elbows with some of the people I had photographed in the poor quarter; I had invited as many of them as I could find. Jack Delano, the FSA photographer whose work had inspired me years before, attended; and the

Rosenwald Fund was represented by Edwin R. Embree, its director, and William C. Haygood, a white Southerner who was his assistant. There were tables full of dainty sandwiches and cocktails with white-jacketed waiters to serve them. It was a grand affair. But my warmest moment came when the little missionary woman I had photographed walked into the gallery wearing her bonnet. Her photograph was one of the largest in the room and, subconsciously, I suppose, I had hung it next to that of the bejeweled lady who thought she resembled her "mammy." It was odd to see the two of them standing beneath their respective portraits with newsmen's flashbulbs popping in their faces. Despite the gathering of beautiful ladies and other affluent people, she was the most sought after. Nearly everyone in the place shook her hand before she finally went home in a taxi I called for her.

Embree and Haygood said glowing things about the exhibition before they left and I went home glowing in presumptuous confidence; then, a couple of days later, realizing they weren't judges, I started to sweat it out. I had done all I could. The question was: had I done enough?

Things gradually returned to normal and I settled back into my daily work. Now and then I imagined myself as a successful Rosenwald fellow, but just as often I felt the pangs of reading the letter that would come one day—saying I had not been accepted. At times I tried to forget the whole business, but this was impossible. Nearly a month had passed when Peter Pollack told me that a jury of photographers, selected to judge my work, had turned me down flat. All this was in strict confidence; the information had been leaked out to Pollack. Terribly disappointed with the news, we sat around for a while, enveloped in gloom. I had given up altogether. "I don't think I'll ever try again," I said, thinking back over the hard work I had put in.

"Just a minute," Pollack said. He was dialing the phone. "Hello. Mr. Haygood, please. Hello, Billy. Pete Pollack speaking. Billy, why in hell did they let photographers judge Parks's work? The man's an artist. Artists should have judged his work." They talked for a few minutes and Pollack hung up. "I have a hunch you'll get another chance. Haygood might put your work before the artists' jury." And for the next few weeks Pollack sweated with me.

Finally one morning an envelope came from the fund. I was still in bed when Sally brought it to me, and I lay there for a few seconds, afraid to open it. "Here," I said, handing it back to her, "give me the bad news." She fumbled with the envelope for a long moment; then, beginning at last to read, her anxious face softened. Then she said weakly, "You made it." She sat down on the bed and we remained there, quiet in our happiness, for several minutes. I wondered about Charlie White, afraid he might not have been so fortunate. I didn't know it then, but he was thinking the same way about me. The two of us were cautiously reserved when I finally got him on the phone.

"Charlie?"

"Gordon?" His voice couldn't hide the joy; and neither could mine.

"We made it! We made it!" we both shouted at the top of our voices.

As Rosenwald fellows we would each get $200 a month for a year. Later that day Billy Haygood came by and warmly congratulated me. I had no difficulty answering him when he asked me where I would like to further my

education as a photographer. "The Farm Security Administration," I said confidently.

"We've already written Roy Stryker asking him to take
you on as a trainee," he said, smiling. "You'd better start
getting packed. We think we know what his answer will
be."

Two weeks later, on a Sunday in December, we were
having some friends in to celebrate Butch's birthday and
our own happy prospects. Sally and I had spent a joyous
week, going about town gathering food, drink and presents
for the coming Christmas. Now the party was under way;
our cheer was underscored by Duke Ellington's music,
which was being broadcast from a local station. Then, in
the middle of "Sophisticated Lady," the announcer's voice
cut in, "We have just received word that the Japanese have
bombed Pearl Harbor! That is all for the moment. Stay
tuned to this station for further news!" It was December 7,
1941.

The news stunned us into silence. It seemed unbelievable;
but then the confirming details began to come through.
After our guests had departed, I stayed up all night listening to reports, trying to decipher their meaning. A great
distance lay between the Kansas cornfields and that fellowship. Now the brightness of my triumph was suddenly
dulled by this disaster. Even before the Japanese attack,
single men were being drafted for service; how, I wondered, would all this affect my immediate future? Self-
concern at such a time was petty, I told myself; but I could
not still my anxiety. The thing I had worked so hard for
was so close; and now it seemed that those years of effort
might be swept away. But the following week an an-
nouncement by the President temporarily deferred married
men with children. And shortly after Roy Stryker wrote

saying he expected me in Washington, D.C., by January 1. I breathed easier. It appeared that in spite of the catastrophe my plans would not be altered for a while. There was lots of work to be done yet, at home as well as at the Art Center. I plunged into it with fervor; and before the month ended I had finished it, packed up and was ready to go. Stryker had found me a place to stay temporarily. I would go ahead, find a house and send for my family later. At last I was on the move.

TWENTY-ONE

I CAME to Washington, excited and eager, on a clear cold day in January. I had been singled out for an unusual blessing. I felt a notch above normal things, bursting with a new strength that would be unleashed upon this historic place. The White House, the Capitol and all the great buildings wherein great men had helped shape the destinies of the world—I would borrow from their tradition, feel their presence, touch their stone. I would walk under trees and on paths where Presidents had once walked. My mind hurried the taxi along to the place where I was to stay. It hastened my unpacking and raced ahead of the streetcar that carried me to the red brick building at Fourteenth and Independence avenues where I would meet Stryker and the photographers of the Farm Security Administration. And I walked confidently down the corridor, following the arrows to my destination, sensing history all around me, feeling knowledge behind every door I passed. I was so uplifted that the plainness of the office I finally entered dumbfounded me. The barnlike room with the plain furniture and bulky file cabinets was as ordinary as any other office I had seen but even more so. No photographs were on the walls and there were no photographers around;

ordinary dust clung to the windows and the air was no different from that I had breathed back in Kansas. I stood waiting, a little disappointed, wondering what I had really expected. I didn't know, I finally realized.

A tall blonde girl who said her name was Charlotte came forward and greeted me. "Mr. Stryker will be with you in a minute," she said. She had just gotten the words out when he bounced out and extended his hand. "Welcome to Washington. I'm Roy," were his first words. "Come into the office and let's get acquainted." I will like this man, I thought.

He motioned me to a chair opposite his desk but before he could say anything his telephone rang. "It's Arthur Rothstein phoning from Montana," Charlotte called from the outer office. The name flashed my thoughts back to the night on the dining car when I first saw it beneath the picture of the farmer and his two sons running toward their shack through the dust storm.

"Arthur? This is Roy."

I'm here, I thought; at last I'm here.

As he talked I observed the chubby face topped with a mane of white hair, the blinking piercingly curious eyes, enlarged under thick bifocal lenses. There was something boyish, something fatherly, something tyrannical, something kind and good about him. He did not seem like anyone I had ever known before.

They talked for about ten minutes. "That was Rothstein." Stryker said, hanging up. "He had bad luck with one of his cameras." The way he said this pulled me in as if I were already accepted; as if I had been there for years. The indoctrination had begun. "Now tell me about yourself and your plans," he said with a trace of playfulness in his voice. I spent a lot of time telling him perhaps more than he bargained for. After I had finished, he asked me bluntly, "What do you know about Washington?"

"Nothing much," I admitted.

"Did you bring your cameras with you?"

"Yes, they're right here in this bag." I took out my battered Speed Graphic and a Rolleiflex and proudly placed them on his desk.

He looked at them approvingly and then asked me for the bag I had taken them from. He then took all my equipment and locked it in a closet behind him. "You won't be needing those for a few days," he said flatly. He lit a cigarette and leaned back in his chair and continued, "I have some very specific things I would like you to do this week. And I would like you to follow my instructions faithfully. Walk around the city. Get to know it. Buy yourself a few things—you have money, I suppose."

"Yes, sir."

"Go to a picture show, the department stores, eat in the restaurants and drugstores. Get to know this place." I thought his orders were a bit trivial, but they were easy enough to follow. "Let me know how you've made out in a couple of days," he said after he had walked me to the door.

"I will," I promised casually. And he smiled oddly as I left.

I walked toward the business section and stopped at a drugstore for breakfast. When I sat down at the counter the white waiter looked at me as though I were crazy. "Get off of that stool," he said angrily. "Don't you know colored people can't eat in here? Go round to the back door if you want something." Everyone in the place was staring at me now. I retreated, too stunned to answer him as I walked out the door.

I found an open hot dog stand. Maybe this place would

serve me. I approached the counter warily. "Two hot dogs, please."

"To take out?" the boy in the white uniform snapped.

"Yes, to take out," I snapped back. And I walked down the street, gulping down the sandwiches.

I went to a theater.

"What do you want?"

"A ticket."

"Colored people can't go in here. You should know that."

I remained silent, observing the ticket seller with more surprise than anything else. She looked at me as though I were insane. What is this, I wondered. Was Stryker playing some sort of joke on me? Was this all planned to exasperate me? Such discrimination here in Washington, D.C., the nation's capital? It was hard to believe.

Strangely, I hadn't lost my temper. The experience was turning into a weird game, and I would play it out—follow Roy's instructions to the hilt. I would try a department store now; and I chose the most imposing one in sight, Julius Garfinckel. Its name had confronted me many times in full-page advertisements in fashion magazines. Its owners must have been filled with national pride—their ads were always identified with some sacred Washington monument. Julius Garfinckel. Julius Rosenwald. I lumped them with the names of Harvey Goldstein, and Peter Pollack—Jews who had helped shift the course of my life. I pulled myself together and entered the big store, with nothing particular in mind. The men's hats were on my right so I arbitrarily chose that department. The salesman appeared a little on edge but he sold me a hat. Then leaving I saw an advertisement for camel's-hair coats on an upper floor. I had wanted one since the early days at the Minnesota Club. It was possible now. The elevator operator's face brought back

memories of the doorman at the Park Central Hotel on that
first desperate morning in New York.

"Can I help you?" His question was shadowed with
arrogance.

"Yes. Men's coats, please." He hesitated for a moment,
then closed the door and we went up.

The game had temporarily ended on the first floor as far
as I was concerned. The purchase of the hat had relieved
my doubts about discrimination here; the coat was the goal
now. The floor was bare of customers. Only four salesmen
stood eying me as I stepped from the elevator. None of
them offered assistance so I looked at them and asked to be
shown a camel's-hair coat.

No one moved. "They're to your left," someone volunteered.

I walked to my left. There were the coats I wanted,
several racks of them. But no one attempted to show them
to me.

"Could I get some help here?" I asked.

One man sauntered over. "What can I do for you?"

"I asked you for a camel's-hair coat."

"Those aren't your size."

"Then where are my size?"

"Probably around to your right."

"Probably around to my right?" The game was on
again. "Then show them to me."

"That's not my department."

"Then whose department is it?"

"Come to think of it, I'm sure we don't have your size in
stock."

"But you don't even know my size."

"I'm sorry. We just don't have your size."

"Well, I'll just wait here until you get one my size."
Anger was at last beginning to take over. There was a

white couch in the middle of the floor. I walked over and sprawled out leisurely on it, took a newspaper from my pocket and pretended to read. My blackness stretched across the white couch commanded attention. The manager arrived, posthaste, a generous smile upon his face. My ruse had succeeded, I thought.

"I'm the manager of this department. What can I do for you?"

"Oh, am I to have the honor of being waited on by the manager? How nice," I said, smiling with equal graciousness.

"Well, you see, there's a war on. And we're very short of help. General Marshall was in here yesterday and *he* had to wait for a salesman. Now please understand that—"

"But I'm not General Marshall and there's no one here but four salesmen, you and me. But I'll wait here until they're not so busy. I'll wait right here." He sat down in a chair beside me and we talked for a half hour—about weather, war, food, Washington, and even camel's-hair coats. But I was never shown one. Finally, after he ran out of conversation, he left. I continued to sit there under the gaze of the four puzzled salesmen and the few customers who came to the floor. At last the comfort of the couch made me sleepy; and by now the whole thing had become ridiculous. I wouldn't have accepted a coat if they had given me the entire rack. Suddenly I thought of my camera, of Stryker. I got up and hurried out of the store and to his office. He was out to lunch when I got back. But I waited outside his door until he returned.

"I didn't expect you back so soon," he said. "I thought you'd be out seeing the town for a couple of days."

"I've seen enough of it in one morning," I replied sullenly. "I want my cameras."

"What do you intend to do with them?"

"I want to show the rest of the world what your great city of Washington, D.C., is really like. I want—"

"Okay. Okay." The hint of that smile was on his face again. And now I was beginning to understand it. "Come into my office and tell me all about it," he said. He listened patiently. He was sympathetic; but he didn't return my equipment.

"Young man," he finally began, "you're going to face some very hard facts down here. Whatever else it may be, this is a Southern city. Whether you ignore it or tolerate it is up to you. I purposely sent you out this morning so that you can see just what you're up against." He paused for a minute to let this sink in. Then he continued. "You're going to find all kinds of people in Washington and a good cross-section of the types are right here in this building. You'll have to prove yourself to them, especially the lab people. They are damned good technicians—but they are all Southerners. I can't predict what their attitudes will be toward you and I warn you I'm not going to try to influence them one way or the other. It's completely up to you. I do think they will respect good craftsmanship. Once you get over that hurdle I honestly believe you will be accepted as another photographer—not just as a Negro photographer. There is a certain amount of resentment against even the white photographers until they prove themselves. Remember, these people slave in hot darkrooms while they think about the photographers enjoying all the glamor and getting all the glory. Most of them would like to be on the other end."

We were walking about the building now, and as he introduced me to different people his words took on meaning. Some smiled and extended their hands in welcome. Others, especially those in the laboratory, kept working and acknowledged me with cold nods, making their disdain obvious. Any triumph over them would have to be well earned, I told myself. Stryker closed the door when we were back in his office. "Go home," he advised, "and put it on paper."

"Put what on paper?" I asked puzzled.

"Your plan for fighting these things you say you just went through. Think it out constructively. It won't be easy. You can't take a picture of a white salesman, waiter or ticket seller and just say they are prejudiced. That isn't enough. You've got to verbalize the experience first, then find logical ways to express it in pictures. The right words too are important; they should underscore your photographs. Think in terms of images and words. They can be mighty powerful when they are fitted together properly."

I went home that evening and wrote. I wrote of just about every injustice that I had ever experienced. Kansas, Minnesota, Chicago, New York and Washington were all forged together in the heat of the blast.

Images and words images and words images and words— I fell asleep trying to arrange an acceptable marriage of them.

Stryker read what I had written with a troubled face. I watched his eyes move over the lines, his brows furrow from time to time. When he had finished we both sat quietly for a few minutes. "You've had quite a time," he finally said, "but you have to simplify all this material. It would take many years and all the photographers on the staff to fulfill what you have put down here. Come outside; I want to show you something." He took me over to the file and opened a drawer marked "Dorothea Lange." "Spend the rest of the day going through this set of pictures. Each day take on another drawer. And go back and write more specifically about your visual approach to things."

For several weeks I went through hundreds of photographs by Lange, Russell Lee, Jack Delano, Carl Mydans, John Vachon, Arthur Rothstein, Ben Shahn, Walker Evans, John Collier and others. The disaster of the thirties was at my fingertips: the gutted cotton fields, the eroded farmland, the crumbling South, the unending lines of dispossessed migrants, the pitiful shacks, the shameful city ghettos, the breadlines and bonus marchers, the gaunt faces of men, women and children caught up in the tragedy; the horrifying spectacles of sky blackened with locusts, and swirling dust and towns flooded with muddy rivers. There were some no doubt who laid these tragedies to God. But research accompanying these stark photographs accused man himself—especially the lords of the land. In their greed and passion for wealth, they had gutted the earth for cotton; overworked the farms; exploited the tenant farmers and sharecroppers who, broken, took to the highways with their families in search of work. They owned the ghettos as well as the impoverished souls who inhabited them. No, the indictment was against man, not God; the proof was there in those ordinary steel files. It was a raw slice of contemporary America—clear, hideous and beautifully detailed in images and words. I began to get the point.

For some time now I had passed the cafeteria in the building without entering. It was not that they wouldn't serve me, because I saw other Negroes eating there. It was the sight of them huddled in the rear that turned me from the door. I knew that I would eventually eat there—but never in the back. Since I was more or less Stryker's responsibility I didn't want to saddle him with any more problems. The agency was already under fire from certain politicians who opposed Roosevelt's New Deal policies. Nevertheless, I knew that when the time came I would not take a seat in the rear.

The test came on the day I met John Vachon. He was the first of the photographers I got to know. He too was from Minnesota and we became friends right away. When he invited me to eat with him that afternoon I was at last deprived of any alibi; so I accepted his invitation. The face of the cafeteria manager turned as red as his hair when we sat down together, but he said nothing. He had decided to lay the problem in Stryker's lap, I found out later that day. But his complaint was met with stern rebuff. "There is no rule that says he has to eat in the rear," Stryker said icily. Then when I entered several days later, the manager openly suggested that I take one of the tables in the rear. But I refused even to answer him. He never bothered me again but I began to collect stares from some of the Negro patrons. One gray-haired, light-skinned Negro gentleman approached me in the corridor one day. "Young man," he said, "you're going to cause trouble for all of us."

"Why?" I asked politely.

"Eating out of your place in the cafeteria. I've eaten in there for nearly twenty years, right back there in the rear, and you should do the same."

"Then I'm very sorry for you, sir," I answered, "but I won't ever eat back there."

"What's the matter? Are you any better than the rest of us Negroes?"

"No, sir. It's just that I don't feel that the whites are any better than me. I won't let them make a place for me."

He looked at me for a moment. Hopelessness was in his eyes. "I just don't understand you young Negroes any more," he said and walked off shaking his head. And I was honestly sad for this old man. But I could no more understand him than he could me; we were centuries apart. And there came a time, that same year, when he ate there in the rear alone. One day someone told me that he had died. And I thought about him during the rest of that week: he was part of the old order that was passing on, and I didn't know how to feel about his death.

Using my camera effectively against intolerance was not so easy as I had assumed it would be. One evening, when Stryker and I were in the office alone, I confessed this to him. "Then at least you have learned the most important lesson," he said. He thought for a moment, got up and looked down the corridor, then called me to his side. There was a Negro charwoman mopping the floor. "Go have a talk with her before you go home this evening. See what she has to say about life and things. You might find her interesting."

This was a strange suggestion, but after he had gone I went through the empty building searching for her. I found her in a notary public's office and introduced myself. She was a tall spindly woman with sharp features. Her hair was swept back from graying temples; a sharp intelligence shone in the eyes behind the steel-rimmed glasses. We started off awkwardly, neither of us knowing my reason for starting the conversation. At first it was a meaningless exchange of words. Then, as if a dam had broken within her, she began to spill out her life story. It was a pitiful one. She had struggled alone after her mother had died and her father had been killed by a lynch mob. She had gone through high school, married and become pregnant. Her husband was accidentally shot to death two days before the daughter was born. By the time the daughter was eighteen she had given birth to two illegitimate children, dying two weeks after the second child's birth. What's more, the first child had been stricken with paralysis a year before its mother died. Now this woman was bringing up these grandchildren on a salary hardly suitable for one person.

"Who takes care of them while you are at work?" I asked after a long silence.

"Different neighbors," she said, her heavily veined hands tightening about the mop handle.

"Can I photograph you?" The question had come out of an elaboration of thoughts. I was escaping the humiliation of not being able to help.

"I don't mind," she said.

My first photograph of her was unsubtle. I overdid it and posed her, Grant Wood style, before the American flag, a broom in one hand, a mop in the other, staring straight into the camera. Stryker took one look at it the next day and fell speechless.

"Well, how do you like it?" I asked eagerly.

He just smiled and shook his head. "Well?" I insisted.

"Keep working with her. Let's see what happens," he finally replied. I followed her for nearly a month—into her home, her church and wherever she went. "You're learning," Stryker admitted when I laid the photographs out before him late one evening. "You're showing you can involve yourself in other people. This woman has done you a great service. I hope you understand this." I did understand.

TWENTY-TWO

MY FAMILY followed me to Washington after a couple of months, and we took a house in a development southeast of the city. It was small, cheap and clean; and we were relatively happy there. But on weekends Butch had to forgo his journey to the heart of town for his big hot dog and malted. He complained, but I couldn't bring myself to tell him the truth; he would know soon enough. And we spent our spare time at the great monuments and in the museums, avoiding the playgrounds that so often erupted with racial hostility. Washington, I knew, was not the place for my children to grow into adulthood. I would attach no sense of permanence to our home there. Again, it was just a stopover; I would move on as quickly as possible.

And now, recognizing more than ever the necessity for knowledge, I threw myself into stacks of books, trying to couple my visual sense with the themes of the more significant writers. Richard Wright's *12 Million Black Voices* became my bible. By now Carl Mydans was covering the war and Walker Evans had gone to work for *Time;* but Lee, Shahn, Delano, Wolcott-Post, Rothstein, Collier, Lange and Vachon came in from field trips from time to time. They were all good people, and in them one felt the compassion that was so evident in their work. Their friendships counteracted the animosity I might have built against all whites—especially at that period. They struck the precarious balance for me.

The first stories Stryker assigned me were exercises in thought, composition and technique. And soon, thinking the entire universe was impatient for me, I became restless; I wanted to show off my newly acquired knowledge and talent. Stryker only pulled the reins tighter, buried me in more problems to decipher. I plunged into a discontent that began to poison my mind against him. He was holding me back, abandoning me to the less-important assignments. Was a secret prejudice of his escaping into the open? I wondered. My discontent surfaced one day when he refused a request for an exhibit of my work to Howard University. "Why not?" I asked heatedly. "Other photographers' works are being shown all over the country."

Stryker looked at me sternly. "Gordon," he said, "you can goddamned well think what you want. No individual photographers have been given shows, and I'm not going to make an exception of you. Furthermore, you're not ready for a show yet—not by a long shot."

"Is that your final word?" I demanded.

"It is. And you can take it or leave it," he answered coldly.

By now John Vachon and I had become fast friends. John didn't talk much, and you got the feeling that he censored each thought before letting it go. But under his calm lay a dry, biting sense of humor. He was lean and long-jawed and, when his sandy hair was uncut, he looked like a Texas cattle wrangler. Since there were so few places we could go together, our families visited each other's homes. One day he came in angry and disheveled, his face dead white. "What's the matter, John?" I asked. But he just kept on walking without reply. Weeks later he told me a white bus driver had cursed and pushed a colored woman, and John had fought with him. Later that same year Marjorie Collins, a young photographer, joined the staff; and since the three of us were about the same age, our friendship spread to her. And we went about the city under stares from some of Washington's white citizens. We were upsetting the established order of things, we knew, but we would not sacrifice our friendship to it. We never spoke to one another about the problem. It belonged to those who invented it inside their own hearts.

The three of us were eating in a Negro restaurant one summer night. We had been to a jazz concert at Griffith Stadium earlier, where Louis Armstrong's orchestra was to have played. The concert had ended in a riot. Some white policemen were showered with pop bottles and Negro policemen had to be rushed in to quell the uprising. The white officers, smarting from the abuse they had taken, roamed the streets that night, looking for black heads to whip. Two of them, plain-clothes men, approached our table after observing us from the doorway. "Well, well, what have we got here?" one of them said, reaching for John's glass.

"A drink," John answered dryly.

"Mind if I have a taste?" he said, picking up the glass.

"I'm not in a habit of letting strangers drink from my glass; but since you're so friendly, go ahead."

The cop took a swallow, set it back down and took out his badge. "Didn't you know the whiskey license in this joint was revoked?" he asked.

"That's the proprietor's business, not mine."

The two of them looked at us for a few seconds, not knowing what to say. Finally, to John, "Are you white or colored?"

"I don't really know. Why?"

"What do you mean you don't know?"

"My parents never bothered to explain it to me."

"Are you three Communists? Let's see your identification."

We showed our government cards, and after a disapproving look he threw them back on the table. Then, having found us a little too secure, they turned upon the waiter who had served us. They cursed, kicked and beat him, pulled him down the stairs and hauled him off to jail. The three of us went to try to bail him out; but they wouldn't allow us to see him. When John went back the next day they had released him. He found the waiter back at the restaurant, his face puffed and swollen from the beating. A surly mood hung over the Negro section the rest of that week, and when John and I went into a Negro restaurant for some barbecue, the owner, a big angry man, took one look at John and ordered him out. "I'll feed you but not him," he said to me.

"But he's all right. He's my friend," I pleaded.

"He's white. That's enough for me. I wouldn't feed him if he was dying from starvation. Get out!"

We walked down the street in silence. "Well, buddy," John said, "now I know what it's like. And that barbecue smelled so damned good."

More and more now the FSA was feeling the strong opposition of Southern conservatives. And Stryker, sensing at last the futility of the fight, warned us that the end might be near. Harried by the mounting obstacles, by the need to preserve the file that had taken so many years to build, he threw himself into a behind-the-scenes struggle to salvage what he could of it.

I saw very little of him during those frantic days. He bounced in and out of the office with officials and politicians who had joined him in his last-ditch fight. Only once did we talk to each other. And that concerned the complaints that were coming in about Marjorie, John and me for being seen together so much. That conversation was halted by an important telephone call Stryker received. "We'll talk about it later," he said. And I walked angrily from his office. How dare he even question our friendship.

The blow finally came. The FSA was to be abolished, but some of us would be absorbed into the Office of War Information—an agency set up in 1942 under Elmer Davis to consolidate domestic and foreign information activities of the government. My situation was depressing, and I felt defeated. I wasn't on the government payroll and my Rosenwald grant would expire the first of January. I didn't feel I had achieved as much as I had hoped to during the year. I had suffered an estrangement from Stryker; and I considered myself to be ignored, only tolerated by him. I couldn't stay in Washington, and the thought of going back to Chicago tormented me. I considered going to Stryker and trying to regain my former status, but my pride warned me that it was too late for that. The harm was done.

Meanwhile, Stryker painfully whittled away at his staff. He sent for me late one Friday afternoon. And, assuming that he was filled with the same venom that had poisoned my feelings against him, I entered resignedly, hoping to get it over with as quickly as possible.

He pushed back in his chair in much the same way he had on that first day I came to his office. He looked drained, ashen and tense from the taxing battle. Suddenly aware of the great strain he must have been under, I felt sorry for him. Everyone knew what that file meant to him—and, more importantly, what it meant to America's history. I wanted to apologize for my actions, but only after our awkward business was settled. I would not take on the role of a beggar; only after he had given me the bad news would I clear the boards.

He started off slowly, too slowly. "Well, by now you know that we've been absorbed by OWI." I wanted to say, "Get it over with, Roy; it's okay; don't make a long message of it." He went on. "We haven't lost everything. There is still a lot here to fight for—the picture file, records and the jobs of as many employees as I can save. I am sure you understand the importance of all this, don't you?"

"I do," I said honestly.

"Well, no individual is more important than all this. This place must somehow go on. No one, two or three persons can place it in jeopardy."

He's thinking of Marjorie, John and me, I thought. And I was right. "Yes," I said, feeling my blood pressure rise.

"You might as well face the fact that this is a Southern city with Southern feelings. And there is only so much you can do about it. I have no personal feelings about your and Marjorie's friendship. It is as natural as day and I am happy to see it. But there are a lot of people around here who don't feel the same as I do. And they feed the flames. Frankly, I want to take you with us into OWI, but . . ."

"But you can't if I continue my friendship with Marjorie Collins. That it, Roy?" I would save him the job. I'd cut my own throat for him, quickly. "You've spent all this time teaching me not to knuckle under to prejudice," I said. "I'm not about to do it now, even if it means I won't be

going to OWI with you." I said it almost without knowing
what I was saying. But it felt right and I was ready to
leave.

A smile suddenly played at the corners of his mouth.
"Well," he answered finally, "you're hired."

Under pressure, Stryker—a strong, dedicated man—had
momentarily weakened, but he had rallied quickly. And in
the clarity of that moment I got a good look at myself. Not
once had I considered his problems. I realized, for the first
time, that my fears had been generously fed by my own
insecurity, that there was far more selfishness in my heart
than I could comfortably live with. I found that praise had
come much easier to my ear than criticism; and, having
grabbed hold of the essence of my problems, I saw that I
hadn't matured so much as I had just grown older. It would
take time to overcome these faults; but at least I was aware
of them. The experience had rescued me from a punish-
ment I was unwittingly inflicting upon myself.

Our move into OWI was smooth, almost unnoticeable.
No physical change took place in the office itself; the
pictorial emphasis was just shifted to industries, people and
institutions involved in the war effort. At this time Edwin
R. Embree, president of the Julius Rosenwald fund, was
writing *13 Against the Odds*, the biographies of thirteen
outstanding Negroes during that period.

At Stryker's suggestion, I offered to photograph some of
the people included in the book. Embree wrote me a letter
of thanks in which he included a passage that was to have
given me a feeling of the text. It read: "In color they vary
all the way from the light cream of Walter White through
every shade of tan and brown to the magnificent ebony of
Mrs. Bethune. They have in their blood all the races of

man. A few may be pure African. Many trace part of their parentage to American Indians. Most of them have much white blood: English, Irish, Dutch, Jewish, French, German—all the strains that have gone into making of the new American people." Then what makes them Negroes? I asked myself after reading the letter. Could the drop of black blood tip the scales so heavily? This passage by Embree had left me somewhat confused. But it didn't really matter. I couldn't wait to meet these Negroes who had overcome generations of slavery, illiteracy and discrimination to gain success.

Eventually I was to meet most of them. And I can't say that I left all of them with a great burst of inspiration. I was too much in awe of their accomplishments to accept the ordinary moments some of them gave me. I had laid to them the impossible feat of proving their immortality in whatever time they spared me, be it ten minutes or an hour.

Walter White, blue-eyed and blond, slight in build, was then the highest officer of the NAACP. He had been chosen, ironically, as an investigator for that organization because his color enabled him to mingle with white crowds and gather evidence about lynchings. He invited me to his office for lunch in the spring of 1943—probably to avoid the strain of finding a restaurant that would have accepted the two of us. He had just returned from Hollywood, and his conversation was full of enthusiasm for it. He said he had sat next to Jane Russell at dinner and found her quite charming as well as beautiful. He mentioned her name several times during our conversation. Because I had expected him to lash out against the whites, I was surprised. I wondered if he thought that his sitting next to the shapely cinema star would impress me more than my eating with him. In any case, I left him knowing more about Hollywood than about the great man to whose feet I had come for wisdom.

I walked slowly back to the office, remembering the stinging accusation the Harlem orator had made against Walter White that night in Harlem. Ten years had passed since then. And in that time his name had epitomized, for me at least, the essence of the black man's struggle for civil rights. Now some banal comments about Jane Russell had caused me to re-evaluate my feeling about him. How stupid of me, I thought; he had just as much right to be thrilled by Jane Russell as I did to be thrilled by him. Nevertheless I was disappointed.

The very next weekend I met Paul Robeson, the renowned baritone and actor. Well over six feet tall, broad-shouldered, dark-skinned, with a deep and commanding voice, he was the exact physical opposite of Walter White. He had been an exceptional scholar, a Phi Beta Kappa and an All-American athlete. He greeted me with a warmth that quickly put me at ease. During that visit, which lasted for over three hours, he spent most of the time asking about my work and ambitions, his manner suggesting that I, not he, was the center of interest. I could feel him studying me with genuine interest. He didn't offer advice, but he congratulated me on my accomplishments. And I felt like a school boy being complimented by his father for good marks. When someone finally came to say that he was an hour late for an appointment, I began apologizing for having taken so much of his time. But he brushed my apology aside. "It was a pleasure," he said. "Come along—I'll give you a lift." I objected, but he insisted in a way that squashed any further protest. He opened the door to a waiting limousine, ushering me in first. As we pulled out I extended our conversation with a trivial question. "Will you be doing any more motion pictures soon?" I asked.

"Not until that industry gives the Negro actor more serious and respectable roles," he answered, "and that may be a long way off." He reached into his pocket and handed me an envelope. "If you have time I would like for you to attend my concert tonight. There are two tickets inside."

We pulled into a long driveway. The building was big and impressive; and as he got out he asked the driver to take me on to my destination. He bade me goodbye and I noted that his huge frame filled the doorway as he entered. He turned, smiled and waved before disappearing into the darkness.

"What building is that?" I inquired of the driver.

"The Russian Embassy," the driver answered; "they are very fond of him there." It was not hard to understand, for, in just a few hours, I too had become fond of this man. And I felt he had left some of his power and strength with me. He had become my hero.

As I walked toward my seat in the stadium that night, applause suddenly filled the air. The audience came to its feet, shouting, "Bravo! Bravo!" Then, before I could turn to see who had entered, Robeson's powerful arm was about my shoulder, weighting me down as we made our way through the cheering crowd. "I'm glad that you could come tonight," he said softly, acknowledging the applause with a broad smile and his free arm. And I was immune to words—consecrated, an adopted prince, moving proudly in the easy, confident strides of my black king.

My appointment with Richard Wright was for a Monday afternoon, but I drove up to New York a day earlier. The August night was hot when I arrived. I pulled out of Central Park and headed up Lenox Avenue, observing people huddled on the stoops and leaning out the windows, trying to get relief from the stifling heat.

Everything seemed quite normal when I reached 125th

242 • GORDON PARKS

Street. I parked my car, took out my bag and headed toward a hotel a half block away. I had no sooner stepped onto the sidewalk than I heard shouting, pistol shots, hooting and jeering. Then all around me people were running, smashing windows, looting; sirens were screaming. The whole world seemed to have gone berserk in an instant. Squad cars were careening in from both ends of the block, their red lights whirling, their tires screeching, emptying policemen into the streets, with drawn guns and billy clubs. I saw an elderly white man raising his arms, trying to ward off blows by two Negro youths who had dropped a radio and typewriter at their feet. A fist finally got to him and he collapsed in a heap. Now a policeman was chasing the two boys, firing over their heads as they cut in and out between the cars. Two women ran past, one with a fully-dressed clothing store dummy, the other with an armful of dresses. I was in the dead center of a Harlem riot.

I tried making my way slowly out of the heart of the melee, hoping that some cop wouldn't take me for a looter. The hope was short-lived, for now one jumped at me, brandishing his pistol and club. "I'm a stranger from Washington! This is my bag!" I yelled above the noise. "I'm trying to get to my hotel! I don't know what's going on here."

"Put that goddamned bag down, you black bastard!" he shouted, pulling back the club. I dropped it and reached for my OWI credentials. And, thinking I was reaching for a weapon, he pointed the pistol at me. "Get your hands to the side if you want to stay alive," he shouted back.

"I just want to show you my OWI credentials!" The word OWI got to him.

"OK, let's see them," he said, keeping the gun pointed at me. I showed him the card and he released me. But I still had a quarter of a block to go. The same situation would meet me further on. I was tempted to drop the bag and leave it, but my camera was packed in the bottom. I wanted to take it out and use it, but the hysteria made such a thought impractical. The police would only think I stole the camera and take it from me.

Boys and girls ran up and down the street with armloads of stolen goods. Two men ran past me carrying small pieces of furniture. Three policemen came after them and they dropped the loot and started to run. A shot rang out; one of the men yelled and sank to the sidewalk. The other man ducked inside a building and ran up the stairs, the cops in pursuit. Now a big woman was beating a policeman over the head with three umbrellas she had taken from a store window. It took two others to subdue her. A policeman was hustling a man past me. The man's face and clothes were drenched with blood from a deep gash across his forehead. The blood glistened like fresh mud in the weird light. Now the cop was pointing me and my bag out to another policeman; and he ran toward me, brandishing his gun. But I hurriedly showed him the OWI card and asked him to escort me to the hotel; he walked me to the edge of the trouble zone. I thanked him and fled across the street. Then I turned to see him clubbing one of three men who were trying to overturn a patrol car.

Wright was sympathetic when I told him about my experience the next day. "My God, man, you could have been killed," he said. But I, in the heat of the riot, had escaped by keeping fairly cool—and asking a cop for help. When I explained this to Wright, he laughed softly. The incongruous picture of a black man asking a white cop for help in such a situation apparently amused him. "I'd never have thought of doing such a thing," he said. He was neat, soft-spoken, well-groomed and scholarly looking, seemingly free of the scars of his terrible Southern boyhood. Yet a sort of terror lurked in his soft eyes. The overnight fame that *Native Son* had brought him two years earlier seemed not to have touched him. He put all his writing aside for me that morning, and we laughed and talked as if we had been friends for years. When I finally left him, I knew I had shared time with a man of courage and deep conviction. He gave me a copy of his novel. The inscription, written in an unruly hand, said, "To one who moves with the new tide." I cherished it, for I had read the passage, taken from *12 Million Black Voices*, many times:

The seasons of the plantation no longer dictate the lives of many of us; hundreds of thousands of us are moving into the sphere of conscious history.

We are with the new tide. We stand at the crossroads. We watch each new procession. The hot wires carry urgent appeals. Print compels us. Voices are speaking. Men are moving! And we shall be with them.

And this was the essence of what he spent that morning telling me.

Mary McLeod Bethune, educator and director of the Division of Negro Affairs of Roosevelt's National Youth Administration, was one of the outstanding women of America and a champion of Negro rights. She invited me to Daytona Beach, Florida, to visit the college that bore her name. Large, dark and square-jawed, she moved about the campus like a mother hen, upbraiding any student who was untidy or boisterous. She had injected an intense religious fervor into the institution; and, knowing that book learning alone could not prepare her students for living in that backward land, she had stressed hand skills. Farming, cooking, sewing and mechanics were placed at the core of each individual's education.

I stayed on for several weeks after photographing her, marveling at the work she had done in that desolate place. But an incident at the very end all but canceled the delight of my stay.

I was leaving the campus with one of the professors. A student had just broken his arm, and he was being sent home after it had been set and put in a cast. A few yards off the campus the professor pulled into a gas station for fuel. He stopped about ten feet short of the pump because an unkempt white man stood in his path, whittling away at a stick. He was looking at the professor's beatup car as though he held a personal grudge against it. We sat there for two, five, ten minutes, the professor nervously tapping the steering wheel.

"Why don't you blow your horn?" I finally said.

"No, no. Please be quiet," he said.

We sat there for another five minutes. I thought I would burst with anger. "That kid's in pain, professor. Go to another station if you don't want trouble with him," I urged.

"Please, please. I'll handle this," he whispered. "You just don't understand." I slumped down in my seat and closed my eyes, trying to shut out the helpless look on the professor's face. At last the professor put the car in reverse and started to back out, only to slam on the brakes when the white man hollered at him. "Don't you want some gas, nigger?"

"Yessir," the professor answered softly.

"Then why the hell don't you ask for it, nigger?" came the reply. I squirmed in my seat. The professor said what I expected him to say. "Please, sir, I would like some gas—please." The man finally stepped aside and the owner, who had observed the whole episode with a smile, came forward. "How many you want, blackie?" he said.

"Ten, sir."

"Ten? Hell, nigger, this goddamned thing'll take more'n ten gallons, won't it?"

"Yessir, it will."

"Then I'll fill the damned thing up." And he did. As we pulled out, the man who had blocked our path spit tobacco juice on the windshield. "You want me to clean off your windshield, nigger?" he asked menacingly.

"No thank you, sir," the professor answered politely. And we rattled off down the dusty road.

"My God, man," I said, shaking my head in disgust, "I don't see how you can take something like that day after day."

He didn't answer me immediately, but after about two blocks he spoke evenly. "Don't think it's easy. All of us teachers down here have to take it, day in day out. If we don't, who'd teach those black boys and girls back there?"

His question took the initiative from me. Who would? I wondered. Certainly not I.

After we had gone about five miles, the professor told me, very calmly, that we were being followed by a policeman. "When he pulls alongside of us, just let me do all the talking. Otherwise there might be trouble." A few seconds later the siren sounded and a big red-faced, cigar-smoking sheriff pulled up and motioned us off the road.

"Just keep calm," the professor pleaded, "keep calm."

The sheriff got out, adjusted his gun and looked our car over. Then he addressed the professor. "Boy, don't you know the wartime speed limits?"

"Yessir. They're thirty miles an hour."

"Well, how fast was you agoin'?"

"About twenty-five, sir—I think."

"Well, if you all is so damned smart, why'n hell don't you go the limits?" The professor had no answer to this one. Then the sheriff had whipped out his gun and pointed it at the student in the back seat. "Take your hand outa your coat, boy, else I'll drill ya!" he hollered. I was astounded, and before the professor could stop me I shouted at him, "He's got a broken arm! He can't take it out! It's in a sling!" He grabbed the boy's arm to make sure he didn't have a weapon. Then he turned on me.

"Whar you from, boy?" he said, waving the pistol in my direction, "and what's all them cam'ras doin' in that seat by ya?"

"Oh, sir," the professor cut in hastily, "he's from a government agency up in Washington. He's been over to our school. He's a guest of Mrs.—of Bethune College."

"Let's see your credentials or somethin' if you come from Washington." I pulled out my OWI card, signed by the President of the United States. He scanned it and threw it back on the seat. "You niggas gittin' mighty important under them Yankee Democrats up there," he said, holstering his gun. "Okay, boy, you drive on more careful else you'll git in trouble down here."

"Yessir, sheriff," the professor answered. And though he tried to get the old jalopy up to thirty miles an hour, she just couldn't make it. So we rattled along at about twenty-eight and a half. And we didn't stop until we reached the college dean's home where, I am sure, the professor was happy to be rid of me. Then he took the boy on home.

America was in its second year of war. And now that I was a part of the information agency, I got an impulsive urge for an overseas assignment. My chief concern had become the Negro soldiers' participation. At first I wanted to join the black 93rd Infantry Division as a correspondent. It had distinguished itself at Bougainville. But when William Hastie, an aide to Secretary of War Stimson, resigned because of "reactionary policies and discriminatory practices against Negroes in the Air Force" my interest shifted to the Air Force.

The 99th Pursuit Squadron, made up of Negroes, was already overseas; and now the initial Negro fighter group, the 332nd, under Colonel Benjamin O. Davis, Jr., was being readied at Selfridge Field, in Michigan. This seemed the logical outfit to join, to show it in training and later in action; and with Stryker's help I applied for my credentials.

On the day that I was accredited, I rushed home to tell Sally the good news. She didn't take it as cheerfully as I thought she would; and I went to bed that night moping at her indifference. The reason came out at the breakfast table the following morning. "Why are you drinking milk instead of coffee?" I asked her.

"The doctor says I should drink milk while I'm carrying the baby."

The news staggered me. How could I possibly leave now? I was disappointed, but I tried not to show it; I forced a grin. "You're pregnant!" I shouted.

But she had caught the hollowness in the false burst of enthusiasm. "It's all right. We'll be okay." She smiled. "You'd die if you couldn't go. You'll be back anyway before it's born, won't you?"

"Well—yes," I said. "I'm sure I will—that is, if you're sure you can make out."

"We'll make out. I'll go stay with Mom until you get back."

"Yes—I guess that's the best thing to do." I didn't really believe it was the best thing, but the very next day we began packing.

The morning before I was to leave for Selfridge Field, I telephoned Stryker, and he asked me to come to the office in the late afternoon. "Nothing's wrong?" I asked nervously. "No," he answered, "just a few odds and ends to clear up. See you later."

It was two days since I had seen my family off to Minnesota. I walked about the nearly empty house, trying to quell my loneliness. Everything that they had left behind multiplied in importance: an old shoe, a pair of faded dungarees, a tablet crammed with my daughter's first ABC's, her fingerprints on the soiled walls. The polka-dot curtains on the kitchen windows hung limply. Sally had made them, and she had been proud of them. Now they were left behind, as if they had been a mistake. The stove smelled of stale bacon grease. And, as I walked up the carpetless stairs, my footsteps echoing in the emptiness, I could hear the unrepaired toilet hissing away. The new tenant would have to fix it. It was no longer a responsibility of mine. Only an old rocking chair remained in our bedroom. Everything else had been given to the neighbors. I sat down, rocking slowly; I began to consider the decision I had made, and, in the quiet of this deserted house, I concluded that I had been rather cold and selfish about the whole thing. If I didn't return, Sally would have to assume the full responsibility for our children. What's more, I had no life insurance. Now I was unsure why I had asked for such a mission. Was it a whim for adventure? Had I been caught up in the excitement of war? I couldn't honestly bring myself to believe that anything I wrote or photographed would alter the conditions that prompted Hastie to resign. Nothing, I began to think, really justified the burden I was placing upon my wife. All this I realized now; but there was nothing to be done about it. The urge was still there. My own restlessness had set the trap—and my impulsiveness had sprung it.

And I sat there rocking myself into the imagined war zone, watching the black pilots roar off to meet the enemy. And I watched them return—tired, dusty, their planes riddled with bullets. And I sat listening to them tell of battle, victory and death. And I put the words in their mouths and took the kind of pictures that would go well above their words. Then suddenly the room was trembling from the strafing and bombing of our position by enemy planes but somehow I survived this and got to England and flying back across the Channel in the bomber squadron I braced my camera against the gun bay and again I photographed the black pilots as they came in their P-38's wingtip to wingtip and I motioned them in closer took my shots as they fell away and rose again around and above us as we roared in over the targets and then the flack was bouncing us all over the sky and someone cried we're hit we're hit and we were going down twisting smoking exploding—and then it was all over. I stopped rocking. The chair let out a tiny squeak as I pushed up from it and I stood until it had rocked itself still. Than I picked up my bags and left the place forever.

And though all this had taken place in my head it had developed out of the sense of possibility. For actually I would spend the rest of training period with the pilots of the 332nd, then accompany them to their overseas base. After a few months, I would join a bomber group; and from inside these B-17's and B-24's, I would photograph the Negro pilots as they escorted us to and from the targets.

The moment I entered the office I knew why Stryker had called me in. The laboratory technicians were giving me a going-away party. Even the red-haired lunchroom manager stopped in to say goodbye. In the beginning I would never have believed that such a thing could happen. But now they were all standing about smiling, drinking, and wishing me good luck. And all the doubts I had harbored were instantly replaced by the joy of this last hour.

TWENTY-THREE

THE HOT air smelled of gasoline and planes when I arrived at Selfridge Field the next morning. Though it was early the sprawling air base was alive with men and all kinds of machines, from jeeps to P-40 fighter ships. A sergeant met me at the gate in a command car; and, as we halted at company headquarters, a squadron of fighter ships thundered up into the hot sky. I stood marveling at the climbing ships, finding pleasure in the fact that black boys were inside them. And, thinking back to Richard Wright's *Native Son*, I recalled the Negro boy's remark when he had witnessed a similar sight: "Look at those white boys fly," he had said in a special sort of awe. Now I was thinking the same thing about these black boys as they flashed above the earth like giant birds.

"That's Wild Bill Walker's squadron taking off," the sergeant said admiringly. "He's one of our best pilots."

Colonel Davis greeted me with a firm handshake that is indispensable to West Point men. He was straight, tall and light brown. His boyish face belied the self-restraint that lay underneath. The son of Benjamin Davis, Sr., the first Negro general, he took his soldiering seriously. He had just returned from overseas, where he had led the 99th Fighter

Squadron into combat. "He goes by the book," one of his officers was to tell me later. "The *Army Manual* is his bible and God help those who disobey it."

We talked for about a half hour; and I am afraid neither of us got much from the meeting. He was neither friendly nor distant, just austere. He asked me orderly questions and I gave him orderly answers; and I left him feeling that he was not a man given to warm friendship. And, in his business, he was probably better off for it, I thought.

The pilots seemed to be a contented group of men. They were at last doing what they had fought so hard to do—fly. They were the best to be picked from the colleges around the country; and there were some excellent pilots among them. The ground officers and their crews were also of the highest caliber. It had the makings of a first-rate fighter group.

I had known the armament officer, Hank Bowman, from Minnesota, remembering him as a gangly kid who used to flip newspapers sideways from his bike as he rode along. He and Tony Weaver, a ground officer on Colonel Davis's staff, soon became my closest friends. And almost immediately they insisted that I discard my civilian clothes and get into my correspondent's uniform. I had wanted to keep it fresh for overseas; but when I awoke the third morning my civvies had disappeared. My officer's cap had been wet down the night before and stuck under my mattress. It now looked as if it had flown a hundred missions. Hank and Tony only smiled when I inquired about my other clothes. I would either have to wear the uniform or go about the base naked. I chose the uniform.

I slept in the barracks with the officers and I ate with them. On the fourth day Colonel Davis granted my flying privileges. Certain pilots were assigned to fly me along on the simulated missions. Most of the time it was Captain George Knox. At other times it was either Gleed, Wild Bill Walker or Wendell Pruitt—all fine pilots and fine men.

Now my days took on an entirely new meaning. I would tumble out of bed at six each morning, shower, eat, jump into my flying suit and hurry to the flight line loaded down with my cameras and notebooks.

There is something about a flying field that makes a heart beat faster; the acrid odor of the petrol has its own way of stimulating the senses, the motors roaring for takeoff, the familiar parrotlike voice of the control tower talking you into position, the barreling down the runway and the final liftoff, the circling for echelon positions; plane *two* comes up and takes position—plane *three*—plane *four*—plane *five*, then *six*. You look across the sky at four o'clock and they are all lined up beside you, men and machines roaring through the upper reaches.

When the bad weather came in, we sat about the ready huts telling jokes and playing blackjack or poker, sniffing now and then at the sky; then, when the clouds lifted enough for takeoff, we would hurry to the ships and fly until chow time. On one such day several of us were gathered in the weather shack when we heard a plane overhead. "Who in hell could be up there in soup like that?" someone said. And we all stopped talking to listen in on the intercom to the tower.

"Redbird to tower—redbird to tower. I'm floundering— bring me in. Over."

"But we're socked in here, redbird. Try to make it to Oscoda. Over."

"Fuel's too low. I've got to come in here. Give me a bearing. Over."

"You're too high and too far north, redbird. Circle sixty

degrees left and start letting down slowly. Over. Come in, redbird. Over."

"It's Jimmy Higgins," someone said. "Where in hell is he coming from?" No one answered.

"Come in, redbird. This is the tower. Over."

Silence.

"Come in, redbird. Do you hear me, redbird? This is the tower. Come in, redbird. Over."

Now a distant whining pierced the damp morning. I glanced at the other pilots. But they were all staring tensely at the floor.

"Redbird—come in. Redbird, this is the tower. Come in. Over!"

The whining was growing louder. We all knew now. He was spinning in. "Get out, Jimmy," someone pleaded softly.

"Redbird, redbird, this is the tower. Are you in trouble?"

The whine was nearing the earth now and after a split second we heard the crash. When we reached the spot several minutes later, there was only a gaping twenty-foot hole filled with twisted metal. A smell of petrol and fresh earth filled our nostrils and we stood helpless on the rim of the hole watching little columns of steam and smoke rise from the rutted earth. Somewhere down in that snarled darkness was Jimmy Higgins.

After such a thing had happened, everyone flew again as soon as possible. It was not good to let fear set in. So no sooner had the clouds rolled back than the squadrons of the 332nd began taking off, flying tighter than ever, diving even more recklessly at the gunnery targets, hedgehopping over trees and executing breath-taking slow rolls. That same afternoon George Knox and I were lumbering along in a trainer toward Oscoda, Michigan. Only the droning motor broke the silence over the peaceful countryside. Far beneath us I could see cows grazing, a tractor crawling over a thin slice of black earth. Now and then we would knife through a patch of white cloud, then we were in the clear blue again; and I began to wonder about Jimmy Higgins falling through space that morning. What was it like to be trapped in a capsule of metal and steel, hurtling toward earth and death? Did he close his eyes and await the impact, or did he die trying to pull out of the spin, hoping for a miracle that never came? Suddenly we were in the midst of a roar; I thought our plane was shaking to pieces. My heart sank and fear shot through my body. But, before I could react further, six P-40's zoomed up and away from us in spiraling bursts of speed.

"You crazy bastards!" George was hollering over the radio. "I'll have every damned one of you court-martialed!" Then he looked around at me and laughed.

"Got any toilet paper, George?" I asked.

"That's Bright and his bunch of clowns. That's what they call giving you a tweeker."

"Well, I'm still tweeking!" I called back. George pointed down to our left. "Look," he said. The planes had regrouped and they were hopping over trees, barns and farmhouses. Chickens were flying through the air. Cows were running along the pasture in fright. George knew, and I knew; it was all a crazy tribute to Higgins.

We spent our weekends in Detroit. And Paradise Valley, a Negro section of the city, opened its arms wide to the nattily uniformed pilots and officers. They were already heroes to these people who had never seen black boys with wings on their chests before. There was no shortage of women; they came from miles around—"in furs, Fords and

Cadillacs," Tony used to crow in delight. The problem was to pick wisely from the multitude. Tony was cocky, proud and brazen with good humor; and he was like a one-eyed dog in a sausage factory after two weeks at the base. A very unpretty woman approached him one night at a bar, but Tony, his sights fixed on something more choice, ignored her. Hours later, when we were leaving the bar loaded and broke, the woman passed us and got into a beautiful new Cadillac. Tony stopped in his tracks. Then, walking up to the woman, he tipped his hat. "Baby," he said, "you look like King Kong, but this car and those furs you've got on are a natural gas. Move over, honey. Let Tony baby drive this thing back to camp." She smiled, moved over and we journeyed out to Selfridge in style.

As the training went into fall, the men's attitude began to change. The fun was about over now. And the talk of women and the joking gave way to more serious things. Racial tensions began to have an effect on their actions and thinking. There were several incidents of white enlisted men on the base not saluting Negro officers. And black soldiers in combat were writing back about being segregated in barracks and mess halls in the war zones. The Negro newspapers were filled with stories about the black men being turned from the factory gates when war plants cried desperately for more help. The Pittsburgh *Courier* carried a long piece about Negro soldiers being assigned to menial labor. And there was a front-page article about an army band playing "God Bless America" when the white soldiers boarded the troopships; then, when Negroes went up the gangplank, the band switched to "The Darktown Strutters' Ball."

And one Sunday night a race riot erupted in Detroit. Fighting spread all over the city; twenty-five Negroes and nine whites were killed and hundreds of both races were injured. The black man was beginning to meet humiliation with violence. White supremacy had become as much an enemy as "blood" and "race" doctrines of the Nazis. Vindictiveness was slowly spreading through the air base. One could feel it in the air, in the mess halls, the barracks and the ready huts.

Once, after I returned from a trip to Washington, I found a note Tony had left for me. It read:

Dear Gordon,

Sorry to miss you but I'm on my way to Steubenville with Judy Edwards' body. As you probably heard, poor Judy spun in and I had to take his body all the way to Detroit because "there are no facilities" for handling Negro dead up there at Oscoda. It's about three hundred miles from Oscoda to Detroit, and in a goddamn army ambulance you can imagine how long it took us to get there. Even as I write this to you, my feelings keep swinging from a murderous rage to frustration. How could anybody do anything like this?

His body was lying wrapped in a tarpaulin in the back of the ambulance; and I had trouble accepting the fact that he was dead, for every time I looked back there, the body seemed to move. I now wonder if the doctors at the hospital had examined him, since this would have required them to touch him too. By the time night had fallen I felt so badly that all I could say was "Judy, I'm sorry. . . . I'm sorry. . . ." We have all suffered some brutal indignities from the whites in this country but this was the final indignity of all. All during the trip I was in an emotional state, alternately talking to the driver and quietly crying for Judy, for his family, for the country and for myself. I felt shame and revulsion for having to wear the uniform I had on. The driver seemed to be caught up in the same mood. We were two of the loneliest soldiers in the world.

I won't tell his folks about this trip because it will just hurt them more. At least to them he was a hero and I'll make sure that when I arrive in Steubenville everyone knows it. The whole dirty business will come into even sharper focus when they lower him into the grave. He'll get an honor guard (a white one), the rifle fire and all the trappings. See you when I get back.

Tony

I stuffed the letter into my pocket and walked over to the airstrip. The night was clear and cold and the stars seemed lower than usual. The fighter ships lined up on the quiet field were ghostly. I walked along beside them, noted the names stenciled in white block letters on the cockpits: Gleed, Pruitt, Tresville, Knox, Bright, Walker and many others. How many of these names will be on little white crosses this time next year? I wondered. At least the 332nd would go into battle with pilots who had faced the enemy before. This would be more of a chance than the 99th Squadron was allowed; for, unlike the white pilots, they had gone into their first battle without one seasoned pilot to lead them. The costly pattern of segregation had arranged a lonely death for some of these men—even over enemy territory. Hitler's Luftwaffe must have laughed when they screamed into the formations of those *schwarze* boys—knowing there wasn't an experienced fighter amongst them.

The next morning Wild Bill Walker, Hank and I ate breakfast together. It was a sparkling day, and we looked forward to some good flying hours. Wild Bill was supposed to have flown me that morning but at the last minute he had been assigned to a trainee from Tuskegee. He was to teach him echelon maneuvers. "Just my luck," he said, "when the gang'll probably be hot riding up to Oscoda." Pruitt flew me instead. And we went up to about fifteen thousand feet waiting for the others to join the formation.

Above us and far to our right we could see Wild Bill taking the trainee through the various turns. "That's a hairy job with new men," Pruitt said over the intercom. We continued to circle, keeping the two planes in sight. Then the unbelievable thing was happening right before our eyes. The trainee's propeller was chewing up Wild Bill's tail. Then came the awful sight of the two broken ships plummeting and spinning toward earth. Pruitt gasped, "They're gone. Poor Bill's gone." He banked steeply and passed over the ships just as they hit the earth; then he called the tower. "Bluebird to tower—bluebird to tower. We're coming in—it's awful—over."

"Come in, bluebird. Come in, bluebird," came the answer. There was sadness in the voice from the tower.

TWENTY-FOUR

A LITTLE after mid-December an order came from the Pentagon halting all furloughs. We knew what this meant. Any day now we would be going overseas. A new tempo hit the base; the men rushed about, restless, patting one another's backs, awaiting moving orders. They came one morning about a week before Christmas. That afternoon Colonel Davis called me to headquarters. "We're about to pull out," he said, "and your traveling papers are not in order."

"What's wrong with them?" I asked.

"You'll have to take that up with Washington. I'd advise you to fly there. We'll probably be leaving before they can get word back here to you."

I packed the battle gear that had been issued to me that morning, took a bus to Detroit, then a plane to Washington; I arrived there late that evening. Stryker had left the OWI by now and had gone to work in New York for the Standard Oil Co. In fact, just about everyone I knew there had gone; the rest were preparing to leave. Besides, it was a weekend and no officials were around. I didn't know where to turn. The one man I did reach had developed a strange case of laryngitis, and was unable to talk, he said. Finally in desperation I tried to reach Elmer Davis, head of the OWI, but he was away on a trip. I fretted through Saturday and Sunday. Then the first thing Monday morning I went to see Ted Poston, a friend of mine in the OWI press section. He had heard the rumors. And Ted put things in their true perspective: "There's some Southern gentlemen and conservative Republicans on Capitol Hill who don't like the idea of giving this kind of publicity to Negro soldiers."

I was shocked—and so was Ted—but there wasn't much we could do about it. The next day I reached Elmer Davis by telephone and told him my story. He listened attentively. When I finished he said, "Don't worry, Gordon, I'll be in touch with the Pentagon this afternoon. You report there tomorrow. I'm sure everything will be all right."

That night, on the Howard University campus, I met Captain Lee Rayford and Lieutenant Walter Lawson, two pilots from the 99th Fighter Squadron. They had returned to the States after completing their required number of missions. Captain Rayford was the holder of the Purple Heart, the Distinguished Flying Cross, the Croix de Guerre, the Air Medal, and the Yugoslav Red Star. He had been shot up over Austria by a Messerschmitt 109. Both of them could have remained Stateside as instructors. Instead they had volunteered to go back to the war zone. We ate dinner together, and since they had to go to the Pentagon the next day we agreed to meet and go together.

We had no sooner boarded the bus and seated ourselves behind the driver than his voice came at us, metallic and demanding. "If you fellas wanta ride into Virginyuh, you gotta go to the rear." We looked at one another questioningly, deciding in our silence not to move. The driver stood up and faced us, a scrawny disheveled man with tobacco-stained teeth and a hawk nose. The armpits of his uniform were discolored from sweat. "You all heard what I said. This bus ain't goin' nowhere till you all go to the back where you belong."

"We intend going to Virginia in the seats we're in," Lee said with finality.

"Okay, if you ain't back there in one minute I'm callin' the MP's and havin' you put off."

"You'd better start calling right now," Lee replied.

Two white Air Force captains and a major were seated across the aisle from us and I noticed that they stirred uncomfortably. Several other whites were scattered in the near-empty bus and an elderly Negro woman sat at the rear. I watched her through the rear-view mirror. She had half risen from her seat; there was courage, dignity and anger in every line of her small body. Her look demanded that we stay there, and I was determined not to disappoint her. The bus had become dead quiet while the driver stood glowering at us.

"Fellows." One of the young white captains was speaking now. "We know how you feel about this," he said, his voice cloaked in false camaraderie, "but the major has an appointment at the Pentagon in a half hour. He wonders if you would mind moving back so that we can be on our way?"

My two friends were outranked. But there were no bars on my shoulders. The American eagle on my officer's cap was as large and significant as his or the major's. I took a good look at the old woman in the rear. She was standing now, gripping the seat ahead of her. Then, borrowing the captain's icy politeness, I stood and addressed the major. "Sir," I said, "as you can see, these men are fighter pilots. They have completed their missions but they have volunteered for more duty at the front. Would you like to order your fellow officers to the rear? They have no intention of moving otherwise." My anger was rising, so I sat back down.

The bus driver stood watching us until the major finally spoke to him. "Drive on," he said. "Can't you tell when you're licked?" The driver cursed under his breath, threw himself into the seat and slammed in the gears and we lurched off toward Virginia. "Hallelujah!" the Negro woman shouted from the rear. "Hallelujah!" Her voice rang with pathos and triumph. "Thank God we don't have to sit in the back of our P-38's," Lawson sighed as we got off the bus.

The three of us parted soon after. "We'll see you on the other side somewhere," Rayford said cheerfully. And I watched the two young men walk away from me at the entrance to the Pentagon, hoping that I would meet up with them again. Our thoughts were already separated from the incident on the bus. We had won; our anger was dead.

The officer in charge of overseas traffic was drinking a Coca-Cola when I entered. I handed him my papers and explained my situation. He scanned them without speaking —all the time sipping the Coke. He took one long swallow, smacked his lips and belched. "Far as I can see, your travelin' papers are in order," he finally said, opening another bottle.

"Then why was I sent back here?"

"Beats me, fellow. I'm just tellin' you far as this office is concerned they're in order."

"Thank you. Now where will I contact the fighter group?" I waited. He was gurgling Coke again.

"I can only give you directions as far as Newport News, Virginia. You'll have to play it by ear from there."

"But if everything is in order why can't you be more specific?"

"I'm being as specific as I can. I'm not allowed to give out the exact location; and that's that." He belched again.

I thanked him as coldly as he had received me and left, feeling that only luck could get me to the group before it sailed.

Our plane took off in a blinding rainstorm—and it landed in another one at Norfolk, Virginia. A taxi took me to the ferry landing where I would cross over into Newport News. I sat there in the waiting room for an hour on top of my battle gear among a boisterous group of white enlisted men. Four Negro soldiers were huddled in a nearby corner. Two of them were propped against each other sleeping. Most of the white boys seemed to be making a festivity of these last hours. But there was a sort of emptiness attached to their laughing and drinking. Obviously they were headed for some departure point. It's all to hide the fear, I thought. Their faces were so young.

We filed out when the ferry whistled. It was still raining and we stood near the edge of the dock watching the boat fasten into the slip. Through the wetness I noticed a sign reading COLORED PASSENGERS and another one reading WHITES ONLY. The four black soldiers moved automatically to the colored side, and so did I. How ironic, I thought; such nonsense would not stop until we were in enemy territory.

After all the outgoing passengers were off and the trucks and cars had rumbled past, we started forward. Then I saw a Negro girl step from the ferry. She had been standing in the section marked for cars; now she was in the direct line of the white enlisted men, who stampeded to the boat screaming at the tops of their voices. I saw the girl fall beneath them into the mud and water. The four Negro soldiers also saw her go down. The five of us rushed to her rescue. She was knocked down several times before we could get to her and pull her out of the scrambling mob.

"You lousy white bastards!" one of the Negro soldiers yelled. "If I only had a gun!" Tears were in his eyes, hysteria in his voice. A long knife was glistening in his hand.

"Soldier!" I shouted above the noise, letting him get a look at my officer's cap. "Put that knife away!"

He glared at me fiercely for a second. "But you saw what they did!"

"Yes, I saw, but we're outnumbered ten to one! You can't fight all of them. Get on the boat!" He looked at me sullenly for another moment, then moved off. We cleaned the mud from the girl's coat and she walked away without a word. Only proud anger glistened on her black face. Then the four of us joined the soldier I had ordered away. He was standing still tense beneath the sign reading "colored passengers."

"Sorry, soldier," I said. "We wouldn't have had a chance against a mob like that. You realize that, don't you?"

"If I've gotta die, I'd just as soon do it where I got real cause to." His tone was resolute. I had no answer. I was tempted to hand him the bit about the future and all that, but the future was too uncertain. The yelling was even louder now on the other side of the boat. "Sons-of-bitches," he muttered under his breath.

"Good luck," I said to them as we parted on the other shore. "So long," they said—except the one I had spoken to—then they moved off into the darkness and rain again. I turned away, feeling I had somehow let him down.

"Colored move to the rear!" The voice met me again when I got on the bus with some of the white enlisted men. Sick of trouble, I made my way to the back and sat down; I was the only Negro aboard. Some of the whites were standing, but I had four empty seats around me. "Gordy! My God, it's Gordy!" a voice rang out above the noise. And suddenly a soldier was rushing back toward me. "Bud!" I shouted, getting to my feet only to be knocked back to my seat by his bear hug. It was Bud Hallender, a husky man I had played basketball with back in St. Paul. Now he was down beside me, slapping my back and wringing my hands.

"You all cain't ride back there with that nigra! Move back up front where you belong!" Bud ignored the command; now he was telling the others I was the co-captain of his basketball team, his friend.

"You all hear me? You cain't ride back there with that nigra!"

"Go screw yourself!" Bud shouted back. "Drive on or we'll throw you off this goddamned crate and drive it ourselves!" Laughter rocked the bus. The driver plopped down into his seat without another word and drove off toward the heart of town. And Bud and I talked excitedly of a time and place where things had been different. Finally, at the terminal we wished each other a jovial goodbye.

I made a thorough check of my map; and, riding a hunch, I wrote out a government order for a bus ticket to a point where I suspected the pilots would be camped. The agent at the window examined it and looked at me suspiciously. "Where'd you get this?" he said.

"It's a government issue slip, for travel."

"I know what it is, fellow, but I ain't neva heard of a nigra writin' one of these things out. I ain't givin' you no ticket. Not me."

"I'm attached to the Office of War Information. I'm my own issuing officer," I explained.

"I don't care what you are. I just don't believe no nigra can write out one of these things without a white man signing it."

"I'm en route overseas. I've got to meet my group before sailing time. I've got to catch the next bus!" My voice had risen now.

"Well, I ain't givin' you no ticket unless you got cash!" His voice was raised one notch higher than mine, and people were gathering around the window. We stood glaring at each other when a door opened on my right. "Can I be of any help to you, sir?" A young man with a pleasant face confronted me. I explained my problem and he asked me to step into his office. "Are you with an air group?" he asked after I had taken a seat.

"Yes. That's right," I answered cautiously.

"I thought so. You don't need that ticket. I have to make a telephone call. Excuse me for a moment." He came back after a few minutes. "It's all arranged. You walk straight down the main street for three blocks, turn left for two more blocks and wait there on the corner. Someone will pick you up within the next half hour."

I thanked him and went out to follow his directions, wondering whether this was a subterfuge of some kind, a way of evicting me from the terminal peacefully. I doubted it; yet such chicanery would come as no surprise now.

It was twenty minutes before an army command car rolled up beside me. A Wac stuck her head out the window and checked my description. "OWI?" she asked.

"That's right," I answered.

"Hop in," she said cheerfully. Another Wac drove the car and they whisked me off to a military barracks where my papers were thoroughly checked again, this time by an army captain.

"Have to be sure," he said; "once you're in there's no getting out." He finally handed them back with a smile. "They're okay. Good luck. Have a safe trip. The Wacs will drive you out to the embarkation base." My spirits leaped ahead of the car as we sped toward Camp Patrick Henry.

The pilots of the 332nd stopped their gambling, letter writing and drinking long enough to give me a rousing welcome. They were all genuinely happy that I had made it. My bunk had been made up and was waiting. And I showed my appreciation with two bottles of Scotch and several cartons of cigarettes which I had wrapped in my battle gear. Aside from women, I knew these were the things they would crave most. Money was useless now. They gambled it away with abandon. The noise kept up far into the night, then into morning. But I slept well, knowing the first leg of my mission had been accomplished. Now, if luck held, I would be at sea within four days.

Tony and I went out for some fresh air the next night. "It's hard to believe but we've had trouble right here on this base," he said as we walked along, "so we'd better stay in this area."

"What kind of trouble?"

"The same old jazz. One of our ground crewmen was beaten up by some white paratroopers night before last. Then they've tried to segregate us at the base's movie house. Everyone's in a hell of a mood." We became suddenly quiet as we circled the area.

A shot sounded nearby and the two of us stopped in our tracks. Then there was another shot. Someone seemed to be returning the fire. "We'd better get in. Sounds like trouble," Tony said. Our barracks had already gone dark when we entered it. Several men were at the windows with guns looking out cautiously into the night. When all was quiet again, the lights went back on and the gambling and the letter writing and the drinking started again. New orders came the following morning. We would take to the boat two days earlier than had been proposed. I was happy about this. There seemed to be less danger at sea than on this troubled base.

Colonel Davis sent for me just before noon. I hurried anxiously to his office. No more trouble, I hoped; it was too close to sailing time. But when he looked up at me his face was calm. It was, after all, some routine matter he would speak about, I thought.

"I'm sorry. Your papers are not in order. A final call from the Pentagon has come through. You will not be able to embark with us."

"This is ridiculous," I said. "Can't you do anything? Someone in Washington is trying to prevent coverage of your group overseas, Colonel. This is the first Negro fighter group. It's history. It has to be covered. Can't you protest in some way, Colonel?"

"There's nothing, absolutely nothing I can do. The orders are from the Pentagon. They cannot be rescinded. I'm terribly sorry."

I had lost. And suddenly anesthetized to the colonel and all that was around him, I turned and started out. "You are aware that you are sworn to the strictest of secrecy about what you have seen or learned here," he was saying as he followed me to the door. "You realize the dangers of any slip."

"Yes. I understand, Colonel."

"It is even possible to detain you until we are overseas under such conditions. But I am sure you won't discuss our movements with anyone."

"I won't. Don't worry. I want to forget the whole thing as quickly as possible." I rushed back toward the barracks, angry and disgusted. I couldn't bring myself to say good-bye to the pilots again. I packed quickly and waited for the command car the colonel had ordered for me.

The pilots were readying themselves for the boat when the car arrived; and I slipped through the rear door without even a backward glance. At five o'clock the next morning, after wiring Sally, I boarded a plane for Washington. I would change planes there and go on in to New York, where I would wait for my wife and children. The thought of even stopping in this city irked me. I wouldn't live there again if they gave me the White House rent free, I thought as the plane roared down the runway.

We began circling over Washington at dawn; and far below I could see the landing field, lying like small strips of cardboard under a wispy patch of cloud. Further out in the distance the monuments of the city shone milk-white in the winter sunlight and the water in the mall sparkled like an oblong jewel between the sculptured trees; there was the Capitol standing quiet and strong on one end and the Lincoln Memorial set on the high quarter of the opposite slope. What a beautiful sight to be wed to such human ugliness, I thought. And as we dropped lower I could see the tops of the stores, theaters and restaurants whose doors were still closed to me.

I thought back to the fighter pilots. They would soon be far out to sea, sailing toward war and death, ignoring, at least temporarily, their differences with the land they were leaving to defend. This was the price for a questionable equality.

We were landing, and the intolerance of Washington came rushing up toward me as the plane roared down toward the strip. There would only be an hour's wait before I took off again. And I would hate that hour; the memories here had been too searing. I just wanted to get out.

I strode into the air terminal, tired, hungry and irritated to a point of fury, my nerves stretched raw. Everyone in the place looked as if he were a member of the Klan. My whole body seemed to be itching for a fight—a last physical protest against the frustrations of these past six days. I walked toward the lunch counter, where only one seat remained unoccupied. The man next to it had a red creased neck, thin lips; his beady eyes, manner and clothing spoke of the deep South. I detested the very sight of him; I knew he would say the words that would set me upon him. I threw my gear on the floor, clenched my fists and sat down beside him—waiting. He was turning now, looking me over. My body tensed. And then he said easily, casually, "Good morning, soldier. Looks like it's going to be a nice day for flying." He pulled out a pack of cigarettes and offered me one, then lit it.

With some difficulty I came to terms with myself. Then I blew out the smoke and confusion in one long breath. "You're right—it looks like a good day for flying," I said, "a very good day." And the two of us ate in peace.

I didn't ask him where he was from or where he was going. It didn't make any difference. It was a nice day for flying. And I said this to the stewardess when I boarded the plane for New York and I said this to the old lady who sat beside me in the plane and I said this to the skycap who helped me with my bags at La Guardia Field and to the cabby who drove me up to Harlem.

A friendly word from a stranger, and a cigarette, had lifted me temporarily from the darkness. As I settled back into the cab, I linked him in my mind with the old trolley conductor who had befriended me on that cold and lonely morning twenty years before, moments after I had thought of robbing him. With a few kind words these two men, like all the others who had helped me, had pushed me a few more inches down the road. Harvey Goldstein, for instance, had given me more than I expected—more, probably, than he could afford. Bill Hunter showed me the value of initiative and of receptiveness to other people. Roy Stryker, with patience and foresight, had given me discipline and a sense of direction. I could, in a way, even be thankful to my brother-in-law and to Barnes, the dining-car steward. Their actions had also propelled me to the point at which I now found myself. It was sad to think that somewhere they still wallowed in unhappiness. My experience had left me scarred and angry at times, but now I was bringing my hopes back to the shadowy ghetto, to see if they would take root in the asphalt of the city streets, would sprout in the smoke and soot, grow in barren days and nights—and at last know fruition. If so, the hunger, hardship and disillusion would have served me well. My mother had freed me from the curse of inferiority long before she died by not allowing me to take refuge in the excuse that I had been born black. She had given me ambition and purpose, and set the course I had since traveled.

As we reached the high point of the bridge, a stretch of dreary rooftops widened on the horizon. I didn't know what lay ahead of me, but I believed in myself. My deepest instincts told me I would not perish. Poverty and bigotry would still be around, but at last I could fight them on even terms. The significant thing was a choice of weapons with which to fight them most effectively. That I would accept those of a mother who placed love, dignity and hard work over hatred was a fate that had accompanied me from her womb.

We left the bridge and rolled into Harlem; and I was among the tired tenements and garbage cans again. They didn't seem strange to me now. When we crossed Lenox Avenue an icy wind was swirling trash up from the gutters. The hawk was over the ghetto—and all around me, black people were buttoned up and hurrying against its fury.